I0127848

Zimbabwe's Military:
Examining its Veto Power in the Transition to Democracy, 2008–2013

Edited by Dr Martin R. Rupiya

The African Public Policy and Research Institute (APPRI) wishes to acknowledge the financial support provided by Trust Africa for this project.

Published by APPRI, 357 Visagie Street, Pretoria 0001

© APPRI 2013

ISBN 978-0-620-56750-3

First published 2013

Editing by Hilda Hermann
Layout by Joan Baker
Production and cover by Bronwen Müller
Printed by Megadigital, Cape Town

All rights reserved. No part of this publication may be reproduced or transmitted, in any form or by any means, without prior permission from the publishers.

Contents

Foreword

Since Zimbabwe's political independence in 1980, the country has been a source of fascination for political analysts, researchers, students, diplomats and others and has invoked mixed but equally interesting perspectives and comments in the international arena. Depending on which side of the fence the observer was on, these comments have swung from condemnation, ambivalence to sympathy and praise by various regional, continental and global actors. This was possibly not only because of Zimbabwe's choice of a neo-Marxist revolutionary post-colonial government in 1980, but also due to the country's protracted liberation war that claimed many lives. Another critical factor that elevated Zimbabwe's status in Africa was its strategic geo-political location and subsequent role in regional and global matters, especially at a time when the United Nations and other international actors had declared apartheid in neighbouring South Africa a crime against humanity.

Thus, this book: *Zimbabwe's Military: Examining its veto power in the transition to democracy: 2008-2013*, adds fresh impetus and new momentum to contemporary debates on the context and peculiarities of the Zimbabwe question. The book is relevant to several audiences with interests in the topics and sub-topics covered by the book, which include civil-military relations in Zimbabwe, and the role of the Zimbabwean military in the country's socio-economic, political and governance systems. In particular, the appeal of the book lies in the fact that it skilfully tackles Zimbabwean civil-military relations, linking this to several issues of varying importance to observers of global political and geo-political dynamics. Such dynamics, which are well-articulated and covered in the book, include peace and security, defence conflict resolution and conflict management, global dispute resolution initiatives and peace-building, the African Union's role in ameliorating conflict in the continent and its part in international politics, diplomacy, intelligence, national party politics, and post-colonial democratisation.

The book's rich variety of authors has enabled it to cover closely-related, complex and diverse topics normally covered in studies of defence, post-colonial land reform and redistribution, the nature of development, natural and mineral resources management, nationalism and the national question, colonialism and *decoloniality*, and violence and identity politics in a post-colonial state. While all these topics have been tackled by various scholars in earlier works, the

iv

main advantage of this book is that it seeks to cater for anyone searching for contemporary information on the role and impact of negotiation, mediation and peace-building in Africa generally, and specifically in Zimbabwe; including related topics and sub-topics that will make the book a favourite reference text for researchers and scholars.

While focusing on Zimbabwe, the book touches expertly on issues affecting many African countries, particularly the Democratic Republic of the Congo, South Africa, Cote d'Ivoire, Burundi, Angola, Botswana, Tanzania, Mozambique, Nigeria and Swaziland. This will make it important to those seeking to understand the advantages and limitations of what is often termed the "African Agenda", African Renaissance and post-colonial reconstruction.

For social scientists and students of other academic disciplines, researchers, experts and students of African international affairs, members of the donor and multi-lateral community, and, of course, Zimbabweans and other Africans of different persuasions and interests in African politics, this book will be a timely companion to enrich the quality of discussions and debates on the issues it covers. The book is also meant for those interested in Zimbabwe's geo-political position as an evolving democratic system with numerous implications for the role of the region and continent in the 21st Century's global political order.

Diplomats working in national, regional or global forums will also find this book particularly interesting, as will policy-makers and global public servants interested in conflict resolution and African perspectives on how to tackle and resolve conflict in the continent.

The authors seek to close several gaps in the Zimbabwean question and have made great attempts to go beyond the usual simplistic or superficial analysis of Zimbabwe's contemporary and past political problems. One of the key contemporary problems that the book examines is the role of the military in influencing various facets of Zimbabwe's socio-economic and political landscape, which is particularly fascinating given the fact that elsewhere in Africa the issue of the military's role in national or domestic politics is still shrouded in mystery at best or, at worst, ignored.

The book showcases the work of reputable scholars and intellectuals from a wide range of academic, research and professional backgrounds whose experiences cover countries including Zimbabwe, Ethiopia, United Kingdom, Germany, to name but a few. Those seeking to understand the latest perspectives on regional economic communities will find this book an invaluable resource.

Finally, as articulated in this book, Zimbabwe's march towards restoring democratic rule is also about human rights and restoring citizens' dignity, restoration of the rule of law and resuscitation of constitutional rule and the establishment of a political system based on free and fair, credible elections that can enhance government's legitimacy and thus assist a country in its path towards democratisation. All these, including the pertinent difficulties that the country has faced since independence, are reflected in different ways in this book. Hence, the book should appeal to politicians, officials of election management bodies, political activists, civil society and non-governmental organisations, African and international think-tanks, governments, political advisors, embassies, and media and political commentators.

Dr Kealeboga J. Maphunye
WIPHOLD-Brigalia Bam Research Chair in Electoral Democracy in Africa,
Department of Political Sciences, University of South Africa (UNISA)

Authors

Associate Professor, Lieutenant-Colonel (retired) **Dr Martin R. Rupiya** is Executive Director of the African Public Policy and Research Institute (APPRI). The Institute, established in 2012, focuses on new African civil military relations and how this relates to national security on the continent that has found itself, since the 1990s, propelled to democratise, replacing the one-party-State systems established in the post-colonial period. Rupiya is currently Visiting Professor and lead facilitator on the Executive Masters Programme, Institute for Peace and Security Studies (IPSS), at Addis Ababa University, Ethiopia. Rupiya's most recent article – "Global issues affecting Africa: Drones over African skies: purpose, impact and implications" in *African Armed Forces Journal* (April 2013) – reflects on the changing nature of warfare. He also co-edited the 2012 book HIV/AIDS and the Security Sector in Africa, published by the United Nations University in Tokyo. Before establishing APPRI, Rupiya had been the Director of Research: Africa at Cranfield University, United Kingdom; Senior Researcher and MilAIDS Project Manager at the Institute for Security Studies, Pretoria, South Africa; Associate Professor in the Department of International Relations, University of the Witwatersrand, South Africa; Visiting Fellow in the Department of Politics and International Studies, Rhodes University, Grahamstown, South Africa; and Senior Lecturer and Director of the Centre for Defence Studies at the University of Zimbabwe.

Dr Charles Abiodun Alao, Senior Research Fellow of the Conflict, Security and Development Group, King's College London, holds a PhD on the Integration of the Zimbabwe Military. Recent publications, which formed the summary of his contribution include *Mugabe and the Politics of Security in Zimbabwe* (2012) and *Natural Resources and Conflict in Africa: The tragedy of endowment* (2007). His twin research interests are the politics of natural resources management in Africa, including land conflicts, and peace and human security dimensions on the continent. Alao is co-editor of a number of eminent journals, including the *African Journal of International*

Affairs and Development (AJIAD) and the *Journal of Global Initiatives*, and co-authored the Concept Paper on the African Union's *Common African Defence and Security Policy*, which was adopted in 2004.

Professor Sabelo J. Ndlovu-Gatsheni is Professor and Head of the Archie Mafeje Research Institute (AMRI), College of Graduate Studies (CGS) at the University of South Africa (UNISA). He has published extensively on Zimbabwean politics and history, focusing on such themes at civil-military relations, relations between nationalist politicians and the military, conflict and violence, identity, nationalism and the State. His main publications include *Do "Zimbabweans" Exist? Trajectories of nationalism, national identity formation and crisis in a post-colonial State* (2009); *Empire, Global Coloniality and African Subjectivity* (2013); *Coloniality of Power in Post-colonial Africa: Myths of decolonisation* (2013); and *Nationalism and African National Projects in Southern Africa: New critical reflections* (2013).

Dr João Gomes Porto is currently Visiting Professor at the Institute for Peace and Security Studies (IPSS) at Addis Ababa University, Ethiopia. He is also Visiting Professor at University of Leipzig (Germany) Institute for African Studies, and Honorary Research Fellow at the Department of Peace Studies, University of Bradford, United Kingdom. From 2002 to 2005, Gomes Porto was Head of the African Security Analysis Programme at the Institute for Security Studies (ISS), Pretoria, South Africa. His most recent academic and policy research publications include "Mediators Not in the Middle: Revisiting the normative dimensions of international mediation" in Engel (ed), *New Mediation Practices in African Conflicts* (2012); "Multipronged Strategies for a Multifaceted Crisis? A critical reflection on EU policy towards Zimbabwe" in Ganzle, Grimm & Makhan (eds), *EU Policy for Global Development* (2012); "Africa's New Peace and Security Architecture: Promoting norms and institutionalising solutions" (2010); and "The African Union New Peace and Security Architecture: Towards an evolving security regime?" in *African Security* 2(2009); "The Mainstreaming of Conflict Analysis in Africa: Contributions from theory" in Francis (ed) *Peace and Conflict in Africa* (2008); and "From Soldiers to Citizens: Demilitarisation of conflict and society" (2007).

Dr Siphamandla Zondi is Director of the Institute for Global Dialogue (IGD), an African foreign policy and diplomacy think-tank based in South Africa, and a Research Associate in Politics and Development Studies at the University of South Africa (UNISA). After his undergraduate studies at the former University of Durban-Westville (now University of KwaZulu-Natal) in South Africa, he pursued his MPhil and DPhil studies at Cambridge University in the United Kingdom, focusing on African agency in Africans' interface with Western modernity. He worked as a researcher at the Africa Institute in Pretoria, South Africa, focusing on southern Africa's regional integration and former liberation movements, before he took the position of head of the Africa programme at the IGD, where he led second-track diplomacy and research teams on Burundi, Cote d'Ivoire, the Democratic Republic of the Congo (DRC), and Zimbabwe. He succeeded Professor Garth le Pere as head of the organisation in January 2010. Zondi's areas of interest are South Africa's foreign policy, with special reference to its pan-African and global dimensions, Africa's international relations and negotiations diplomacy, and the question of development in Africa and globally. His latest publications include "African Union Audit and the State of Continental Integration: An analysis" in *Africa Insight – African Union at 10 Years Special Edition*; "Is the Seoul Consensus on Development an Alternative to the Washington Consensus? – A critical perspective from Africa" in *Africa Review* (2013); and "Common Positions as African Agency in International Negotiations" in Brown & Harman (eds) *African Agency in International Politics* (2013).

Professor Dr Ulf Engel, whose 1994 DPhil (Hamburg University) was on "The Foreign Policy of Zimbabwe", is currently Director of Studies, African and European Masters at the Global and European Studies Institute, University of Leipzig, Germany. He is also Professor Extraordinaire at the Department of Political Science, Stellenbosch University, South Africa, while also serving as Visiting Professor at the Institute for Peace and Security Studies, Addis Ababa University, Ethiopia. Among his numerous related and most recently published works is "New Mediation Practices in African Conflicts" available at http://www.univerlag-leipzig.de/article.html;article_id,1344.

Acronyms

ACHPR	African Commission on Human and Peoples' Rights
ACP	African and Caribbean Pacific
AIPPA	Access to Information and Protection of Privacy Act
AMU	Arab Maghreb Union
ANC	African National Congress
ASEAN	Association of South East Asian Nations
AU	African Union
AUPSC	African Union Peace and Security Council
BMATT	British Military Advisory and Training Team
CCM	Chama Cha Mapinduzi (Tanzania)
CFSP	Common Foreign and Security Policy
CIO	Central Intelligence Organisation
COMESA	Common Market for Eastern and Southern Africa
COSATU	Congress of South African Trade Unions
DA	Democratic Alliance
DRC	Democratic Republic of the Congo
EAC	East African Community
ECCAS	Economic Community of Central African States

ECHO	Humanitarian Aid and Civil Protection Department of the European Commission (previously known as the European Community Humanitarian Office)
ECOWAS	Economic Community of West African States
EDF	European Development Fund
EISA	Electoral Institute for Sustainable Democracy in Africa
ESAP	Economic Structural Adjustment Programme
EU	European Union
FLS	Frontline States
GDP	Gross Domestic Product
GNU	Government of National Unity
GPA	Global Political Agreement
HRW	Human Rights Watch
IBRD	International Bank for Reconstruction and Development
ICG	International Crisis Group
IGAD	Inter-Governmental Authority on Development
IMF	International Monetary Fund
JHC	Joint High Command
JOC	Joint Operations Command
JOMIC	Joint Monitoring and Implementation Committee
KAR	King's African Rifles
LAA	Land Acquisition Act
LHA	Lancaster House Agreement
LRRP	Land Reform and Resettlement Programme
MDC	Movement for Democratic Change
MDC-M	Movement for Democratic Change – Mutambura
MDC-N	Movement for Democratic Change – Ncube
MDC-T	Movement for Democratic Change – Tsvangirai
MOU	Memorandum of Understanding
NAM	Non-Aligned Movement
NAO	National Authorising Officer
NCA	National Constitution Association
NCA	National Consultative Assembly

NEC	National Economic Council
NEPAD	New Partnership for Africa's Development
NGO	Non-Governmental Organisation
NIP	National Indicative Programme
NSC	National Security Council
OAU	Organisation of African Unity
OPDSC	Organ on Politics, Defence and Security
PAP	Pan-African Parliament
POSA	Public Order and Security Act
PVOA	Private Voluntary Organisations Act
RF	Rhodesian Front
RISPD	Regional Indicative Strategic Development Plan
SADC	Southern African Development Community
SADC-PF	Southern African Development Community – Parliamentary Forum
SROC	Standing Rules on Orders Committee
TPDF	Tanzanian People's Defence Force
UDI	Unilateral Declaration of Independence
UK	United Kingdom
UMP	Uzumbe-Maramba-Pfungwe (District)
UN	United Nations
UN-Habitat	United Nations Human Settlements Programme
UNISA	University of South Africa
UNSC	United Nations Security Council
USA	United States of America
WB	World Bank
YCLSA	Young Communist League of South Africa
ZANLA	Zimbabwe African National Liberation Army
ZANU-PF	Zimbabwe African National Union Patriotic Front
ZAPU	Zimbabwe African People's Union
ZCTU	Zimbabwe Congress of Trade Unions
ZDF	Zimbabwean Defence Forces
ZEC	Zimbabwe Electoral Commission
ZESN	Zimbabwe Election Support Network

ZHRC	Zimbabwe Human Rights Commission
ZIDERA	Zimbabwe Democracy and Economic Recovery Act
ZIPRA	Zimbabwe People's Revolutionary Army
ZNA	Zimbabwe National Army
ZNLWVA	Zimbabwe National Liberation War Veterans Association
ZUM	Zimbabwe Unity Movement

1

Introduction

Martin R. Rupiya

The march towards democratising the African state and subjecting the same to a multiparty, competitive environment is a recent phenomenon, only going back to the end of the Cold War during the 1990s. Before this, the lack of democratic progress had been the result of collusion between an international security system dominated by the superpowers, which had carved the globe into spheres of influence, and a dominant one-party-state system on the continent. In Samuel Huntington (1991:15) citing the three periods 1828–1926, 1943–1962, and the final beginning during 1974, Africa has missed becoming part of this international growth, not least because of stifling international security and the stilted economic system whose advantage is tilted against the continent.[1]

When forces of democratisation were unleashed, the African political terrain was almost totally unprepared. In the first decade of multiparty democratic experiment, 47 African countries, mainly from sub-Saharan Africa, attempted the exercise. The result: 38 countries regressed, with 12 States experiencing military coups, further forcing the already fragile African state to implode.[2] A new phenomenon of collapsed States has haunted Africa ever since. Countries such as Togo, the former Zaire (now the Democratic Republic of the Congo), Somalia, Ivory Coast, Malawi, Zambia, Kenya, Zimbabwe and Madagascar fall into this category of facing democratisation challenges. In response to this Africa-wide political phenomenon, the African Union (AU) developed an intervention, a conflict mechanism instrument in which key mediators would be appointed to rapidly engage key actors and seek to put together a political power-sharing agreement, captured in a document to which the protagonists would append their signatures. The import of the document would be to act as a framework for conduct and processes during a preferably defined transitional period before free and fair elections were held.

During the transitional period, key areas of contestation appear to have emerged in most case studies around:

a) the need for a new constitution, usually to dilute the centralised powers of the presidency

b) reform of the electoral commission – again, usually appointed by the incumbent, therefore unable to exercise independence and perceived to be unfairly beholden to this office

c) the opening up of media space, allowing other voices to be heard and to reach out to the rest of the population, and

d) transformation of the security establishment to assume a national character from what was, as we saw in the Tanzanian Chama Cha Mapinduzi (CCM) case, an instrument of the ruling party that performed in a manner viewed as partisan by other players.[3]

Tanzania was but one example of a country that experienced this phenomenon, but was able to successfully weather the transformation. During the 1990s, the country's Constitution banned the existence of any political party other than CCM. This meant that, for multiparty democracy to be a feature in Tanzania, first the country's Constitution had to be amended.[4] In effect, Tanzania had to institute what became popularly known as the "Forty Laws" in the old Constitution, designed to decouple the party from State institutions, including the civil service, in order to prepare the country for multiparty democracy under The Presidential Commission on Single Party or Multiparty System in Tanzania, 1991: Report and Recommendations of the Commission on the Democratic System in Tanzania, led by Chief Justice Francis Nyalali, popularly known as the Nyalali Commission.[5]

The next challenge is around institutions of government and, for our purposes, focusing on security and defence organs.[6] In Tanzania, after the perceived military mutiny by the inherited regiment of the King's African Rifles (KAR) in January 1964, put down with the assistance of Nigerian and British military intervention, the old units were summarily disbanded and a new Tanzanian People's Defence Force (TPDF) was created.[7] Fast-forward to 1991 multiparty democratic transformation: the TPDF, aligned and associated with CCM, was called to assume a more national character and distanced itself from the political party.[8]

It is therefore true to say that the era of democratisation has created new peace, development and stability challenges, given the near total collapse of existing polities and the introduction of unpredictable, highly competitive and conflictual power struggles destabilising the fragile political systems around the African state. In most instances, institutions that are a precondition for robust, democratic political stability under the new culture are either absent or seriously compromised, resulting in yet another phase of fundamental political, ideological and security reorientation on a scale similar to the 1960 "Wind of Change" phenomenon.

In southern Africa, a region that had to take up arms in order to wrest African majority independence as evidenced in Angola, Mozambique, Namibia, Zimbabwe and South Africa, assisted by Nigeria, Tanzania, Zambia, Lesotho, Swaziland and Botswana under the Frontline States (FLS) auspices of the Organisation of African Unity (OAU) Liberation Committee, the dynamics are slightly different when it comes to decolonisation and the new democratisation agenda. In the first instance, for liberation movements to succeed in wresting power from unwilling and unrelenting dominant settler and colonial powers, enjoying international support gives them a particular moral edge of being the true proponents and advocates for democracy. Hence, when calls for democratisation are made, this point must not be lost. The second feature is that, in subsequent and current debates, made possible only after the superpowers had abandoned their spheres of influence posturing, any contributions from the superpower quarter has to be viewed with a taint of scepticism. This is significant if one takes into account the agencies calling for political and economic reform – ensconced within the World Bank (WB), International Monetary Fund (IMF) and other international organisations – through which former colonial and imperial powers are now pursuing this as a foreign policy agenda.[9] The essential thrust of the World Bank's *Sub-Saharan Africa: From Crisis to Sustainable Growth* (1989) was to provide a link between aid and governance that translated to political reform for global, capitalist economic management.[10] The impact of this Washington consensus on the unsuspecting Third World was devastating.[11] Mark Duffield wrote *Symphony of the Damned: New discourses, complex political emergencies and humanitarian aid* after more than 30 African countries opened up their political and economic environments to almost inevitable collapse.[12]

The point to take away from this discussion is that the democratisation agenda continues to be pregnant with residual and continuing subjective restructuring of the global political and economic dominance by those sitting at the top. In direct contrast, when it comes to political crises in the FLS region and elsewhere, Africa and the sub-regions have invested in the decolonisation of the continent, including the liberation of southern Africa. In any political contestation, the continent seeks to shore up its gains rather than lay itself bare to experiments that are likely to make Duffield's work recur.

Although we may argue that Africa is entering a new phase, for liberation movement-informed regions, the residual effects of former colonial and imperial machinations seeking to re-engineer a comeback through other means has not been discounted. Hence, in the complex, multi-layered and multifaceted Zimbabwean debates, the charge against Western powers seeking "regime-change" fall into this rationale and is accepted as one of the challenging realities that has continued to colour the crisis.

In Zimbabwe, the poll defeat of the then ruling Zimbabwe African National Union Patriotic Front (ZANU-PF) during the harmonised elections of March 2008, heralded the first time that a former liberation movement faced political oblivion when it lost political popularity at all three levels: local government, parliamentary and presidential. Significantly, in the disputed presidential run-off that followed, it is common cause that the security establishment played a decisive, violent but partisan role to block democratic transition – a position acknowledged by the AU, Southern African Development Community (SADC) and the SADC Parliamentary Forum – that led to the creation of the Government of National Unity (GNU) in February 2009 under the auspices of the Global Political Agreement (GPA) signed on 15 September 2008. This decision by both the AU and the SADC recognised the complexity of the political situation over the destiny of Zimbabwe, including: an international agenda to remove ZANU-PF from power; phases of misgovernance by ZANU-PF, such as the 1980s' Matabeleland massacre ("Operation *Ghukurahundi*") and the 2005 "Operation *Murambatsvina*" (Drive Out the Filth); an obvious trend of general political decline in popularity and early interventions by the SADC, such as the March 2007 Dar es Salaam mandate for then South African President, Thabo Mbeki, to head up the facilitation role on the Zimbabwean crisis; the existence of grievances from organised labour unions under the Zimbabwe Congress of Trade Unions (ZCTU) umbrella, which then succeeded in creating an opposition political party, the Movement for Democratic Change (MDC).

Research question

The discussion and debate aimed at developing a better understanding of the veto power of the military within the complex Zimbabwean political crisis, began with a series of dialogues among key participants, bringing together particular knowledge and perspectives on the character and nature of the crisis. Whereas the finished chapters of only some colleagues are featured here, we also wish to acknowledge the contributions made by: Thomas Deve, an academic, former journalist and activist on the democratisation of the country, whose main import was that any discussion on security sector reform of the "Red Army" was viewed as part of the regime change agenda; Professor Andre Mangu, Head of Civil Law at University of South Africa (UNISA), who critically examined the SADC's intervention efforts – not only in Zimbabwe, but also in the Democratic Republic of the Congo (DRC) – that tended to ignore citizens' aspirations. Both Deve and Mangu made short but insightful presentations that enriched the debate. The first chapter titled "Who wields the command and control authority for the Zimbabwean security sector: 2008–2013?" aims to provide a sense of how the military establishment executed its role during the GNU and examine the extent to which this entity conducted itself during this transitional, power-sharing period. The measurement for this discussion is the SADC Agreement on Zimbabwe, commonly referred to as the GPA, and subsequent SADC communiques on the role of the security establishment that were issued during that period. A major conclusion, which was obvious since the inauguration of the GNU in February 2009, was that ZANU-PF, in true revolutionary and Marxist terms, had not only captured the State and transformed State institutions into its own image (as was seen in post-colonial Tanzania), but deployed the State beyond the reach of the GNU. Despite the enacting of the National Security Council (NSC) Act by the new parliament in March 2009, defence and security issues remained outside cabinet, parliament and even the more informal Monday principals meetings. The issues around policy, management, and command and control of the security establishment therefore remained located within the presidency, the politburo and party-mandated ministers, commanders, a select group of senior civil servants and other functionaries, all of whom were not subject to the diluting integration of the GNU power-sharing agreement. A single ministry, Home Affairs, was allowed to be subject to co-division with two ministers: Kembo Mohadi

4

from ZANU-PF and Giles Mutsekwa from the Movement for Democratic Change – Tsvangirai (MDC-T), who was later replaced by Theresa Makone. The key objectives of this desired isolation and almost total exclusion from contamination by the GNU and its implications during this period are examined in this chapter.

This is followed by a summary of the recently published book by Charles Abiodun Alao, an academic at Kings College London, who did his PhD research on the challenges of integration of the Zimbabwe National Army (ZNA), in a chapter titled: "Governance and the politics of security". Alao takes an interesting approach in his analysis, arguing that, since independence, President Robert Mugabe and ZANU-PF have viewed security and, by extension, sovereignty and independence as the sacrosanct products of the struggle around which everything falls into place. Given the opening comments of the cockpit from which we find the contemporary democratisation agenda – that of the Washington Consensus, concerned with re-ordering the world subjectively for a single economic power to rule – one finds resonance with this spirited interpretation and approach to safeguarding security. In his discussion, Alao tries to conflate the personality and character of Robert Mugabe with that of the revolutionary movement, to emerge with a single, cohesive ideology and a military organisation prepared to defend it. In this, the political opposition is anything but appendages of Western and former imperial protégés bent on reversing the gains of the armed struggle around land reform, minerals acquisition and ownership, and economic policy options that have Zimbabweans at the centre. Discussed as someone who is at the tail end of his long political career, exactly how the ideology and purposeful direction relates to other players is at the heart of Alao's discourse.

In "A perspective on the ethnic, regional and ideological dimensions and its implications", Sabelo Ndlovu-Gatsheni examines the increasing militarisation of the State and, by extension, its attendant reality of intervention in the country's politics. He reflects on the nature of the composition of the forces, sufficient to then resonate with the political aspirations of the elite in an unquestioning relationship that has been detrimental to domestic ethnic relationships, such as the pogrom witnessed against the Zimbabwe African People's Union (ZAPU) and the Ndebele in the Midlands and Matabeleland generally. The main reason for this development, in his view, is the quest by ZANU-PF and President Robert Mugabe to continue to safeguard the State from neo-colonial destabilisation. To this end, the gravitation of the military, even as an ethnic-dominated group, had become possible in the nature of constituencies within a neo-colonial State, where this identify found favour with the dominant political power. This is an analysis that resonates with Alao's point of view, with authors viewing the debates between ZANU-PF and the MDC as actors who are talking past each other on the question of why and where the military is located in the Zimbabwean crisis.

Siphamandla Zondi's chapter, "South Africa and SADC mediation in Zimbabwe: Still at the crossroads?", attempts to locate the crisis within the broader regional and pointedly South African interpretation, providing an overview of the evolution of the peace process and conflict resolution through mediation. A sense of exhaustion and fatigue has emerged, perhaps showing that the earlier signs of perceived ripeness,[13] in which actors were expected to make concessions that would result in the erosion of privileges and legitimacy, may actually have been a premature view. From 2003 to 2006, before South African President Thabo Mbeki arrived on the scene as the SADC's lead facilitator, former President Joaquim Chissano of Mozambique, and Ali Hassan Mwinji and Benjamin Mkapa of Tanzania had been leading the mediation, with similar inconclusive results.

Zondi's sub-regional discussion is followed by Ulf Engel's discussion on foreign policy and relations. For Engel's PhD thesis on Zimbabwe's post-colonial foreign policy, he had the most interesting experience, engaging in dialogue and one-on-one interviews with most of the key players in the Zimbabwean State at a time when independence had just been achieved. They were anxious to share their views of the world and the international relations they sought to forge, based very much on the success of the liberation struggle. While this emphasised cementing relationships with the East, there was also the realisation that comprehensive global relations required engaging and working with former enemies in the West. Engel has titled his chapter "International dimensions of the Zimbabwe conflict: Past interventions, future prospects".

The final chapter is that of João Gomes Porto: "Multipronged strategies for a multifaceted crisis: A critical reflection on European Union policy towards Zimbabwe, the sanctions debate and the political role of the security sector". It reviews the impact of targeted sanctions, otherwise called restrictive measures, 11 years after they were imposed. His findings are illustrative, exposing the limits of sanctions as an instrument of economic isolation, and as leverage to force adjustment or change in political behaviour and conduct. In his research, Gomes Porto cites the disconnect between the absence of an international sanction mandate, such as a resolution from the United Nations Security Council (UNSC), and the intentions of a multi-membered and sometimes divided EU. In his submission, there appears to be little evidence of change in behaviour or form by President Robert Mugabe or ZANU-PF on the imposition of the measures, whose impact was dented by timing, the gradual nature of their implementation, and the difficulty of coordinating the individual, bilateral actions of the 27 EU members in their relationship with Zimbabwe. Further, Gomes Porto notes that action by the USA, Canada, Australia and the EU did not find favour with the AU or the SADC, resulting in the diluting of intentions to isolate those targeted and influence their political conduct. On the ground, Mugabe and ZANU-PF successfully turned the sanctions issue into a badge of honour, adopting a victim stance among Pan Africanists, who did not distinguish between the targeted and full sanctions mantra. For them, sanctions were sanctions, and a statement of acknowledgement of their revolutionary quality and zeal. In his conclusion, writing for an EU audience, Gomes Porto finds that the sanctions issue and decision on Zimbabwe was something of a failed agenda.

These papers form the basis of detailed and analytically informed research that seeks to enhance our understanding of the dynamics that surround African states on the questions of democratisation and, in this case, specifically post-colonial liberation Zimbabwe. Already, in examining the focus of the papers selected for this book, consensus is split and the complexity of this case study becomes obvious. What is not obvious, however, is whether this is evident in the actions of the facilitators, including the AU and SADC, and what leverage these entities have in order to create conditions for peaceful co-existence of the parties in conflict within Zimbabwe.

There are some hard questions to be answered on the challenges that characterised the main contours of the crisis.

Without this type of research, both those for and against a particular party or dimension of the crisis will never fully understanding why actor A is adopting a given posture compared to actor B, who may also be behaving in a manner that is incomprehensible to the other. The work of analytical research is, therefore, to lay bare the facts in a detailed and chronological manner, in the hope that, politically and sociologically, we can draw useful lessons that can be used in similar case studies elsewhere.

---

[1] Significantly, Huntington also cites reverses, occurring in the periods 1922–1942 and 1958–1975.

[2] Bassett & Strauss (2011).

[3] For examples, see the *Lusaka Accord of the Democratic Republic of the Congo 1999*, the *Zimbabwe Global Political Agreement 2008, and the SADC Agreement on Madagascar 2009*, amongst others.

[4] This process that was successfully concluded through the Chief Justice Francis Nyalali Commission, which held countrywide consultations. Curiously, while the Commission's recommendations were for the continued maintenance of the one-party system, government chose to ignore this and adopt multipartyism.

[5] Rupiya (2006:31).

[6] Tungaraza (1988:291).

[7] During the East African colonial period, Britain had a single Brigade, with its regiments for this region deployed in Uganda, Kenya and Tanzania. This was the "in" place at independence during the 1960s. As President Julius Nyerere later admitted, the mutiny, happening close to a meeting of the again-perceived competing labour unions, had been erroneously viewed at the time as a well-calculated and coordinated coup attempt.

[8] Rupiya (2006); Lupogo (2001).

[9] The first salvo for Africa to "democratise" was fired by the World Bank policy document: *Sub-Saharan Africa: From Crisis to Sustainable Growth* in preparation for Washington taking over, "unfettered", the management of the global economy after the departure of Moscow's competing ideology. *See* Rupiya (2006:34).

[10] *See also* Shivji (1996).

[11] Mulikita Njunga (2003:105–115).

[12] Duffield (1996). *See also* Rupiya (2006:35).

[13] This argument was informed by the well-established doctrine and cliché of I.W. Zaartman, which led to the SADC Extraordinary Summit on Zimbabwe in March 2007.

2

Who wields the command and control authority for the Zimbabwean security sector: 2008–2013?

Martin R. Rupiya

Already, we are a militarised party ... So it must not come as a surprise that we assign people from the military to run public institutions.

President Robert Mugabe[1]

Executive summary

After losing the harmonised election of March 2008, the undiluted command and control of the security establishment is the single most important element that the Zimbabwe African National Union Patriotic Front (ZANU-PF) has been able to rely upon for political survival. In a symbiotic politico-military relationship that has endured with a single leader since 1977, President Robert Mugabe managed to capture the State and deploy this outside the inclusive government during the transitional period, while allowing complete reign of the military in the critical areas of: managing the security environment within the country in favour of his party while constraining all else; conducting an aggressive foreign policy abroad that served to have on side the Pan African community, Russia, China and India, among other key international players, against Western and former colonial detractors; managing the Electoral Commission, the registrar and the voters' roll; managing the media to translate into a single liberation narrative; and linking serving and retired war veterans, militia and customary chiefs to the intelligence, police and armed forces under Joint Operations Command (JOC) to serve a single and party line.

Diamond revenue in an economy controlled through licensing and in an environment facilitating lack of transparency, given existing Western sanctions, emerged as the game changer during the second half of 2009. Not only did the easily and cheaply secured alluvial diamonds provide much-needed resources, but they also acted as an important reference of what other global players coveted in Zimbabwe: its minerals.

This is the key role that the security establishment played that resulted in a landslide victory, aided and abetted by what Roger Riddel (2013) has described as "the political failures of the opposition – entranced by being in government – even if they were not in power".

The challenge that faces Zimbabwe, the Southern African Development Community (SADC) and the African Union (AU), now that it has been acknowledged that a militarised operation secured the exit to the Government of National Unity (GNU), is: What is the nature of the political crisis likely to be as we go forward? There is also a related challenge for ZANU-PF: What and when will be the right time to put the sword back into the sheath and allow the process of nation building to proceed?

As some Zimbabweans engage in muted isolated celebrations and others heal from the devastating heartbreak – with measurable shock being the common denominator – it is time people take stock of the past elections to draw hard lessons for the future.

Nhlanhla Ngwenya[2]

Introduction

As 31 July 2013 drew close, a date that heralded the end of the GNU, global attention was transfixed on the Zimbabwean harmonised election.[3] A select group of international observers were on the ground, including those from the AU, SADC and SADC Parliamentary Forum – the three key groups that had condemned the June 2008 election result.

At the beginning of July 2008, at its 11th Ordinary Summit hosted in Sharm el-Sheikh, Egypt[4] the AU adopted Resolution 1 (XI) on Zimbabwe, based on the consensus reflected in the three mission observer reports of the AU team from Addis Ababa, Ethiopia; the cross-political parties represented in the SADC Parliamentary Forum, with its offices in Windhoek, Namibia; and the submission on behalf of the SADC Secretariat, based in Gaborone, Botswana.[5] All had agreed that the harmonised election held in Zimbabwe in March 2008, soon followed by the presidential run-off on 27 June, was deeply flawed, characterized by a severely restricted political environment, closed media and partisan institutions, including a violent security sector that had committed serious human rights violations, ultimately succeeding in undermining the poll result in favour of the incumbent president under "Operation *Mavhotera Papi?*" (Where Did You Vote?)[6] This was akin to what Tom O'Connor has cited as a veto coup – violent repression blocking democratic transition "undertaken by high-ranking officers" organised as the JOC in Zimbabwe.[7] To be fair to the generals, their objective in blocking the transfer of power to the Movement for Democratic Change – Tsvangirai (MDC-T) was to provide an opportunity for President Mugabe and ZANU-PF to re-organise themselves and win the election, whereupon the military would relinquish its hold.

A couple of days after the election closed, the results coming out were interesting, with President Robert Gabriel Mugabe securing an overwhelming 61.09% of votes against Morgan Richard Tsvangirai's 33.94%. ZANU-PF captured 76% of available seats, sufficient to change the Constitution without the support of any other party, defying all pundits, scenario predictions and some significant perceptions – or, shall we say, expectations – on the ground.[8]

The element of surprise was total and the impact devastating, leaving the "enemy" – political parties competing against ZANU-PF and President Mugabe – shell-shocked. This bombshell left constituencies unsure whether to laugh or cry, as Nhlanhla Ngwenya has aptly captured above.

In reality, however, the election result was clearly the product of a well-resourced military operation executed with audacity, guile, aggression; conducted with utmost secrecy, with an unwavering, ideologically grounded single-mindedness; centrally and tightly calibrated against an unsuspecting "enemy", which was left in "shock and awe", confused and completely overwhelmed.

How was this achieved? We can begin to understand how this was crafted, planned and executed partly by looking at the command and control of the military during the transitional period. To this end, this discussion is not about technical or tactical military insights, but rather focuses on the broader process and political implications of the role of the military in a multiparty context. It is therefore merely a retrospective of why we think it happened the way it did and how it was possible. Finally, the discussion attempts to offer some thoughts on the implications of such an operation by the military wing of ZANU-PF and how this is going to translate into the delivery of socio-economic and political demands by citizens in the future. Stated differently, the challenge is how the ruling party is going to reconcile itself with the aspirations and domestic governance grievances that have seen the party lose popular electoral appeal, now that it has secured the sweeping vote and mandate for the next five years.

It is undisputed that Zimbabwe's exit from the AU and SADC-inspired Government of National Unity (GNU) was not through a free-and-fair election, as had been provided for under the GPA, but rather the result of a well-planned, adequately resourced, tactically multifaceted, aggressive and audaciously executed military operation. The objective of the military operation was to secure a political goal, the legitimacy of ZANU-PF, against other competing political parties, without necessarily abandoning nominal commitment to the GPA. To this end, exclusive command and control of the military during the transition was critical and a precondition for success.

Why was it imperative for ZANU-PF to adopt a military approach for political survival? And how did ZANU-PF succeed in gaining exclusive command and control of the military in a transitional, power-sharing arrangement in order to achieve its singular goal? To this end, to what extent is this only temporary? In other words, now that ZANU-PF has taken the internal and structural gamble of reversing its symbiotic, politico-military relationship to one of dominance, in order to successfully confront competing political parties in the 2013 election, what is the future for democratic political competition in Zimbabwe? Stated differently, what policy, institutional and political conduct is required to right the ship after this unprecedented event? Finally, with a militarised State in power, to what extent is it likely to respond to it citizens' political and economic grievances?

While several authors have tried to explain why and how President Robert Mugabe and ZANU-PF were able to secure a landslide victory in the recent election, there has been little acknowledgment of the central role played by the military. Riddel (2013) provides five reasons why ZANU-PF succeeded, and in three – ideological and security power projection that secured an environment in which the judiciary and media upheld a single ZANU-PF liberation narrative; the challenges of the Zimbabwe Electoral Commission (ZEC) and the voters' roll; and the command and control of the chiefs and traditional leaders in controlling the rural vote – the role of the role of the military is referred to almost by default.

This paper argues that the electoral win was the result of a military operation subject to effective political control by ZANU-PF during the transitional period. However, it is also noted that a delicate, internal, structural and ideological shift of balance of forces may have occurred, tilting in favour of the military arm and political hardliners against the more moderate political faction that acknowledges political work still needs to be done to reconnect the party with grassroots and national popular support. The point has to be emphasised that, what has transpired is not necessarily political competition that settles the differences between the parties representing different constituencies; instead, the election result is but a supra-national and sub-regional closure of the more definitive edges of the crisis. The more fundamental domestic challenges remain, but may be dormant in the short to medium term.

- Why was it imperative for ZANU-PF to adopt a military approach for political survival?

   After President Robert Mugabe and ZANU-PF secured a precarious and partial stay in office, through AU and SADC intervention in 2008 calling for the creation of a GNU, the next step was to restore full legitimacy at the end. It was a "must win" for a number of reasons examined below associated with the command and control of the security sector during this period. While some of the key reasons encompass ideological, historical, personal and structural interests, the question of succession within ZANU-PF, security, and a sense of historical ownership and investment in the independence project, the presentation does not reflect a hierarchy, but points towards how some of these feed off and reinforce each other.

   The first reason must be the tacit but never publicly acknowledged challenge that confronted the AU and SADC: a president and his military who had seized power after losing elections in Zimbabwe. Given the investment Pan Africa had made in the independence of the country, any public citing of the reality facing the continental bodies would again open up the situation to outside intervention. The lesser evil was therefore to confine this situation within the African solution, even if this short-changed the electorate, and suggest a power-sharing GNU leading, yet again, to free-and-fair elections. In other words, with an aggressive ZANU-PF still holding onto the reins of power, the AU had little choice but to accept this reality, unable to voice its objections or invoke the isolation of a Zimbabwe under military rule.

The second reason was also a default reality for ZANU-PF: accepting the position of the security establishment in control of the State after it had had stepped in and blocked the democratic transfer of power following the comprehensive electoral loss of March 2008.[9] This event was not without warning as ZANU-PF's political popularity had been in serious decline since the loss of its preferred position in the February 2000 Referendum and the near routing in the June 2000 parliamentary election when the party was returned with a wafer-thin five seat majority. Sensing an acceleration of this trend, ZANU-PF threw the first military dice on 9 January 2002, when commanders appearing on public television vowed not to recognise or allow anyone to occupy the presidency, even if they won the elections, unless they possessed liberation credentials.

However, even as these platitudes continued to be made, the political situation continued to deteriorate. The first SADC intervention came through the forum of former presidents Joaquim Chissano of Mozambique, and Ali Hassan Mwinyi and Benjamin Mkapa of Tanzania, during the period 2003 to 2006. This quiet diplomacy appeared to fail as, in March 2007, a SADC extraordinary meeting in Dar es Salaam publicly appointed then South African President Thabo Mbeki as the region's facilitator.

The third factor that galvanised ZANU-PF to rely on the military for political survival is the fear of domestic and international retribution and even trial. In its own words, when refusing to publish the Chihambakwe Commission of Inquiry report, the State argued that this would result in sections of Zimbabwean society degenerating into open conflict. Post-colonial Zimbabwe has experienced pogroms, admitted to have been the result of mistaken assessments, but subsequently lacking in the adoption of genuine reconciliation, compensation and rehabilitation. The evidence put together by the Catholic Commission for Justice and Peace after massacres during "Operation *Gukurahundi*", and later by UN-Habitat's Anna Tibaijuka, referring to "Operation *Murambatsvina*", offer insight on the internal use and abuse of State organs on citizens.

- How did ZANU-PF succeed in gaining exclusive command and control of the military in a transitional, power-sharing arrangement in order to achieve its singular goal?

The how, while explicit in some areas, remains shadowy in others. Given the nature of military operations, not all the evidence is likely to be known for a while yet.

ZANU-PF succeeded in retaining exclusive command and control of the military during the transitional, power-sharing period by engaging in an early and coherent strategy for political survival in which the same institution was going to play a decisive role. This was possible, even against a repeatedly intrusive SADC facilitation process that demanded the separation of the military from civilian affairs.[10] When the SADC demands became explicit, ZANU-PF became bellicose, questioning the "authority" of the SADC over its perceived sovereignty and even serving notice that it would leave the organisation. The SADC had no capacity to go beyond comments made in diplomatic corridors and occasional restraining communiqués.

Operating as a State within a State, ZANU-PF was able to forge effective foreign military relations, breaking the sanctions imposed on the military by the West during early 2000. This was significant in providing much needed war material, training and access to modern technology. In point of fact, the sanctions imposed on the military when the country was fighting a war in the Democratic Republic of the Congo (DRC) were counterproductive in the eyes of Pan Africanists, who correctly read Western duplicity in the move, culminating in an even closer relationship between the institutions and the party. At the time, various reports, including conclusions from the UN, cited Ugandan, Rwandan and Burundian forces as having invaded the Congo, yet these were not sanctioned.

As Riddel (2013) asserts, even before the establishment of the GNU, the lure to government posts for the political opposition and later serving in government, "even if they were not in power, unwittingly aided and abetted" ZANU-PF machinations. Against this background, even where the security establishment continued to hound and harass the political opposition, supported by the Attorney General's office that was supposed to have been addressed as one of the outstanding issues of the GPA, this behaviour did not disappear throughout the four-year transitional period. The effect of this was to create a sense of permanent fear, intimidation and insecurity in those seeking to challenge the status quo and limit the impact of those few "allowed" into the artificial inclusive government. In practice, the security establishment then set to work the various stages of the electoral system in favour of the former ruling party, ZANU-PF. Elements were deployed in the Electoral Commission and Air Vice-Marshal Henry Muchena was appointed ZANU-PF Elections Director, with the responsibility of revamping the political party structures. He also had the authority to allocate serving military, war veterans, chiefs and other customary leaders, as well as youth militia members, areas of operation during the election period (*see* Map 1). More importantly, prospective ZANU-PF candidates had to be vetted by the Central Intelligence Organisation (CIO) before the Elections Director received and appointed them in the party structure. In other words, the military exercised complete control over the electoral machinery and the outcome for ZANU-PF.

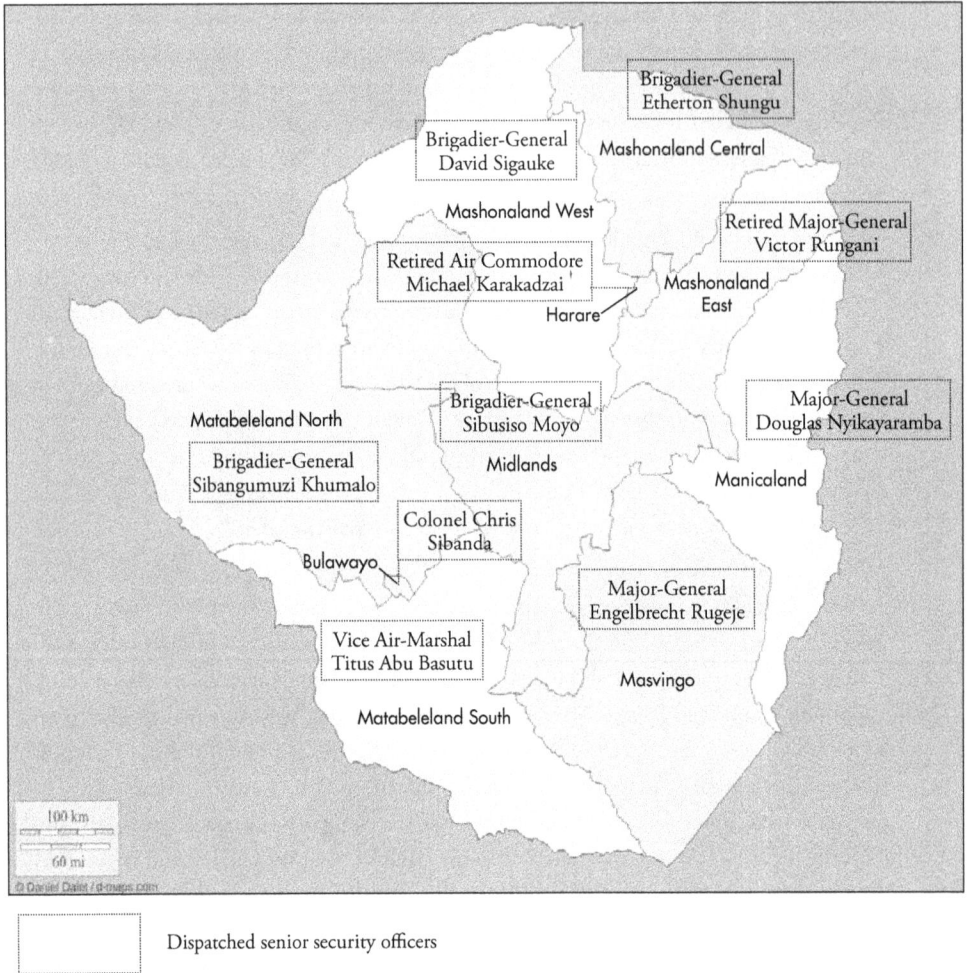

Map 1: *Joint Operations Command preparations to despatch senior officers*

Next, attention was paid to the Registrar's Office, responsible for the voters' roll and the registration of new voters. At the time of writing, unsubstantiated evidence questioning the validity of the voters' roll appears central to the surprise that greeted Nhlanhla's citizens.

A final caveat was the entry of unimaginable resources – the discovery of alluvial diamonds in Marange-Chiadzwa – that brought almost instant wealth in millions per month into the coffers of the State within a State, and not directly into Treasury. Estimates calculated minimum revenues from the diamonds at anything between US$1.7 to 2 billion per year.[11] The hosting of the Ministry of Finance by the MDC-T's Tendai Biti, and the sanctions regime in place that sought to seize and block any transactions conducted by Zimbabwe, provided license for the Ministry of Mines and Mining Development, and other actors, to shield the proceeds and revenues from diamonds. However, this brought immediate relief

14

to the quest for resources, which had nearly brought down the government and resulted in unprecedented levels of hyperinflation.

- ## The impact of diamonds on military operations

In any military operation, resources and time are major constraints. In the Zimbabwean case study, the flood of limitless revenues opened up at precisely the right moment for the event to succeed. The fact that the country remained under sanctions provided the opportunity to keep transactions under wraps.

The first acknowledgement of ZANU-PF positioning in the command and control of the security establishment during the transitional period occurred before the GPA was signed on 15 September 2008. Although directly mentioned by the AU and SADC, during negotiations, the issue of the security establishment was successfully argued to be left out for separate treatment in the GPA. Once the document was signed, however, the former incumbent moved swiftly to seize ministerial control of all the coercive institutions and departments, including Foreign Affairs, the Minister of State in the Presidency (also responsible for the CIO), the Ministry of Defence, and a shared Ministry of Home Affairs, with the MDC-T confined to co-ministerial positions, permanent secretaries and departments such as Prisons and National Parks.

While the GPA provided for a National Security Council (NSC), enacted in March 2009, this was packed with serving senior civil servants, diluting the impact of policy makers. This approach has been repeated in the *Draft Constitution* (Chapter 11, sections 206 and 209), in which membership of the NSC, chaired by the president, continues to have the commanders in the same room.

At a party congress hosted in December 2009, the president and ZANU-PF simply stated that management of the security establishment was not going to be open to the inclusive government. Instead, the party's politburo and other structures were isolated and kept apart from the governing structures of the transitional government such as cabinet.

- ## Implications and conclusions

A well-planned, adequately resourced and well-executed military operation delivered a political landslide for President Robert Mugabe and ZANU-PF in the 31 July 2013 harmonised election. However, the political crisis that began during the mid-1990s and was exacerbated in the next decade-and-a-half still needs be addressed. Be that as it may, for reasons of posterity and what still needs to be done for a comprehensive response to the country's political crisis, this paper considers some of the military dimensions necessary to achieve the minimum political result, examines select elements of how this was done, and identifies some implications for the future.

In the domestic crises in which the AU and SADC have had to intervene, Zimbabwe and a potentially embarrassed former liberation movement, ZANU-PF, presents a unique case study for exiting the GNU. Election success was secured by a landslide, but prevailing SADC Principles and Guidelines were violated in relation to excluding the diaspora, refusing to restore the rule of law and the central participation of the military in politics. Sub-regional bodies have, for now, elected to go along with and sanction the vote. However, this leaves the country, its citizens and security institutions clearly unprimed to peacefully co-exist in a multiparty political democracy over the next five years. Both the AU and SADC may later be surprised at being invited, yet again, to intervene in the Zimbabwean political crisis, should the situation deteriorate among still deeply divided and irreconcilable constituencies.

---

[1]   "Be presidential not partisan" commentary in *News Day*, 27 August 2013.

[2]   "Self-assessment by media key to correcting mistakes" commentary on Nehanda Radio, 26 August 2013.

[3]   The 11th Ordinary Session of the African Union Summit, Resolution on Zimbabwe Assembly/AU/Res.1 (XI) that culminated in the Global Political Agreement (GPA) on Zimbabwe (September 2008), provided the framework for power-sharing arrangements while defining what needed to be done during the transitional period. The GPA was resulted from the appointment of a SADC facilitator, then South African President Thabo Mbeki, at the SADC Extraordinary Summit on Zimbabwe hosted in Dar es Salaam in March 2007.

[4]   African Union 11th Ordinary Session, 30 June – 1 July 2008, Sharm el-Sheikh, Egypt, at http://www.africa-union.org/au/root/conferences/2008/June/Summit/dec/pdf. Accessed 2 July 2013.

[5]   Assembly/AU/Res. 1 (XI), p. 1.

[6]   Important we grasp the nature of governance in the crisis; characterized by military operations.

[7]   "The Coup D'état African Patterns" at http://www.drtomoconnor,com/3160/3160lect07.htm. Accessed 27 June 2013.

[8]   This is not to ignore the Freedom House report and other sentiments expressed.

[9]   Results released after five weeks revealed that Tsvangirai had secured 47% against Mugabe's 43%, but lost control of parliament and was swept from local government councils.

[10] Such as the Livingstone and Maputo Communiqués, 15 June 2013.

[11] Towriss (2013:99–117). *See also* Partnership Africa Canada (2009).

3

Governance and the politics of security[1]

Charles Abiodun Alao

Right from independence, it was obvious that the management of Zimbabwe's security would be its most important security challenge. Apart from having to contend with the expected challenges facing a newly liberated country, the new nation also had to contend with the domineering presence of apartheid South Africa, always lurking in the background, striking fear in the heart of any neighbouring country that tried to raise any response to its apartheid policy. There were also other key issues as to how the new national army was to be formed through the amalgamation of former enemies and former rivals, and how to address inter-group and inter-racial relations that everyone expected to be acrimonious. Although considerable goodwill greeted the entrance of the new country into the committee of nations, there was serious apprehension as to how the country would address these new challenges, with many thinking that the new leader's future security strategy would be known through his policy on key security issues.

More than three decades into his administration, the whole world now seems to have seen how President Mugabe handles Zimbabwe's security challenges. Ironically, the verdict seems to be that he did actually start well, extending hands of friendship to all former enemies and former rivals, but ultimately changed, allowing the desire of self-perpetuation in office to take precedence over national interest. This chapter takes a deep look at how Mugabe handled Zimbabwe's security, especially during the period in which he held exclusive control of the country. Specifically, the chapter looks at his management of domestic and regional security.

Handling the immediate security challenge: The establishment of a new national army

Most analysts have identified the establishment of the new national army as one of Mugabe's most important achievements – and there may be some justification for this. Indeed, at the time of independence, it was thought that forming a new national army from the crop of guerrillas and the former Rhodesian army would be a difficult task. Quite rightly, Mugabe was able to identify the British government as the best candidate for the assignment, and this was effectively handled, despite a few hiccups. However, a close look at the way Mugabe went about establishing the new national army revealed a number of things: first, throughout the period under study, the Zimbabwean defence and security institutions found the distinction between "regime" security and "national" security severely blurred. This is possibly because the nature of the war of liberation and the close link that existed among guerrillas during the war made the separation of the "military" from the "political" particularly difficult. Many of those in the military remained active political players and vice versa. Second, and consequent of the first, the Zimbabwean defence institutions were the greatest tool subsequently used by Mugabe to ensure his effective hold on power. Finally, some of the key security issues that became particularly important in Zimbabwe, like the controversies surrounding the activities of the "war veterans" and the use of the defence forces to address domestic security issues, all emerged because of the ways the Mugabe government managed the politics of the defence and security forces.

In the process of forming the new national army, the Mugabe administration made a number of concessions to its former "enemies" (the Rhodesian Forces) and its former "rivals" (Zimbabwe People's Revolutionary Army (ZIPRA)). With the Rhodesian security forces, the administration invited Lieutenant-General Peter Walls, Commander of the Rhodesian Army, to remain as Army Commander of the new Zimbabwean National Army (ZNA). It also allowed former members of the Rhodesian security forces who wanted to remain in the army to retain their old ranks, despite the fact that many of them allegedly gave themselves accelerated promotions shortly before independence. For ZIPRA, the government ensured some form of parity among the first set of Zimbabwean officers appointed in the country. Rex Nhongo (later to become Solomon Mujuru) and Lookout Masuku, former heads of the Zimbabwe African National Liberation Army (ZANLA) and ZIPRA respectively, were made Lieutenant Generals. Their deputies, Josiah Tungamirai and Jevan Maseko became Major Generals. This created a sort of parity between ZANLA and ZIPRA at the apex of the ZNA.

However, a close look at these decisions shows that they were more pragmatic than they were indicative of openness and fairness in the way the government intended to run the security forces. For example, when viewed very closely, the government had no choice but to make concessions to the Rhodesian Forces. First, the new army was to be woven around conventional soldiery, an area in which Mugabe's ZANLA guerrillas were largely inexperienced. This made it imperative for the new administration to put aside any historical differences. Second, all the structures to be used for the new national army belonged to the Rhodesian Forces, an advantage the government could not ignore. Third, it could have been suspected that giving some form of recognition to the Rhodesian Forces would discourage its members from undertaking sabotage activities on the installations around which the new national army was to be built.

The concessions granted to ZIPRA can also be explained on the grounds that the force, though numerically smaller than ZANLA, was more experienced in conventional soldiery. The Mugabe administration may have felt it advisable to have on board a guerrilla force with some knowledge of conventional soldiery, thus preventing a situation that would make the new army completely beholden to the former Rhodesian Army. Secondly, Mugabe would not want to give any indication that he was willing to ditch the Zimbabwe African People's Union (ZAPU) so soon, especially as many African countries considered the decision to fight the election separately as not being in the spirit of the efforts that led to the formation of the Patriotic Front. It is important to point out that many of these countries were giving particular attention to how the Mugabe government would address the formation of the army, regarding this as an indication of how well the administration was willing to accommodate ZAPU.

The first set of military appointments also exhibited considerations that reflected the strategy of Mugabe to hold on to control of the military. Mugabe needed Walls to stabilise the situation, especially amid rumours of a military coup being planned to overthrow his government. The rumours were taken seriously by Mugabe and became a major factor in his thinking as he prepared to assume office. It was even believed that he appealed to the British government to allow Lord Soames stay on for an extra year, to dissuade possible coup plotters.[2] Although there could have been those who wanted to plot a coup, at least two factors would have made this unattractive. First was the resounding nature of the Zimbabwe African National Union Patriotic Front's (ZANU-PF) political victory at the election, which showed clearly that the party had enormous popularity in the country, a condition that was enough to dissuade any forceful removal. The second was the nature and extent of international involvement in the elections, and the immediate recognition that was given to the new government by external actors.

Despite the concessions granted to both the Rhodesian Army and the former ZIPRA, some of the early policies adopted by the Mugabe administration showed signs that the new prime minister was determined to hold tight to issues concerning the country's defence forces. For example, before the integration of forces commenced, the government disbanded some segments of the Rhodesian security forces which it considered unacceptable. Among them were the Selous Scouts, the Auxiliary and the Guard Force. In addition to disbanding ad hoc units of the Rhodesian Army, the administration did not extend the parity between ZANLA and ZIPRA beyond the rank of General. Of the eight new Brigadiers, ZANLA had five; and it had 11 of the 17 new Colonels.[3]

The formation and early development of the national army suffered a number of political hiccups, three of which are of particular importance. The first was the discovery of arms caches at several locations in the country. These caches, widely believed to have been made by ZAPU, affected the trust between ZANU and ZAPU, resulting in the removal of key ZIPRA leaders from the Joint High Command (JHC), especially Lookout Masuku and Dumiso Dabengwa.[4] From this moment, Mugabe's grip of the national army was out in the open and no longer assumed a façade. The second political hiccup in the army establishment process involved a number of armed clashes between ZANLA and ZIPRA during the integration exercise in Entumbane.[5] The clashes were so profound that the government had to rely on former members of the Rhodesian Security Force and flying war planes, to bring them under control. Apart from the resulting destruction, what was particularly disturbing from a military integration point of view was that some of the units that clashed were those already integrated, and as such expected to show signs of harmony and camaraderie.

Another early development that reflected the determination of the Mugabe administration to act outside the box in managing the national army, manifested in the role of external actors in its establishment and early developments. Again, while it was widely believed from the onset that only the British Military Advisory and Training Team (BMATT) would take charge of the integration of the new national army, the Mugabe administration found ways of diluting the monopoly of the British by bringing in soldiers from North Korea and China, former supporters from the liberation war era. Of the two countries, however, the relationship with North Korea was the more controversial. The reason for the controversy, as will be discussed later, did not concern the training team itself, although this too was significant, but largely involved the activities of the brigade they trained.

While the integration exercise was taking place, a major problem emerged in the relationship between the Mugabe administration and Lieutenant-General Peter Walls. This led to the latter's dismissal as chairman of the JHC and his expulsion from Zimbabwe. The Walls crisis had two major effects on the integration exercise. The first was that it contributed to the mass exodus of white officers (over 250 resigned) from the army, most of whom migrated to South Africa, while the second left the question of how to fill Walls' seat as the chairman of the JHC. Alan Page, the Secretary of Defence, became acting chairman for some time, before Emmerson Mnangagwa, Minister of State for Defence in the Prime Minister's Office, took over the post and saw the reorganisation of the military to its conclusion.

The handling of the demobilisation exercise in Zimbabwe created considerable dissatisfaction, largely because expectations could not be met and temporary alliances that had existed between the guerrillas and the party leadership could no longer be sustained. The manner in which Zimbabwe went about its demobilisation exercise was crucial to a number of subsequent security developments in the country, evidenced in the activities of the "war veterans". The first thing the government did in terms of facilitating voluntary demobilisation, was to announce what it called a "demobilisation package". This was a programme of assistance comprising four main elements: further education, technical training, business advice and a demobilisation allowance.

Further education was meant for those who had not completed their education, especially those below secondary school level, and others who would like to continue with the studies they abandoned for the liberation cause. This free education programme was in addition to other opportunities.

The technical training aspect of the package was designed for those interested in starting a new career upon leaving the armed forces. A number of technical colleges were established to provide crash programmes for ex-soldiers. Some former guerrillas undertook automotive engineering, welding, and other technical and commercial courses; some attended teacher training courses; and others were trained as nurses and medical assistants. Special centres were set up to train former soldiers as customs and immigration officers.

The third element of the demobilisation package dealt with advising and assisting discharging soldiers, especially those seeking employment or wishing to be self-employed. This was offered regardless of whether they had benefited from the education and training programmes. Soldiers were encouraged to pool their earnings into co-operatives, to enable them embark upon small-scale ventures by themselves.

The final element was the granting of a demobilisation allowance, which was regarded as the most attractive component of the entire demobilisation package. All soldiers who opted for voluntary demobilisation were promised a monthly allowance of Z$185 (about US$150 at the time) for two years. This was sufficient to keep many of the unmarried guerrillas gliding on an euphoric cloud for some time, and why the government thought many of them would be encouraged to demobilise. Each soldier leaving the army under the demobilisation programme was entitled to the demobilisation allowance, regardless of whether he had taken advantage of the education, training or other parts of the package. Despite all these attractive features, the government's programme of encouraging voluntary demobilisation did not achieve much success as many ex-combatants were unwilling to risk certainty for uncertainty.[6]

Of all the aspects of the post-independence military reorganisation in Zimbabwe, the demobilisation exercise and the treatment accorded to former guerrillas opened the government to justifiable criticism. The complaints arising from the demobilisation exercise were complex and multi-dimensional. For a start, many ex-ZIPRA guerrillas argued that they suffered more than their ZANLA counterparts, and that they were more involuntarily demobilised than former ZANLAs. Statistically, more ZANLA troops were demobilised, but this may not highlight the full picture as there were more ZANLA troops than ZIPRAs. When one considers proportional representation, ex-ZIPRAs appeared more affected than ZANLAs – a situation that caused fundamental disaffection in subsequent years. The second set of complaints came from everyone who was demobilised, irrespective of the side they belonged to. Many complained about their demobilisation payment, which they said was either inadequate or not paid at all. Many also complained about the treatment they received regarding their plans to return to civilian life. The complaint that the demobilisation payment was inadequate rested on the argument that the extended family system invariably brought huge responsibilities, which the amount could not sufficiently address. Thus, many ex-combatants wanted the allowance increased and the two-year duration extended. Although some people did not receive their demobilisation money, the former Chief of Army Staff, Major-General Zvinavashe, claimed that most in this category did not complete the necessary forms,[7] and that there was therefore no way for the government to know that they existed. Nevertheless, it is equally fair to add that, after the affected people had regularised their demobilisation papers, it took quite a while before things were put in order.

The way ex-combatants were treated in their desire to return to civilian life has been one of the most controversial issues in post-independence Zimbabwe, with many Zimbabweans arguing that the government signed them off from the military without doing much to integrate them back into the society. Most of the efforts the government made in this regard were either inadequate or completely ineffective. Finding a home in neither a civilian nor a military community made things extremely difficult for many ex-combatants.

From the time of independence, Mugabe made it clear that he would maintain an effective grip on all affairs relating to national security. The first indication of this was that there was no substantive Minister of Defence and Mugabe combined the position with his role as prime minister. A trusted and loyal lieutenant, Emmerson Mnangagwa was made Deputy Minister of National Security.[8] With this appointment, Mugabe was well situated to oversee all security decisions in the country. Although in theory the Constitution is supposed to handle all issues relating to defence – with parliament having major roles to play in key issues such as organisation, administration, discipline and budgeting – the situation in Zimbabwe, as indeed, in many African states, highlights a major gap between these ideals and reality.

Two crucial questions have attracted concern since the establishment of the Zimbabwean Defence Forces (ZDF). First is the extent to which there remains typologies of behaviour, which parallel the divisions of the past; and second is the extent to which the force has stayed out of local politics. Although, to a large extent, most of the ZIPRA–ZANLA divisions have been eliminated, especially as the pool of those who joined from the war of liberation is fast dwindling, some of those in service still argue that residues of this division remain. Some ex-ZIPRA guerrillas in the army still argue that they are sometimes discriminated against in granting promotions, and that the allocation of responsibilities during external military engagements has never been to their advantage. While divisions along the pre-independence divide may be reducing, others have emerged between senior officers and the rank and file, especially after 1998, when access to and distribution of the "proceeds" from Zimbabwe's involvement in the war in the Democratic Republic of the Congo (DRC) further widened the gap. Since 1993, the pay and living conditions for the military have deteriorated, and up to 40% of personnel live outside barracks because of a lack of proper accommodation. The salaries of all security forces were doubled at the beginning of 2002, but many interpreted this gesture as an attempt by the government to buy the loyalty of the military because of the then impending elections.

Right from its formation, the extent to which the ZDF could be effectively kept out of politics was a crucial issue. Because of the peculiarity of its formation and the historical links between politicians and the military during the struggle for independence, the activities of the defence forces have always been influenced by politicians. Indeed, as far back as 1990, Major-General Zvinavashe, confirmed that it would not be possible for Zimbabwe to have a completely apolitical army until all those who shared the "bush" experience had completely disappeared from the political and military scene.[9]

The reality of this became visible when political opposition against President Mugabe and the ruling party, especially from the MDC, resulted in the military leadership declaring that it would not recognise, respect, or even salute any president that had not shared the war of liberation experience with them. This declaration was made by Major-General Zvinavashe in January 2002, and, possibly to give the effect of consensus of this decision among the security forces, he made the declaration in the company of the commanders of the army, air force, prisons and the much-dreaded Chief of the Central Intelligence Agency. All of these individuals were comrades-in-arms of Mugabe, and their stance was a clear message to the leader of the opposition Movement for Democratic Change (MDC), Morgan Tsvangirai, who spent his younger days furthering his studies and did not join the liberation struggle. A central issue that has continued to plague the security dynamics in Zimbabwe is how the armed forces have been used to advance the political agenda of Mugabe and ZANU-PF.

From the time the Unity Accord was signed in 1987, uniting ZANU and ZAPU, the process of "Zanuisation" of the national army began in earnest. Former ZIPRA elements in the army realised the futility of launching any opposition, especially as those they could have looked to for encouragement, such as Dumiso Dabengwa, seemed to have been browbeaten into conformity and had joined the government. Even after the signing of the Unity Accord, preferential treatment for former ZANLA guerrillas in the national army allegedly continued on issues relating to appointment and promotion. This, however, reduced over time, especially as new recruits were enlisted into the army. For example, all the commanding officers after the Unity Accord were former ZANLA combatants, and as old ZANLA officers retired from the army they were replaced by equally trusted ZANLA officers. A major example was the retirement of Josiah Tungamirai, an officer considered by many as very professional, from the leadership of the air force. He was replaced by Perence Shiri, who headed the Fifth Brigade operating in Matabeleland. With this appointment, the leadership of the army and the air force fell into the hands of trusted allies of Mugabe, and this was to remain the case throughout much of this controversial period of Zimbabwe's political history.

After the effective removal of ZAPU as a political force, the Mugabe administration effectively tightened its grip on the army. The first opposition party that emerged after the eclipse of ZAPU, the Zimbabwe Unity Movement (ZUM) under the leadership of Edgar Tekere, did not have much political clout, and the government did not have to consider the possibility of unleashing the military might of the State on the organisation. Indeed, the influence of Tekere and his party did not spread beyond Manicaland and some local support from Mutare. There was also no external sympathy for the party. Consequently, it was easy for the government to dismiss it as being of mere entertainment value that did not justify using the considerable force of the military. The fact that Tekere had been a member of the ruling party also meant that caution would be exercised in deciding to use force against him.

There has been considerable academic interest in the politicisation of the army. According to Knox Chitiyo, this seems to have come in three phases.[10] The first may be said to have started with the Entumbane riots, up to around 1998. This was the first major development that reminded members of the national army of old allegiances, and inculcated into their thinking the old divisions. The second phase started around 1998 with the deployment of the ZNA to the DRC. The deployment generated considerable public debate and the armed forces openly discussed the pros and cons of the engagement. Indeed, there were sections of the armed forces that openly expressed disaffection at the engagement. To address this, the government embarked on the process of reassessing loyalty within the military. A number of people considered vocal in their opposition were quietly removed from the army, while senior officers were "bought" with juicy contracts in the DRC. During this period, the first set of anti-government officers were removed from the military. The third phase came after 2000. This time, the government tried to get the armed forces into all segments of society, and virtually all boards and parastatals in the country had retired or serving members of the armed forces on their board.

When the MDC emerged to offer a major challenge to the Mugabe administration, the government saw the need to unleash the security institutions on the opposition. There were indeed cases where the top echelons of the armed forces openly declared that the army would not accept any person other than Mugabe as their commander-in-chief. Specifically, army top-brass told its rank and file that they were not allowed to join the opposition party.

The role of the armed forces in advancing the interest of the Mugabe administration has been widely recorded. There is really no doubt that the security apparatus was used to intimidate those opposed to the Mugabe administration. Paramilitary forces like prison services joined in the suppression, which also included the intelligence services. So profound was the extent of the extent of the abuse of the security apparatus that the Global Political Agreement (GPA) that brought in a Government of National Unity (GNU) in 2009 specifically recommended the need for security sector reform. This was, however, later rejected by ZANU-PF at its congress in December 2009, when it declared that "ZANU-PF as the party of revolution and the people's vanguard shall not allow the security forces to be the subject of any negotiation for a so-called security sector reform [because] the security forces are a product of the national liberation struggle".[11]

In looking at the evolution of Zimbabwe's security forces and the way Mugabe has used these institutions, a number of things are noticeable. First, Mugabe ensured that all the key institutions were held by trusted and loyal hands – mostly those who shared the war of liberation experience with him. Very rarely does Mugabe remove the old brass in the hierarchy of these institutions, ensuring that they are well looked after and that minor misdemeanours are overlooked if these do not threaten his hold on power. These key individuals thus ensured that those promoted to seniors positions, even if they did not share the war of liberation experience, were loyal and trusted officers. With this, the loyalty of the security institutions to Mugabe has always been guaranteed. Second, Mugabe has always ensured that the balance of the command structure has tilted in favour of former ZANLA guerrillas. This was a strategy adopted from the commencement of the integration exercise. When Mugabe realised that some form of parity should be attained between former ZANLAs and ZIPRAs in the command structure of the military, the strategy was constructed in such a way that a strong ZANLA officer was made the head and a weak Ndebele, close to retirement, was made the deputy. In this way, former ZANLA officers' hold on the defence institutions has remained a constant feature of the Mugabe presidency. Third, throughout the period, Mugabe held complete control of the affairs of Zimbabwe. A constant issue in the management of the armed forces is the subtle rivalry between the Karanga sub-ethnic group of the Shona (where key officers come from) and other sub-ethnic groups of Shona. Consequently, Mugabe has spent much time balancing the politics and intrigues that exist between these two sub-ethnic components. Finally, Mugabe has always ensured that senior officers in the armed forces have unrestricted access to wealth and opportunities, which has reinforced their loyalty to him.

On the whole, Zimbabwean defence institutions have been at the centre of the politics and diplomacy of security in the country. What this chapter has done thus far is place the establishment and early development of the defence forces within the wider framework of Mugabe's self-perpetuation agenda. As the years passed, and as the political situation in the country assumed diverse and more complex ramifications, the activities of the defence forces assumed more controversial dimensions. Nowhere has this been more profound than in the affairs surrounding domestic politics, which will constitute the focus of discussion in the next section.

Managing domestic security

Domestic security has been one of the most controversial issues in post-independence Zimbabwe. Since independence, a number of key issues have emerged and Mugabe's handling of them has been quite important. Some of these are listed below.

Meeting the immediate security legacies of the war of liberation

Against the background of the war of liberation that preceded Zimbabwe's independence, there were, at the time of independence, a number of firearms in the possession of unauthorised holders. Addressing this was an issue of immediate concern. The Zimbabwean parliament passed the Firearms Recovery Act, under which the government gave a general amnesty to all holders of unlicensed arms who handed them over to the government within five months, after which it became an offence to hold on to the arms illegally. The minimum penalty for the offence was five years imprisonment.[12] All licenses issued by the previous administration were revoked, and those who possessed weapons under this relaxed arrangement were ordered to submit their weapons and re-apply for new licenses. The law was widely publicised, with posters and pamphlets distributed in Shona, Sindebele (the language of the Ndebele people) and English. The Ministry of Home Affairs liaised with the Ministry of Information to give the law publicity through the Zimbabwean Broadcasting Corporation. Although there were mild controversies, especially with the issue of the mandatory five-year jail term for contravention of the Act, the majority of the population regarded the promulgation of the law as justified.

Other major security legislations were enacted to address the consequences of the war of liberation. The most striking thing about security legislation during the early years of post-independence Zimbabwe, was the retention of some of the laws that had sustained Ian Smith's minority regime. It is ironic that the new government retained some of the laws against which arms were taken up in the first place. This may not be as much of a contradiction in principle as it appears on the surface. The tense situation that emerged after the war was such that it became necessary for the government to promulgate certain laws to meet exigencies. However, the extent to which the laws could be said to have been appropriately or judiciously applied, depended largely on individual perception. Immediately after independence, the government sought an "emergency power" regulation from parliament that would place the country in a State of Emergency and, simultaneously, enable the government to enact legislation unilaterally. These regulations first manifested in the country's politics in 1965, introduced by Ian Smith as part of the efforts to get over the challenges confronting the Unilateral Declaration of Independence (UDI). They remained in force throughout the 13 years of the UDI and during the short period of Abel Muzorewa's administration.

The arms cache controversy

The arms cache controversy has remained a major security issue in post-independence Zimbabwe. While the government was contending with the recovery of firearms in the immediate post-independence setting, secret arms caches were discovered in areas of Bulawayo. This discovery, which was first announced in February 1982, was one of the most controversial domestic security issues in Zimbabwe. In the first place, it led to the dismissal of Joshua Nkomo from Mugabe's administration and a breakdown in Zimbabwe's coalition government. It also marked the beginning of a chain of security problems, which engulfed the entire country, and subsequently brought Zimbabwe back into the limelight of international attention. Arms caches were discovered on two sites: Ascot farm near Bulawayo, and Hampton Ranch in the Midlands, not far from Gweru. Both sites were owned by a private company, Nitram, which Nkomo had helped to set up shortly after independence.[13]

The discovery was interpreted as an attempt by ZAPU to overthrow the government, and it was alleged that the party had established links with the South African government in the perceived plot. Peter Walls, then living in South Africa after his expulsion from Zimbabwe, was said to have participated in this attempt to overthrow the Mugabe administration. This was denied emphatically by Walls[14] and the government produced nothing to support the allegation. The first step the government took was to expel Nkomo and a number of ZAPU ministers from their public positions. Those affected by the expulsion were: Nkomo; Minister of Transport and Vice-President of ZAPU, Josiah Chinamano; Minister of National Resources and Water Development, and Secretary General of ZAPU, Joseph Msika; and Deputy Minister of Mines, Jim Mtuta. Two weeks after the expulsion, Lookout Masuku, former ZIPRA commander, and Dumiso Dabengwa, former ZIPRA chief of security, were also arrested and detained. All property and companies owned by ZAPU were confiscated by the government, irrespective of whether arms were found on them or not.[15] It was further alleged that the arrested ZIPRA leaders had been recruiting guerrillas for secret training in South Africa, and had been in contact with the Soviet Union's KGB to plan against the government. When the case was heard in court, two ZIPRA officials were ordered to be released for lack of evidence, but immediately re-detained under the emergency power law.[16]

There are two main theories about the arms cache crisis. The first, prevalent among ZANU members, was that the discovery genuinely surprised Mugabe and ZANU, undermining whatever trust they might have had in Nkomo. The caches were interpreted as proof that Nkomo's ZAPU was bent on launching a coup sometime in the future. The second theory was that the existence of the arms caches had been widely speculated,[17] and thus should not have been a surprise to the ZANU leadership. However, ZANU simply decided that the time was ripe for Nkomo to be thrown out of government in order to consolidate ZANU power and force the pace of "Zanuisation" of the country, leading eventually to a *de facto* one-party state. This, as one would expect, was ZAPU's position.[18] Just as the arms cache crisis had its antecedent in the armed clashes, similarly it had an extension in one of the most controversial events in post-independence Zimbabwe: the unrest that engulfed Matabeleland for five years from 1982 to1987.

The Matabeleland unrest

What came to be known as the Matabeleland unrest was a set of civil disturbances and tension that engulfed the Matabeleland province of Zimbabwe – the province occupied by Sindebele-speaking people, the smaller of the two major ethnic groups in the country – between 1982 and 1987. During this period, the "dissidents" – an amorphous amalgam of disaffected ex-combatants, disillusioned radicals and common criminals – waged a campaign of killing, terrorism and economic sabotage to undermine the government of Robert Mugabe.[19] The government reacted in various ways that were not only controversial, but also created more problems than they attempted to solve. The Matabeleland unrest occupies a unique place in the history of post-independence Zimbabwean security because it highlights, more than any other defence legacy of the war of liberation, the major politico-military variables that emerged during the birth of Zimbabwe.

The prevailing economic and social conditions lent another important background to the crisis: the expectations of independence gradually began to appear unfulfilled, not so much because the government was not trying to fulfil these expectations, but because most of the people had a misleading concept of what independence meant, and thus felt dissatisfied with the pace of developments. Economic hardship was more prevalent in Matabeleland, which was defectively affected by racial land distribution during the minority regime. Apart from the land factor, other non-agricultural sectors did not fare any better. Although there had been considerable increases in the wages of Zimbabweans, the cost of living had also gone up. This was particularly significant as some of those who took part in the dissident operation did so for economic reasons.

However, what provided the most important background to the Matabeleland crisis was the situation in the military between the period of independence and the take-off of dissidence in 1982. Many former ZIPRA officers objected to the administration of the army and had a strong urge to do something to rectify the situation. The second Entumbane crisis turned out to be a major turning point in this regard. It resulted in the first *en masse* desertion of ex-ZIPRA combatants from the new National Army and it revealed to those ex-ZIPRA combatants who chose to remain in the army the dangers and consequences of any attempt to seek redress through revolt.[20] Thus, at the time the Matabeleland unrest began, there were pent-up emotions waiting to erupt.

What triggered the actual unrest was the discovery of the arms cache and the punishment meted out by the government in response. When the arms cache issue first came up, the general opinion in Matabeleland went along predictable lines. As noted earlier, many Ndebele people believed that both ZANLA and ZIPRA had hidden arms, and that the government's claim that only ZIPRA caches were "discovered" was a clear pretext for getting rid of Nkomo. Many further argued that, despite the "discovery", the real onus rested on the government to prove that there was actually a plot to overthrow Mugabe.[21]

When the government dismissed Nkomo and others, many Ndebele people, both within and outside the army, interpreted it as a clear indication that they were being schemed out of government. These fears appeared to be confirmed when Masuku and Dabengwa were detained. The expulsion of Nkomo, Chinamano, Msika and Mtuta was seen as a move to deprive them of proper representation in government, while the detention of Masuku robbed them of their main voice in the military. As indicated earlier, some of those who stayed behind after Entumbane largely did so because of the respect and admiration they had for Nkomo, Masuku and Dabengwa.

However, what seemed to affect the ex-ZIPRA guerrillas most was the confiscation and freezing of accounts of ZAPU companies. In fact, any attempt to consider the Matabeleland unrest must give special attention to this issue. Many ex-ZIPRA guerrillas had invested in some of these companies, especially Nitram, while others who opted for demobilisation worked on ZAPU-funded farms after investing their demobilisation gratuities in business ventures. Government's confiscation meant a loss of investment for those who had shares in these companies, and a loss of investment and/or jobs for ex-guerrillas working on the farms. Many argued that confiscation of properties across the board (running into dozens) was unjustified, especially as arms were discovered on only two of them. Their disenchantment prompted mass desertion from the army, which was deemed the most appropriate way of expressing their opposition to government. The Entumbane experience, during which many ZIPRA soldiers were killed, had taught them the dangers and consequences of any attempt at revolt from within the army; and since the dismissals and detentions that followed the discovery of the arms caches provided a disenchanted operational base, many ZIPRA soldiers deserted the army and joined the dissidents. By June 1982, the number of deserters was put at 2 700, and by August, it had increased to about 4 300.[22]

Disturbances began in the early months of 1982.[23] The dissidents embarked on an extensive campaign of murder, mutilation, kidnapping and other acts of terrorism. Although there is little doubt that the unrest was started by ex-ZIPRA troops, other groups later joined in the mayhem. The dissidents fell into three categories: ex-ZIPRA, who took to dissident activities for the abovementioned reasons; the South African-sponsored "Super ZAPU", believed to comprise mostly Muzorewa's disbanded auxiliary force; and common bandits for whom the new order was an asperity, either because they expected too much from independence and believed that the government was not doing enough, or because their social attitude simply motivated such tendencies.[24] However, it is interesting to note that these groups of dissidents did not work together – a fact that could be attributed to their lack of common purpose. In fact, the ex-ZIPRAs and the "Super ZAPU" were occasionally engulfed in skirmishes when they met in the bush.[25]

After intense negotiations, the Zimbabwe National Unity Accord was signed between ZANU and ZAPU in December 1987.[26] The main outcome of the Accord was the merging of the two political parties, which led to ZAPU's re-admittance into the corridors of power. Another important element of the Accord was the granting of amnesty to all dissidents in the bush, provided they gave themselves up within a stipulated period.[27] Interestingly, all that the Unity Accord offered over the dissident issue had been proposed more than four years earlier in parliament. Senator Oatt of the Rhodesian Front (RF) had made a speech to this effect on 15 March 1983, suggesting the need to set up an impartial Commission of Inquiry, in addition to the withdrawal of the Fifth Brigade from Matabeleland, the reincorporation of ZAPU into government, and the granting of amnesty to dissidents.[28] All these suggestions, which attracted unfavourable interjections during the speech, were adopted by the government four years later.[29]

The Unity Accord eventually solved the dissident problem. The amnesty was accepted by about 135 dissidents who came out of hiding, and it was astonishing to discover that it was only this number that had brought untold hardship to the country for more than five years. Another source of surprise was the relatively organised command structure among the dissidents, a far cry from the disorganised gang of bandits the government and many others had expected. As part of the amnesty deal, Mugabe (who had become president) freed 75 members of the security force serving jail terms for murder. The dissidents who had killed missionaries in Esigodoni were also freed unconditionally.[30] However, the release of these people raised considerable criticism as many felt they needed psychiatric treatment before they were released back into society. Thus, unlike the post-civil war situation in Nigeria, and more like the amnesty offer for RENAMO dissidents in Mozambique, general amnesty in Zimbabwe meant general amnesia.

"War veterans" and the land "invasion" controversy

Undoubtedly the most important domestic security issue faced by the Mugabe administration was the controversy surrounding land invasion by "war veterans".[31] Three phases of the controversy can be identified: first was the period immediately after independence, when concern was more on how to obtain enough land for blacks from the white minority, both to ensure equitable distribution and to satisfy the aspiration of blacks who equated the armed struggle with land redistribution.[32] The second phase came after the government had acquired some land from whites, and concern shifted to how it would ensure equitable redistribution among the population; while the third phase came when political opposition to the Mugabe administration brought the land issue to the forefront of national political debate.

At the core of this Zimbabwean controversy are three main actors: government, white commercial farmers, and the local population. Despite ephemeral alliances, which sometimes bring segments of these groups together, in reality there has been no love lost between them. During the first phase, the battle line was drawn mainly between white commercial farmers and the government, with the local population supporting the government. The main issue during this phase was how much land whites were willing to give up and how they were to be compensated for it. The government rejected any claim for compensation on the grounds that a country coming out of the throes of war could not afford to pay the huge compensation demanded by white landowners. An undeclared position though, was the belief in many government circles that the initial acquisition of land by whites was illegal, and as such there were no moral grounds to discuss compensation. On the contrary, however, the position of white commercial farmers – one that was shared by foreign governments and international financial institutions – was that the law of property rights applied to commercial farm land, and that market-value compensation had to be paid in the event of acquisition. The local population did not see land strictly according to the economic perception of either the government or white farmers, but their inclination to get more land forced them to support the government.

The second phase came in the early 1990s. It should be noted that, by 1990, the constraints of the Lancaster House Agreement (LHA) expired and were soon followed by the Land Acquisition Act (LAA) of 1992. This, in theory, gave government the right to compulsorily acquire land for redistribution and resettlement. Despite this, the process of land redistribution was slow and minimal. By 1997, when the first phase of the land reform and resettlement programme ended, the government had only resettled 71 000 families out of the targeted 162 000 on almost 3.5 million hectares of land. Of these, only 19% was classified as prime land, the rest being either marginal or completely unsuitable for grazing or cultivation. By 1999, 11 million hectares of the richest land were still owned by about 4 500 commercial farmers.[33] Dissatisfaction among black Zimbabweans at the speed with which the government was tackling the issue of land redistribution, brought land to the forefront of public interest, forcing the government to promulgate the LAA. The government's argument for effecting this promulgation was that a law was needed to disentangle it from the legal encumbrances that made land redistribution difficult. While this was in itself controversial, as some saw it as an attempt to forcefully recover land from whites, greater controversy came when it was realised that the land acquired was allegedly distributed among senior members of the ruling ZANU party, cabinet ministers and others close to Mugabe.[34] This increasing concern over land came at a time when domestic opposition against Mugabe was rising, particularly because of the depreciation of the Zimbabwean economy. The land problem also fed on (and into) other aspects of domestic politics. After 1993, black Zimbabweans began to revise their views about the government's land policy as white farmers and political opponents of Mugabe began an informal alliance that was to develop later in the land saga.

In February 2000, land politics in Zimbabwe reached another phase when the ruling ZANU-PF lost a national referendum.[35] Although the referendum was on constitutional reform, land issues played an important part in the government's campaign and the subsequent outcome. The government based its campaign for a "Yes" vote for constitutional reform on the need to acquire more power to complete its land reform. It claimed that it intended to acquire approximately five million hectares of the 12 million then held by whites.[36] However, the opposition argued that the referendum was a political ploy by government to divert attention from the country's political situation, and that the process was being managed by a government department whose competence and independence were widely questioned.[37] The opposition further argued that the clause "was bad in law and calculated to sabotage [the] country's economic prospects".[38] The referendum brought together an unlikely alliance: white farmers and radical black politicians, united in their opposition to Mugabe remaining in power. The outcome was a defeat of the government – the first in 20 years. With this, Mugabe and the ruling ZANU-PF realised that the parliamentary elections, which were three months away, could not be taken for granted. As a result, from the moment of the electoral defeat, the government brought the land issue more fully into politics.

In a way, the emergence of "war veteran" activities can be traced to the dichotomy between politicians and the military. It is now believed that what propelled the veterans was an implicit indictment levelled against politicians by a serving military officer, Gibson Mashingaidze, then a brigadier in the ZNA. At the funeral of popular war veteran, Mukoma Musa, Mashingaidze said politicians were corrupting themselves while veterans who fought the war suffered. He specifically said that ZANU-PF had forgotten them.

An unprecedented turn came on 26 February 2000, when a group of people describing themselves as "war veterans" began seizing white farms. Although they had been active in Zimbabwe before the referendum, and had indeed been campaigning for land reform,[39] the increase in their activities and the level of violence after the defeat of the government in the referendum were viewed by many as a ploy by Mugabe to intimidate the opposition ahead of the May 2000 elections. It was also seen as a means of breaking the alliance between the opposition MDC and white farmers. Mugabe gave open support to the takeover of farms, even after the country's High Court declared the occupation illegal.[40] By the end of March 2000, the situation was such that many believed Zimbabwe to be on the road to anarchy. On 6 April 2000, the first white farmer in the spate of controversy gave up his land and immigrated to Australia,[41] and on 15 April the first white farmer casualty occurred. By the end of May 2000, the government had produced a list of 804 farms to be seized without compensation.[42] The situation continued to deepen racial tensions within the country, and the consequent food crisis further compounded the unstable political situation. Although Mugabe conceded in May 2004 that some mistakes had been made in the land controversy,[43] he maintained that he had no regrets.

Understanding the events in Zimbabwe between March and April 2000 is a difficult task. It was alleged that government and army trucks were used to transport "war veterans" to white farms, and that government kept the veterans supplied with food while they were on the farms.[44] Having lost the referendum, Mugabe's and his party's cloak of invincibility seemed to disappear, placing future elections in a precarious position. The takeover of the farms was almost certainly designed to intimidate white farmers and browbeat them into conformity. It was also clear that most of those who took part in the farm seizures and intimidation were not actual "war veterans", as many of them were too young to have participated in a war that had ended 20 years before.[45] Obviously included in the group were party thugs loyal to Mugabe and ZANU-PF. Even the credentials of the leader of the group, Chenjerai Hunzvi, were questioned, as it was revealed that he did not fight in the war of liberation.[46]

There was also an irony to the entire controversy as Mugabe, who later became the champion of the landless, had been forced a few years earlier to act on the land issue. Indeed, there were those who opposed Mugabe politically, but nevertheless supported the forceful occupation of land.[47] Many black Zimbabweans wanted land and few were interested in how land redistribution would come about. In many parts of the country, land occupation was described as *Chimurenga* 3.[48] The intimidation carried out against whites also had racial undertones. The frustration felt by black Zimbabweans at the racist behaviour of some of white farmers cannot be ignored. While some whites were kind and considerate to their black staff, there were those who grossly maltreated them, considering their employees no better than hired chattels. Consequently, it is believed that the resistance by some black workers was not to save their white employers, but to ensure, in the eventuality of the exit of white farmers from the country, the land would not go to "war veterans". By early 2003, another distinct phase seemed to have emerged in the Zimbabwean land saga, with Zimbabwean elites, especially those close to Mugabe, allegedly driving landless black Zimbabweans away from the lands they occupied.[49]

The land controversy in Zimbabwe shows the problems that arise from the accumulative effects of defective natural-resource governance. The structure inherited by the country at independence was unsustainable because of its glaring racial imbalance, but attempts by the Mugabe administration to create new structures were also sectional, defective and unhelpful. The outcome was the general confusion that has characterised the country's land sector. Nevertheless, beyond all the media euphoria, the Zimbabwean land crisis raises four important themes: first is the nature and extent to which resource conflicts can be exploited by the incumbent administration for political advantage; second is the extent to which resource conflicts in Africa can attract western political interest, even at short notice; third is the impact resource conflicts could have on socio-economic and political developments in a country; and fourth is the consequences such conflicts can have on regional stability.

Faced with serious economic difficulties, Zimbabwe began to modify its position by mid-2005. Indeed, government officials like vice-presidents Joseph Msika and Joice Mujuru pointed out that the war against white farmers was over, and that farmland was to be given to farmers on a 99-year lease. Indeed, the Governor of the Reserve Bank, Gideon Gono, added that white farmers would be provided with guarantees of uninterrupted tenure backed by government security forces.[50]

Land politics in Zimbabwe created panic in other countries with similar ethno-racial land arrangements, especially South Africa, Kenya and Namibia. In South Africa, for example, the Rand fell by 3% in the period following the crisis in Zimbabwe. South Africa's land situation, although less controversial, equally had a potentially explosive ramification. Indeed, by mid-2001, some form of land invasion had been attempted in the country.[51] In South Africa, about 60 000 white farmers own more than 200 million acres of land, with 1.2 million black farmers eking out a living on 40 million acres. However, a number of reasons give South Africa some respite, even if temporarily. First, the African National Congress (ANC) government is determined to ensure that the situation is peacefully managed, especially to protect racial harmony in the country and safeguard the investments and foreign respect it has earned since the peaceful transition from apartheid. Second, unlike Zimbabwe, South Africa has other natural-resource endowments, thereby reducing the economic and social pressures on land. Third, international interest in South Africa is such that the country is in a better position to obtain external support to address its economic problems, and provide a cushioning effect on some social problems that can aggravate existing land crises.

The MDC, Mugabe and domestic security

Once the government was able to intimidate ZAPU into signing the Unity Accord and eclipse ZUM, there was no major domestic opposition to ZANU-PF until the MDC arrived on the Zimbabwean political scene. The first hint the government received of the strength of the MDC was the loss of the referendum on land reform held in 2000. The MDC campaigned with the white minority party against the government and won. This alliance revealed to the Mugabe government the dangers that could come from the alliance of the white opposition and the MDC, and from that moment, the government decided to do everything to break the growing power of the MDC.

The Mugabe administration adopted a two-pronged method in dealing with the MDC challenge. The first was to intimidate the party and its leadership. This was the most pronounced method used by the administration. Tsvangirai was physically assaulted and imprisoned a number of times, as were many others of the party leadership. The second strategy was to infiltrate the MDC and engage in a divide-and-rule method. This achieved some success as the MDC later broke into two factions, but the break-up did not affect the strength of the opposition that had emerged against Mugabe – one that would be tested during the upcoming elections.

The first election conducted after the formation of the MDC was won by the ruling ZANU-PF amid allegations of brutality against the leadership and membership of the MDC. The alleged irregularities and brutality in the elections were to result in Zimbabwe's suspension from the Commonwealth. The same method was employed in the 2008 elections, where opposition supporters were brutalised and the military made it clear that they would not support the victory of the opposition MDC. It was, indeed, the suppression of opposition supporters that resulted in the withdrawal of the MDC from the run-off conducted after the first election.

Discussions that ultimately resulted in the formation of a national government between ZANU-PF and the MDC were delayed and almost cancelled because of the disagreements between the two parties on control of the security apparatus. Tsvangirai refused the position of prime minister unless he was given control of the ministry of Home Affairs, which controls the police. Already, Mugabe had made it clear that he would maintain control over the national army. Although it was not specifically stated, one of the reasons why the MDC insisted on controlling the police was that it was the strongest institution used to suppress opposition party members. Indeed, just a few weeks before the official commencement of the new government, many key members of the MDC were still being held in custody.[52]

Responding to regional development

Right from Zimbabwe's independence, Mugabe had realised the need to put his relationship with the country's immediate neighbours under close watch. Of all these, the relationship with South Africa has been the most complex. Put broadly, this relationship would seem to have undergone four different phases: Phase one occurred between Zimbabwe's independence in 1980 until the attainment of majority rule in South Africa in 1992; phase two was the period covering the independence of South Africa and Zimbabwe's involvement in the DRC; phase three covered the period of obvious rivalry between the two countries over the DRC; while the fourth phase was one that saw South Africa deeply involved in efforts to address Zimbabwe's domestic political and security challenges.

On its part, the relationship with Zimbabwe seems to have undergone three phases. First was the tactical ambiguity phase, between independence and the signing of the Unity Accord with ZAPU in 1987. During this phase, Mugabe watched Zambia at a respectable distance, largely because of the role the country played in supporting Nkomo during the war of liberation. This was followed by what may be termed the "reconciliatory phase". This came after ZAPU had been incorporated into the GNU and there were no grounds for suspicion of those countries that had supported the party during the liberation war. The third phase may be termed the "openly critical phase", when Zambia joined other countries in criticising Mugabe's domestic policies.

In the case of Botswana, Mugabe's security diplomacy would also seem to have come in three phases. The first was when both sides suspected each other and the relationship was cold. At independence, as was the case with its relations with Zambia, the attitude of Harare towards Botswana was not as warm as that with Tanzania or Mozambique. However, what complicated the issue in Botswana's case was that, while Zambia was ready to co-operate and re-adjust its policy to suit the prevailing realities in Zimbabwe, Botswana was alleged to have continued with an "open door" policy towards ZAPU. In fact, Botswana was alleged to have offered military bases at Pikwe for "Super ZAPU".[53] Zimbabwe complained to Botswana that most of the refugees at Dukwe camp were dissidents. Initially Botswana denied these allegations, and the divergence of opinion over the status of the residents at Dukwe camp marked the beginning of tension between the two countries.[54] The tension reached a critical level on 8 November 1983, when the ZNA entered Botswana, a few kilometres into the border town of Maitengwe. The troops were accompanied by helicopters and spotter planes to hit the bases of "dissidents" and "anti-government" guerrillas operating from Botswana.[55]

On 20 December 1983, a Zimbabwean soldier was shot dead in Botswana by members of the Botswanan army after he allegedly pursued "dissidents" about two miles inside Botswana. This resulted in an emergency meeting between Zimbabwean and Botswanan officials at Plumtree, Zimbabwe, on 22 December 1983. The issue was resolved amicably, and from then on it appeared that both sides were able to better understand each other's positions on the issue. By the end of July 1984, Botswana had repatriated more than 1 200 Zimbabweans from Dukwe camp. Of this number, about 300 were said to be former ZIPRA combatants.[56]

The second phase was the "relatively harmonious phase", during which both countries tried to establish a cordial relationship. Once the security problem emanating from the hosting of dissidents was removed, both countries explored ways of ensuring genial relations, with many Zimbabweans travelling to and living in Botswana, which was one of the most economically viable countries in sub-Saharan Africa. However, it was not long before grounds for tension re-emerged in Botswana-Zimbabwe relations.

The last phase came after the domestic situation inside Zimbabwe forced Botswana to take a position on Mugabe's government's policies. Indeed, unlike any other country in the region, Botswana made a clear stand that it was against what it saw as Mugabe's dictatorial tendencies in Zimbabwe. The president of Botswana, though not openly supporting the MDC, was critical of Mugabe's policies. Unlike Zambia, which limited its criticism to Mugabe's treatment of the MDC and avoided the land invasion controversy, Botswana made clear its objections to both land invasion and of the suppressive policy towards the MDC. It is important to point out that Botswana has had a fairly stable democracy and the country found Mugabe's sit-tight policy somewhat difficult to countenance. President Ian Khama declared openly that he would not recognize the 2008 election in Zimbabwe, claiming that the Mugabe regime was just "limping along and there is a real danger that the whole thing could collapse".[57] President Khama was to maintain the same position when he took sides with the winner of the Ivorian election, Alassane Ouattara, and invited him to visit Botswana. As in the case of Zambia, Mugabe was disappointed and Zimbabwe angrily described Botswana's action as "extreme provocation" designed to "pick a quarrel with Zimbabwe". Zimbabwe also accused Botswana of training a rebel army for Tsvangirai to overthrow Mugabe.

Between independence and 2009, Zimbabwe's security relationship with Mozambique was one of the most important. The relationship comprised two phases: the first saw the two countries openly displaying friendship that bordered on an alliance, while the second saw Mozambique maintaining a respectable distance from Zimbabwe. Phase one was the era of "boisterous camaraderie", when both countries exhibited friendship because of their close affinity during the war of liberation and their mutual desire to fight the Mozambican dissident movement RENAMO.

When the domestic situation in Zimbabwe assumed a difficult dimension, Mozambique's policy towards Harare became somewhat cautious. While Maputo was never at any time openly critical of Mugabe, it did not support him while he was being criticised for his domestic and sub-regional policies. Having come out of a bitter civil war that had its origin in its involvement in the war in a neighbouring country, Maputo saw the need for some form of caution on the development in Zimbabwe. Apart from this, Maputo was already winning accolades for sustaining its democracy and good governance. Indeed, its former president was later to win the coveted Mo Ibrahim Award for good governance. To now be seen openly fraternising with a government with questionable credentials, was not in line with the country's growing democratic reputation. At the same time, however, it did not want to join the growing critics of Mugabe.

Mugabe could have been slightly disappointed with Mozambique for not showing greater support while he was being criticised for his domestic policies. Specifically, there was no support for Mugabe's farm invasion policy. However, it appears that after Chissano left office in 2005, the crop of leaders with whom Mugabe had fraternised during his war of liberation days had also left Mozambican leadership, and another set, less inclined to celebrating the heroic past, had assumed power in Maputo. While relationships with immediate neighbours were important in understanding Mugabe's security strategy, the country's relationship with the South African Development Community (SADC) was also important to get a complete sub-regional picture.

The first expression of open disagreement between Mozambique and Zimbabwe on the issue of security came with Mugabe's controversial intervention in the DRC in 1998, under the auspices of the SADC. Mozambique felt that the intervention was illegal and inappropriate, and the country joined South Africa in calling for the removal of Mugabe from key positions in the security protocol of the SADC. While Mugabe would have interpreted Mozambique's position as indicating a new low-time level in their relationship, he was, nevertheless, willing to go ahead with his position, especially as he would have realised that Maputo was unlikely to go further than this in its objection to his intervention. Another issue that created some subtle concerns was the treatment of Zimbabweans at the Mozambique border. Because of the downward plunge in the Zimbabwean economy, the historical migration to Zimbabwe had, by 2003, reversed, with Zimbabweans now going to Mozambique in search of better life. Many complained of harsh treatment by Mozambican immigration officials.[58]

Conclusion

The politics surrounding the management of security in Zimbabwe have been very complex. However, all the policies that were adopted have been linked to Mugabe's desire to use both domestic and regional developments to hold on to power. Indeed, throughout the first 28 years, Mugabe's main objective has always been to exploit every domestic and sub-regional security opportunity to consolidate his grip on power, while continuing to exploit the legacies of the past to satisfy the desires of the present. Immediate neighbours became involved in this calculation, and they had to strike a policy balance that would take into account internal developments within Zimbabwe, respect for the country's sovereignty, protection of their own borders from the consequences of any possible upsurge in Zimbabwe's domestic challenges, and the desire to give an outward impression of friendship, even if there were internal concerns of apprehension.

[1] This is an abridged version of sections of my book, *Mugabe and the Politics of Security in Zimbabwe* (2012).

[2] Meredith (2007:14).

[3] The ZANLA Brigadiers were Sheba Gava (later to become Sheba Zvinavashe), Dominic Chinenga, Edzai Chanyinka, Frederick Mutanga and Agnew Kambeu.

[4] Masuku was a Lieutenant General in the army, in his capacity as former head of ZIPRA, the armed wing of ZAPU, while Dabengwa was former head of ZAPU's intelligence wing.

[5] Two clashes took place in Entumbane. The first was in November 1980, which was sparked by a comment allegedly made by radical ZANU leader, Enos Nkala, that the party would deliver a blow against ZAPU. This lasted two days. The second was in February 1981. This was particularly serious as it spread to Glenville and Connemara in the Midlands.

[6] There were cases of ex-guerrillas who took advantage of the package and handled their demobilisation payment well. For example, some ZIPRA ex-combatants came together in 1983 and formed the "All-Are-One" Co-operative, with Z$45 000. By 1989, the co-operative had a turnover of over Z$3.7 million, and was judged the best-run service co-operative in the country. *See African Concord* (Lagos), 1 October 1990, p. 23.

[7] Personal interview with Major-General Zvinavashe, Chief of Staff (General) of the ZNA, Harare, Zimbabwe, 21 March 1990.

[8] Emmerson Mnangagwa was among the guerrilla fighters that launched the first attack on Rhodesian installation at the beginning of the war. The attack failed and he and others were sentenced to death. He, however, escaped the gallows because of a faulty medical examination that categorized him as being under-aged.

[9] Personal interview with Major-General Zvinavashe, Chief of Staff (General) of the ZNA, Harare, Zimbabwe, 15 March 1990.

[10] Discussion with Knox Chitiyo, September 2011.

[11] http://www.nation.co.ke. Accessed 20 December 2009.

[12] *See Hansard* (Zimbabwe), 30 June 1981, pp. 152-162.

[13] Immediately after independence, Nkomo made a number of significant purchases, especially farmland. He claimed that the purchases were made to provide jobs for ZIPRA guerrillas who would not be able to be integrated into the new national army.

[14] Three days later, Walls denied, through his lawyer, that he had arranged or attended any meeting between Nkomo and the officials of the South African security force. He also denied allegations that he had planned or was taking part in any activity detrimental to the Zimbabwean government.

[15] In all, about 52 ZAPU properties, worth about Z$20 million, were confiscated by the government.

[16] The ZIPRA commanders were charged but acquitted, then swiftly re-arrested under the emergency power regulations. Masuku was released in March 1986 when his health started to fail, and he died the following month. Dabengwa was released in December 1986.

[17] This is largely true. In fact, *Africa Confidential* had, as far back as June 1981, stated that "…there are numerous caches of arms throughout the country particularly in the Ndebele country". *See Africa Confidential*, Vol. 22, No. 13, June 1981.

[18] *See African Confidential*, Vol. 23, No. 5, March 1982. This position was still prevalent in Matabeleland during the author's visit in March 1990. Those with whom the author discussed the issue insisted that stockpiling arms was widely done by both ZAPU and ZANU. One described the entire practice as "a permitted offence". When asked if any of them could tell the author about any of the sites used by ZANLA, one simply retorted: "How can we know? Ask them, and if they are honest enough with you, they will tell you where they kept them."

[19] The term "dissidents" rather than "bandits" seems to be used more for the people who unleashed terror on Matabeleland. Even government officials referred to them as "dissidents". This is in contrast to the situation in Mozambique where, until recently, the anti-government troops were simply described as bandits when efforts at resolving the war in the country forced the government in Maputo to use less strong terms to describe Resistência Nacional Moçambicana (RENAMO). A "dissident" (as opposed to a bandit) presupposes some justification for the need to dissent. It is not known the extent to which the Zimbabwean government believed that those who took up arms in Matabeleland had justification for their actions.

[20] An ex-ZIPRA combatant who is still in the army told the author that, after Entumbane, he felt convinced that total confusion was a distinct possibility. According to him, many of those who stayed back did so because of pressure from Nkomo, Masuku and Dabengwa. He said that, after the conflict, many ex-ZANLA combatants were in the habit of floating another ruthless suppression if soldiers from ZIPRA dared to embark on another revolt. It is only fair to add here that this was denied by an ex-ZANLA officer with whom the author discussed the matter informally.

[21] *See African Confidential*, Vol. 23, No. 11, 26 May 1982.

[22] These figures are from *Keesing's Contemporary Archives*, July 1983, p. 32241.

[23] Early 1982 is the time usually regarded as the beginning of the dissidence. However, there is a claim by Wilf Mbaya, a South Africa-based Zimbabwean journalist with the *Johannesburg Star*, that dissident operations began in May 1980. See "Ndebele rebellion gathering force" in The Star (Johannesburg), 23 July 1980.

[24] The author is aware of an attempt to add a fourth category to the group of dissidents: ZNA pseudo operations. These were members of the ZNA alleged to have taken part in dissident activities, either to discredit ZAPU, or possibly for the fun of it. Although the author heard this from a number of sources, no evidence could be found to support the allegation. The only place where the allegation was documented was in Paul Moorcraft's book, *African Nemesis: War and revolution in Southern Africa* (1990:305), where he cited South African sources. While one may not categorically dismiss this claim, its authenticity may be questioned.

[25] Many ex-ZIPRAs who accepted the government's amnesty marking the end of the unrest said in interviews that there was no working relationship between them and "Super ZAPU". Some ex-ZIPRA dissidents claimed that some of the weapons they used to prosecute their dissident operations were captured from "Super ZAPU". According to them, their reasons for fighting "Super ZAPU" was because they could not countenance anyone receiving arms from South Africa to fight against Zimbabwe. It is unclear whether this was a pretext or genuine intention not to have anything to do with South Africa.

[26] For more information on the Accord, see chapters by Willard Chiwewe, Didymus Mutasa, Joshua Nkomo and Robert Mugabe in Banana (ed) (1989).

[27] Many dissidents envisaged an amnesty following an accord between ZANU and ZAPU, and they had planned to give themselves up after such amnesty. This was understood from an interview granted by some of them before the Accord was signed. See Rukumi (1987:34).

[28] *See Hansard* (Zimbabwe), 15 March 1983. This was published in *The Herald* of 16 March 1983. His words were quite prophetic: "Strong arm tactics by the Fifth Brigade will only serve to exacerbate, rather than cure the situation".

[29] In February, one of the expelled ministers, Josiah Chinamano, suggested that unity with ZANU would be a good idea. However, he did not make the type of extensive suggestions Senator Oatt made. *See Hansard* (Zimbabwe), 2 February 1983, column 1173.

[30] At that time they had not been formally charged, but some had been arrested.

[31] The history of the nation's land politics has been recorded in several instances, such that a brief recap will suffice. For more on the land dispute in Zimbabwe *see* Kibble (2001), Nelson (2003) and Zhou (2002).

[32] Evidence supporting the fact that many guerrilla fighters saw the war in land terms could be seen in many of the *Chimurenga* (Liberation) songs. They were also encouraged in this belief by the leaders of the liberation movements.

[33] Human Rights Watch (2002:6, 7).

[34] An anecdote in Zimbabwe shows the extent of alleged corruption and irregularities in the land reallocation exercise. A key cabinet minister was said to have spotted a huge expanse of land during a drive through the suburbs of Harare, and immediately told his driver that he must acquire the land, to which the driver allegedly responded that he had only just acquired it the previous week.

[35] The referendum had its roots in the Constitutional Commission set up by the government in May 1999 to gather the views of the people on a new constitution, and to submit a report to the president within six months. The draft was submitted on 29 November 1999 and gazetted on 2 December 1999.

[36] On the first day of the two-day referendum, the State-owned *The Herald* ran the front-page editorial comment: "Let us all vote for land, peace and a democratic future" (*The Herald* (Harare), 12 February 2000). The issue divided the country's newspapers, with The Herald supporting the government and other newspapers like the *Zimbabwe Independent* and *The Standard* supporting the opposition.

[37] Discussions held with Zimbabwe's opposition members in April 2000.

[38] "Let us vote 'no' to dictatorship" in *Zimbabwe Independent* (Harare), 11 February 2000.

[39] The author was in Zimbabwe during the period and this sentiment was clearly noticeable.

[40] There seems to be disagreement within ZANU-PF over land occupation. For example, the Home Affairs minister declared on 10 March 2000 that farm occupation had served its purpose and should end. Mugabe, however, contradicted him by declaring that the occupation must continue.

[41] BBC News, 6 April 2001.

[42] *The New Vision* (Kampala), 3 June 2000, p. 12.

[43] In an interview Mugabe granted to Sky Television on 24 May 2004, he conceded that some mistakes had been made, but that they did not affect the principle behind the action.

[44] Meredith (2002:167).

[45] The author is aware of the *mujibars*, the young intelligence gatherers who took active part in the war of liberation, but most of those who took part in the land-invasion exercise were too young to have been *mujibars* during the war.

[46] Although Chenjerai Hunzvi's estranged wife, Wieslawa, made this allegation, nothing has been done to deny that he was a medical student in Yugoslavia during the war of liberation. Hunzvi died of cerebral malaria shortly after the land occupation crisis assisted him in securing a seat in parliament.

[47] A list of those who benefited from the forceful acquisition of land shows a number of people hitherto known for their radical socio-economic and political views.

[48] *Chimurenga* is the Shona word for "struggle", which has been used in Zimbabwean history to describe the war against foreign control. *Chimurenga* 1 was the war fought to resist the establishment of imperial control. *Chimurenga* 2 was the war of liberation that resulted in the political independence of the country in April 1980.

[49] *See African Confidential*, 21 February 2003, Vol. 44, No. 4.

[50] Thompson, C. "Return to hell" in *The London Line* (London), 2 June 2005, p. 9.

[51] "South Africa: Space invaders" in *The Economist*, 14 July 2001, p. 62.

[52] Seven key members of the MDC, including Gandhi Mudzingwa, an adviser to the MDC leader, and Chris Dhlamini, the head of security for the party, still had charges against them for an alleged bomb plot.

[53] *Africa Now* (London), December 1983, p. 25.

[54] Dr Knight Maripe, chairman of the Botswana People's Party, one of the three parties in the Botswana parliament, confirmed while on a visit to Zimbabwe that the refugees at Dukwe camps were not dissidents. Later, the Botswana minister of Public Service and Information, Daniel Kwelagobe, gave a detailed explanation of Botswana's stand on the issue in the Botswana parliament on 26 March 1983. He confirmed that Botswana was not harbouring dissidents and blamed the Zimbabwean press for making remarks that could strain relations between the countries.

[55] There had been previous accusations by Botswana of Zimbabwean incursions into its territory. In April 1981, the Botswana government claimed that veterinary officials were abducted by the Zimbabwean army, but were later released. Again, in October 1981, the government claimed that the Zimbabwean army crossed its borders and beat up a village headman who refused to give information about Zimbabwean dissidents. It was, however, the Maitengwe incident that was confirmed by Harare.

[56] *See The Herald* (Harare), 17 July 1984.

[57] *See* "Botswana: Khama set to win elections, vows not to recognise Mugabe as Zimbabwe president" in *The Zimbabwean*, 17 October 2009.

[58] Discussions with Zimbabweans resident in southern Africa.

A perspective on ethnic, regional and ideological dimensions of the composition of the Zimbabwean military and their implications

Sabelo J. Ndlovu-Gatsheni

One of the puzzling realities of current Zimbabwean politics is the increasing militarisation of State, and the threat and reality of intervention of the military in politics. This reality has been interpreted at two levels. Firstly, the Zimbabwe African National Union Patriotic Front (ZANU-PF) has embraced it as part of safeguarding the nationalist revolution and defence of the nation from neo-colonial forces of destabilisation. Secondly, the Movement for Democratic Change (MDC) formations have interpreted this as an open threat to democracy that portends a serious danger of the emergence of a military junta in Harare, in violation of the national constitution. The key question is: Why has the Zimbabwean military assumed a veto power and the status of king-makers since 2002? This chapter responds to the question by delving deeper into the constitution of the Zimbabwean military, with a specific focus on its composition, identity and ideology. The paper posits that four core issues need to be fleshed out and understood if one is to fully comprehend the recent behaviour of the Zimbabwean military. The four variables are composition, ideological orientation, identity, and generational outlook.

Since Zimbabwe attained political independence in 1980, the military has not been insulated from the negative effects of national competitive politics on their *esprit de corps* (honour and professionalism). This was partly because of the reality of the emergence of the post-colonial army from elements that had participated in the 15-year-long war of independence and partly due to the fact that the victorious political party (ZANU-PF) made deliberate efforts to create a military that was imbued with its political philosophy.[1] This came out clearly during debates on why Zimbabwe was creating the Fifth Brigade at a time when other members of the army were being demobilised. The prime minister's justification for the creation of the Fifth Brigade was that they needed a military formation that was inculcated with ZANU-PF political philosophy.[2]

ZANU-PF leadership was fully aware that it was inheriting highly politicised and opposing armed groups. The bringing in of the British Military Advisory and Training Team (BMATT), which worked in collaboration with war-time commanders of the Rhodesia Forces, the Zimbabwe People's Revolutionary Army (ZIPRA), and Zimbabwe African National Liberation Army (ZANLA), was tasked to integrate these contending forces into a professional Zimbabwe National Army (ZNA) loyal to the post-colonial State.[3] The challenge was compounded by the fact that the complex processes of the constitution of the ZNA became inextricably intertwined with the equally complex twin-projects of State-building and nation-building and, as such, could not be fully insulated from vicissitudes of national politics and political party competition for power. As early as 14 May 1980, the Zimbabwean parliament noted that "the most difficult and pressing problem in State-building and nation-building – the integration of the army and air force – … was also the key to stability, enabling the new government to proceed with reconstruction and resettlement".[4]

Driven by imperatives of security and regime survival, ZANU-PF pursued a peculiar State-building and nation-building project, which Norma Kriger (2003:73–75) described as "party-state" and "party-nation". What Kriger was referring to is a process of elevation of the ruling party into the centre of the State and the nation, to the extent that State and national agendas became indistinguishable from those of the ruling party. This process can simply be termed "Zanufication" of the State and the nation. It entailed the use of party symbols as though there were national symbols. It also had direct implications for the constitution of the military. As the nation and the State underwent "Zanufication", the constitution of the military witnessed "Zanlafication". This unfolded as process of strategically positioning ex-ZANLA cadres into dominant positions within the military, while at the same time side-lining ex-ZIPRA and ex-Rhodesian military forces.[5] "Zanlafication" entailed witch-hunts for ex-ZIPRA within the ZNA.

The broad discursive terrain within which the processes of "Zanufication" and "Zanlafication" took place, was that of the ideology of *Chimurenga*, which formed the foundation myth of the post-colonial State and nation as a by-product of nationalist revolutions dating back to 1896. ZANU-PF and ZANLA placed themselves at the centre of *Chimurenga*, making them complimentary forces with the historic task to not only safeguard the "nationalist shrine" of Zimbabwe, but also to claim primal political legitimacy cascading from active participation in the liberation struggle.[6]

This brief background is important in understanding the recent behaviour of the military and why ZANU-PF leadership is not railing against the increasing interference of the military in national politics. This chapter is specifically focused on four issues considered important in understanding the behaviour of the military today: the composition of the military, the identity of the military, ideological orientation and generational composition. These issues must be fully understood as Zimbabwe struggles to institute security sector reform before the next elections.

The ideological orientation of the Zimbabwean military

The guiding ideology which shapes the Zimbabwean military is that of nationalism traceable to the time of the liberation struggle. It is a nationalism that is backed by what Ranger (2004) has termed "patriotic history". At the centre of this patriotic history is the hagiography of ZANU-PF, ZANLA and President Robert Mugabe, which has been elevated into national history.[7] Within patriotic history, liberation war credentials become the source and qualification for anyone to occupy political office in Zimbabwe. Mugabe emerges in this history as the "father figure" of the post-colonial nation, as well as the alpha and omega leader of the country.[8] Cascading from the liberation war tradition, glorification of the leader of the State, who is also the commander-in-chief of the armed forces is inculcated on the military. Ranger (2003:1–37) sought to find the historical roots of the ideological orientation of the post-colonial leadership of Zimbabwe, particularly its authoritarian and commandist practice in the history of nationalism and the liberation war. He argued:

> ... *Perhaps there was something inherent in nationalism itself, even before the wars and the adoption of socialism, which gave rise to authoritarianism. Maybe nationalism's emphasis on unity at all costs – its subordination of trade unions and churches and all other African organisations to its imperatives – gave rise to an intolerance of pluralism. Maybe nationalism's glorification of the leader gave rise to a post-colonial cult of personality. Maybe nationalism's commitment to modernisation, whether socialist or not, inevitably implied a commandist state.*

The Zimbabwean military has played an active role in violent post-colonial State practices. What emerges poignantly is that, within the top leadership of the military, there is deliberate conflation of loyalty to the State, along with loyalty to ZANU-PF and individual loyalty to President Mugabe. Since 2002, the top brass of the Zimbabwean military has increasingly expressed direct loyalty first to "the leader" (Mugabe) and to the party (ZANU-PF). Addressing soldiers under his command, before the 2008 elections, General Constantine Chiwenga had this to say:

> *Our comrade, defence forces chief, our leader President Mugabe and comrade in arms will romp into victory. We say so because we have no apology to make to any house nigger and puppets.*[9]

A bizarre mixture of such ideologies as *Chimurenga*, Marxism, Maoism, Leninism, Nkrumahism and Nyerereism combined tendentiously to produce Mugabeism, which is manifest in the thinking of the top leaders of the Zimbabwean military.[10] Why the Zimbabwean military has not hesitated participating in violence against all those identified as a threat to ZANU-PF regime security is explainable by delving deeper into violent legacies of colonialism and nationalism. The prosecution of the liberation struggle enabled legitimation of authoritarianism, militarism, violence and intolerance as markers of being revolutionary. On this reality, Ndlovu-Gatsheni (2003:107) has observed:

> *It was during the liberation struggle for Zimbabwe that the party leader and the party itself were glorified in such slogans as* Pamberi Ne Zanu, *(Forward with ZANU-PF),* Pamberi Na Robert Gabriel Mugabe *(Forward with Robert Gabriel Mugabe) … The glorified and worshipped nationalist leadership developed tough talk and sophisticated propaganda and political rhetoric. It also developed arrogance and self-confidence. The African patriarchal ideologies were combined with nationalist authoritarianism to produce a father figure in the nationalist leader.*

So, ideologically, the Zimbabwean military still seems to drink from the historical cup of African nationalism with its borrowings from *Chimurenga* warrior instincts, laced with its lionisation of the leader and religious loyalty to the party. This mentality explains why, soon after winning the 1980 elections, ZANU-PF was eager to create partisan and highly ideological military units like the Fifth Brigade, which journalist and military historian Paul Moorcraft (2012) has depicted as:

> *Trained by North Korea, it was marked by its fanatical ideological loyalty to Mugabe and its incredible brutality … the Fifth Brigade was run from the prime minister's office and was answerable only to Mugabe.*

During the liberation struggle, leading nationalist politicians, including those considered moderate such as Bishop Abel Muzorewa and the Reverend Ndabaningi Sithole, found it necessary to create military wings that were loyal to them as they competed for the position of first black leader of the post-colonial State. Military historian, Martin Rupiya, amplified this argument:

> *At least three important groups competed in the struggle. The Rhodesia regime banned both ZANU and ZAPU while it created institutions whose mandate was to maintain the status quo. Meanwhile both ZANU and ZAPU proceeded to establish military wings whose focus was to challenge not only the Rhodesian regime but, by default, also each other … In the prosecution of the war these fought each other whenever they met in the operational zones.*

From what Rupiya says, it is clear that both ZANLA and ZIPRA were created first as party armies and not as national armies. It appears then that in the DNA of the Zimbabwean military, the party and the party leader are still the mobilising points and foci of all loyalty. There perhaps have not been strong enough processes of "nationalising" the military and orienting them towards national agendas. This is why I have argued that, in terms of ideological orientation:

> *The Zimbabwean armed forces are deliberately indoctrinated with the values of ZANU-PF as a party. All the high-ranking members of the military forces are expected to be members of ZANU-PF. As it stands today, the military is led by those who passed though the nationalist liberation war and who are thoroughly indoctrinated with ZANU-PF nationalist ideology. National service militants are another group of indoctrinated people who are now being recruited into joining the army and police.[11]*

Clearly, loyalty to the party, experience of the liberation struggle, subscription to party ideology and lionisation of the person of the president, are the credentials of value in the Zimbabwean military.

At this juncture, this chapter will branch to pay attention to the identity of the personnel who populate the higher echelons of the Zimbabwean military, with a view to gleaning observations on how their identity impacts on their words and deeds as to what is supposed to be a national army, but has turned out to be a personal militia and an armed partisan detachment. So far, the deployment of the Zimbabwean military to the Congo, just like the deployment to Matabeleland of the Fifth Brigade were not in the national interest, but in the party, personal-political and financial interests of the executive and the elite in the party.

The identity and ethnic makeup of the Zimbabwean military

Close examination of the identity of those holding key positions in the security sector reveal worrying indications of ethnocracy. According to Nederveen Pieterse (1997), ethnocracy arises in a situation where the distinction between nation and ethnicity is eliminated. In an ethnocracy, nationality is defined in terms of majority ethnicity. In an ethnocracy, the State undergoes deep ethnicisation and "nationality itself is often defined in terms of the majority ethnicity". If what appears as the criteria of deployment at the top level of Zimbabwe's military is anything to write home about, then there is something worse than ethnocracy at play. There is clannism and home-boyism, if not nepotism. Chris Maroleng (2005:5) observed that Zimbabwe was governed by a Zezuru clique and elaborated:

> The failure of leadership in independent Zimbabwe has created patronage systems based on region, ethnicity and political affiliation. These have completely undermined both advancement based on merit and market economics … Zimbabwe has become a nation of accomplices joined together by ethnicity, region and political affiliation, and war credentials. Government, among other vices, specialises in covers and cover-ups. It is for this reason that a justice system manned by kinsmen and party cadres is as evil as the Rhodesian system which was constructed along racial lines.

If one closely examines the identity of those who are at the top of the Zimbabwe military, what emerges is something beyond "Zanufication" and "Zanlafication" of the security forces. While it is clear that the Zimbabwean army today is dominated by the Shona ethnic group, there is also "Zezurisation" of the top leadership through deployment of those hailing from Mugabe's Zezuru ethnic group. It would seem the logic is to create an enduring loyalty to the party and its leadership derived not only from ethnic affiliation, but also from clannism and home-boyism.[12]

It appears that "Zezurisation" of the top echelons of the Zimbabwean military happened within the context in which ZANU-PF was increasingly rocked by factionalism that threatened Mugabe's power. Therefore, for purposes of guaranteeing political survival, Mugabe decided to ensure the military was headed by close associates hailing from his tribal group – the Zezuru. The table below shows the current constitution of the Zimbabwean military, with unmistakably Zezuru dominance.

President Robert Mugabe	Commander-in-Chief	Zezuru
Emmerson Mnangagwa	Minister of Defence	Karanga
General Constantine Chiwenga	Commander of Defence Forces	Zezuru
Lieutenant-General Philip Valerio Sibanda	Commander Land Forces	Karanga
Air Marshal Perence Shiri	Commander of Air Force	Zezuru
Didymus Mutasa	Minister of State Security	Manyika
Augustine Chihuri	Commissioner of Police	Zezuru
Paradzai Zimondi	Head of Prison Services	Zezuru

Only Mnangagwa, Mutasa and Sibanda are not of the Zezuru sub-Shona ethnic group. Are these just coincidental appointments based on merit? Like Shiri, who was commander of the Fifth Brigade that committed atrocities in Matebeleland and the Midlands in the 1980s, Mnangagwa was Mugabe's security chief during the same period and seemingly passes the loyalty test. It must also be observable that this line-up not only responds to ethnic dynamics in Zimbabwe, but also reflects ethnic and political factionalism that besets ZANU-PF internally. Only Sibanda is from the ZIPRA military side. Is this evidence that Zimbabwe's military has not fully recovered from liberation war mode, where ZIPRA and the Rhodesian forces were considered enemies?

At another level, it seems the guilt of the *Gukurahundi* atrocities and the primitive accumulation of wealth beginning with diamonds from the Democratic Republic of Congo (DRC) in 1998, the allocation of land under the *Third Chimurenga*, right up to the looting and trading of diamonds from Marange, have bound the executive and the top echelons of the military in one tight jacket of common fear, common interest and common destiny. It is a sort of "brothers in crime" or *Mafioso*-type loyalty that cannot be easily broken.

The generational outlook of the Zimbabwean military

In generational terms, the Zimbabwean military is heterogeneous rather than homogenous. It is constituted by what one could call "the old guard" and a "born-free" generation of soldiers.[13] This is a layer that further complicates the ex-ZANLA, ex-ZIPRA and ex-Rhodesian cleavages. The "born-free" generation is complicated by the cohort coming from Border Gezi's National Youth Service training programme, in which "the old guard" made a concerted effort to reproduce itself through highly partisan and ideologically indoctrinated soldiers loyal to ZANU-PF rather than the post-colonial State and nation.[14]

The graduates of Border Gezi's National Youth Service training, who are disparagingly known as "Green Bombers" in Zimbabwe, were said to be preferred as recruits for the military and other public-service positions. However, the military has also been recruiting those with advanced level and university education into its ranks. One, therefore, remains unconvinced of the fact that those top commanders of the military, who have expressed their loyalty to Mugabe alone and threatened a military coup if someone considered to have no liberation war credentials wins an election, have the backing of the rank and file within the military.

Conclusions and policy reflections

One issue that stands out clearly is that, according to the Zimbabwean Constitution in general and the Defence Forces Act specifically, the Zimbabwean military has no veto power and no basis to masquerade as king-makers. Therefore, the political utterances of Zimbabwe military establishment commanders who threaten to prevent any elected leader without liberation credentials to lead the country is an open violation of Zimbabwean law. It is also a violation of the standing clauses of the African Union (AU) and the Southern African Development Community (SADC), which are very clear on their opposition to the illegal takeover of State power in post-colonial Africa.

What is worrying is the silence of the executive, in the shape of the presidency, in responding to this threat to Zimbabwean constitutional order. Instead, the executive has been complicit in endorsing militant and partisan political statements of what are ordinarily supposed to be guardians of State and national security and not party or what could be called regime security. The silence of the executive has seen leaders of the Zimbabwean military establishments, including Zimondi, openly addressing officers under his command, telling them:

> If the opposition win the elections, I will be the first one to resign from my job and go back to defend my piece of land. I will not let it go … I am giving you an order to vote for the president [Mugabe]. Do not be distracted … I will only support the leadership of President Mugabe.[15]

Zimondi's commitment to defend his "piece of land" speaks to how the ZANU-PF regime has used pay-offs to buy the loyalty of the top leadership of the military establishment. Under normal democratic circumstances, Zimondi's words would have attracted at least censure or discipline from the powers that be, but there was deafening silence, notwithstanding that his words were a direct challenge to the national Constitution and military ethic. Noticeably, however, is that Mugabe stated:

> The war veterans came to me and said, President, we can never accept that our country which we won through the barrel of the gun can be taken merely by an "x" made by a ball-pen. Will the pen fight the AK rifle? Is there going to be a struggle between the two? Do not argue with a gun.[16]

Coming from the Head of State, these are utterances that gesture to endorsement of war veterans and military officers meddling in party politics, and fly in the face of the national Constitution and the well-understood democratic principles of military neutrality in politics. Clearly there are indications that the presidency of the country condones the unconstitutional and unprofessional behaviour of the military that offends democratic principles.

Hope for Zimbabwe lies in the AU and SADC making a strong statement against the Zimbabwe military's threats to subvert constitutional order in a member state. One also remains hopeful that the few top leaders of the military establishment who have been reckless in their statements might just be a misguided, politically overzealous minority, who will not be able to mobilise the rank and file of the military to back them on this illegal interference in national politics. The heterogeneity of the Zimbabwean military might be a safety guarantee against the will of less professional members of the military dragging the nation into a crisis and the possibility of a military takeover of the State.

The final point is that those members of the military who have openly revealed themselves as loyal supporters of ZANU-PF and Mugabe, include those who have taken a leading role in committing atrocities, such as Shiri. The continuation of ZANU-PF and Mugabe in power constitutes a shield from possible prosecution. This fear of prosecution over human rights' violations, including crimes against humanity, is poised to stand in the way of transitional politics in Zimbabwe. What is difficult is to strike a balance between allaying the fears of those who committed atrocities who are in charge of the current State, and avoiding betraying the interests of those who experiences the atrocities who are crying for justice to prevail. Perhaps a truth and reconciliation commission is the best way forward, which might culminate in reconciliation and forgiveness.

---

[1] At birth, the ZANU-PF regime was understandably concerned about its security and survival. This concern made the new government establish some military outfits that were considered loyal to ZANU-PF, such as the Presidential Guards, the Fifth Brigade and People's Militia. These groups were deliberately politicised in favour of the ruling party.

[2] Chan (2011:32) had this to say about the Fifth Brigade: "These were not fighting soldiers: they were not trained to fight against an enemy who would fight back. They were suppressors."

[3] Rupiah (1995).

[4] Zimbabwe Parliamentary Debates: First Session, First Parliament, 14 May 1980.

[5] The opening chapter of Kriger's *Guerrilla Veterans in Post-War Zimbabwe* provides details of the "Zanlafication" process.

[6] Mugabe (2001). *See also* Ranger (2004:215–234).

[7] Tendi (2010).

[8] Ndlovu-Gatsheni (2009).

[9] *The Herald*, 23 June 2008.

[10] Ndlovu-Gatsheni (2009: 233–298).

[11] Ndlovu-Gatsheni (2006:76).

[12] Ndlovu- Gatsheni (2006:75).

[13] The cohort of "born-free" soldiers includes the Sixth Brigade and others who were recruited into the army after 1980. Those constituting the Sixth Brigade were born prior to 1980, but have no liberation war credentials.

[14] For details on National Youth Service training, *see* Solidarity Peace Trust (2003).

[15] Paradzai Zimondi, Head of Prison Services: *The Herald*, 29 February 2008.

[16] Robert Mugabe: *The Herald*, 23 June 2008.

5

South Africa and SADC mediation in Zimbabwe: Still at the crossroads?

Siphamandla Zondi

For nine years, Zimbabwe descended into an abyss of political-cum-economic crisis. This led to a gradual decline of the economy, political polarisation and the disintegration of the State in Zimbabwe. For all this time, neither loud diplomacy by the West nor "quiet" diplomacy by African states succeeded in leading Zimbabwe out of the conflict. With the signing of the Global Political Agreement (GPA) between the Zimbabwe African National Union Patriotic Front (ZANU-PF) and the two factions of the Movement for Democratic Change (one under Morgan Tsvangarai and another under Arthur Mutambara – the MDC-T and MDC-M respectively) in September 2008, Zimbabwe finally edged very close to finding a long-elusive political settlement, and a formula for establishing a new political and economic dispensation. Four months earlier, Zimbabwe had witnessed relatively free and fair elections for the first time in many years, only for the situation to degenerate again into an orgy of political violence and intolerance in the run-up to the presidential run-off elections in June 2008.

Thus, the positive atmosphere of the run-up to the 29 March 2008 elections was replaced with a resurgence of political conflict, prompting the Southern African Development Community (SADC) to intensify its diplomatic moves to find a negotiated political settlement. As the SADC envoy, former South African president, Thabo Mbeki, pushed the parties in

49

intensive talks behind closed doors, the economy continued to sink, with inflation and the prices of consumer goods rising fast, to the detriment of livelihoods in villages and townships. The humanitarian situation also worsened, with ongoing collapse of the social and physical infrastructure, a decline in public services, and loss of income as unemployment rose to over 80% of the population. The cholera epidemic which broke out around October 2008, and continued well into early 2009, affected thousands of poor Zimbabweans, generating more negative news headlines on Zimbabwe. As an indication of the serious deterioration of State capacity, basic services collapsed.

However, the peace negotiations remained on course and some progress was registered with the formation of the bi-partisan monitoring mechanism and the decision by the MDC-T in late January 2009 to join the inclusive government. Both factions of the MDC remain integral parts of the inclusive government, and trust among the parties has grown over time.

This chapter provides a comprehensive overview of the evolution of the peace process in Zimbabwe. It argues that, although the process of conflict resolution through mediation has stalemated a number of times, and even collapsed on some occasions, it was the best way towards peace and democracy in Zimbabwe. Mediated peace processes are usually slow and drawn-out, as was the Zimbabwe process. We argue that progress came about partly because of the skill of the facilitation team and partly due to the fact that the conflict was ripe for a negotiated settlement. The stalemate was no longer bearable for the political elite because it eroded their privileges and legitimacy before significant constituencies.

Dynamic stalemates: a conceptual framework

The fundamental conceptual point underpinning this chapter is that conflict resolution and the onset of peace is facilitated by the ripening of the conflict and political stalemate and the damage it causes to the interests, resources and standing of parties involved. This draws largely from the work of William Zartman who, in his magisterial book, *Ripe for Resolution* (1985), argued that the timing of the resolution of conflict is just important as the quality of proposals. The dominant thinking on conflict resolution has emphasised the quality of peace diplomacy in, among other things, persuading parties to a peaceful settlement, focusing their attention on the root cause, and making peace more attractive than continued conflict. The ripeness school of thought sees the quality of diplomacy as critical and productive only when the time is right – in other words, when the moment is ripe for resolution. A key ingredient of ripeness, it is argued, is that conflict begins to hurt the core interests and resources of the parties to the conflict; another is when unilateral means of exiting conflict, through either suppression or resistance, are blocked and parties feel they are in a costly and uncomfortable predicament. Actually, this school of thought contends that ripeness of time or stalemate is the basic essence of diplomacy, because good diplomacy is about doing the right thing at the right time. The underlying assumption is that parties in conflict are rational actors who, when their unilateral pursuit of satisfactory results are blocked, seek alternative ways out of the impasse. Mediation, arbitration and other diplomatic interventions are attractive alternatives to perpetual and mutually hurting stalemate and conflict. This school of thought makes room for objective referents, including the ability of the mediator to highlight the ripeness and to alert the parties to the hurt that the stalemate causes them and their surroundings (Zartman, 2001:3). This is because ripeness is only a condition, necessary but not sufficient, for the initiation of negotiated settlements. It must be seized upon, either directly by parties to the conflict or through the persuasion of a skilful mediator.

Ripeness is difficult to foretell and, for this reason, in protracted conflict such as in Zimbabwe, a number of propitious conditions for negotiations were missed many times before the SADC started its mediation under Thabo Mbeki in March 2007. These included the efforts by former presidents Joaquim Chissano of Mozambique, Benjamin Mkapa of Tanzania and Bakili Muluzi of Malawi on behalf of the SADC between 2003 and 2006. Therefore, not all ripe moments lead to reduction of conflict – in fact, in some cases ripe conditions lead to escalation of conflict as parties resist the inevitability of a peaceful settlement. This was the case in Zimbabwe when ZANU-PF resisted the efforts of the Commonwealth troika of Mbeki, Nigeria's Olusegun Obasanjo, and Australia's John Howard, leading to its collapse and an intensification of internal conflict. It is no irony that the ripe moment in Zimbabwe was signified by the State's intense clampdown on radical civil society and leaders of the opposition in March 2007.

The premise of our analysis is that the conflict is Zimbabwe is complex and structural. The recent conflict is an artefact of structural continuities going back to the colonial period, including the nature and conduct of the State, the dual nature of the economy (abject poverty alongside obscene wealth), erroneous International Monetary Fund (IMF)/World Bank (WB) austerity programmes, counter-productive economic measures by the Mugabe government, and an oppressive political culture. It has manifested itself in dictatorial tendencies on the part of the political elite that captured the State after colonial rule; antagonistic relations between the ruling and alternative parties; hostilities between the State and a large portion of politically active civil society, including white farmers; and tensions between the ZANU-PF government and Western powers. The conflict escalated with the formation of the MDC in 1999 as the opposition to ZANU-PF out of a coalition of critical interests that included trade unions and advocacy groups. It also worsened as the MDC increased its powerbase and posed a serious threat to ZANU-PF's long-held power.

Early indications of the Zimbabwe crisis

A key feature of post-colonial Zimbabwe is the failure of new rulers to transform the State and economy inherited from colonial predecessors. In part, the Lancaster House Agreement (LHA) at independence frustrated reforms because it had provisions that bound government to willing buyer-willing seller principles of land reform, entrenched private property rights, and protected white civil servants.[1] This imposed limits on how far State and economic reforms could be undertaken, and made radical land redistribution impossible, at least in the first decade.

Important among these limitations were clauses that bound the independent government to keep civil servants from the older order in their posts, maintain economic policies and maintain the land profile. As a result, unfair land distribution could not be changed drastically. About 5 600 white commercial farmers had access to 15.5 million hectares of land, while over 780 000 smallholder farmers had to subsist on 16.4 million hectares of land.[2]

At independence in 1980, Zimbabwe's new government maintained the macroeconomic controls inherited from the Rhodesian government. Within the framework of a command economy, the government also introduced redistributive objectives that necessitated a large public sector and increased government spending on health, education and other social welfare programmes throughout the 1980s. While the country's average growth rate was a good 4.3% per annum in the 1980s, this was jobless growth.[3]

Secondly, it sought to forge alliances with former colonial settlers in the hope that doing so would help avert external interventions and, instead, attract foreign aid for the rebuilding of Zimbabwe. Mugabe was quoted as saying: "If yesterday I fought you as an enemy, today you have become a friend and an ally with the same national interest, loyalty, rights and duties as myself."[4] He went on to appoint former Rhodesian politicians into his government – for instance, David Smith, who had served as a deputy to Rhodesian prime minister Ian Smith, and the Commercial Farmers Union's Denis Norman were appointed as his first ministers of Commerce and Industry, and Agriculture, respectively. Rival Joshua Nkomo's Zimbabwe African People's Union (ZAPU) was also allocated four cabinet posts and three junior ministerial positions.

The Mugabe government committed itself to dealing with the legacies of colonial rule through a programme of social reforms called "Growth with Equity", officially adopted in 1981. This policy envisaged balanced development through equitable distribution of income and productive resources, with special reference to mining, and human resource development through ambitious educational and health programmes, worker participation and extending social services to black Zimbabweans. The positive impact of these measures on social services – especially health, education and food security – was immediate, making Zimbabwe the envy of the whole of Africa for high levels on the Human Development Index (HDI).[5]

However, the politics of redistribution began to hurt the economy from the onset; high social expenditure deepened the budget deficit and, combined with two major droughts, pushed the economy into recession. There were two problems in the main: one was the government's attempt to balance keeping a healthy relationship with the major economic players (Western powers and international financial institutions) and the need to radically change the lives of ordinary people for whom independence meant better services. The second was the general climate under which this balancing act took place, especially in the first two decades of independence. Economically speaking, the 1980s were a difficult period for Zimbabwe and other developing countries. The world economy was in recession, making it difficult for the new government to find gratuitous resources for eradicating the socio-economic backlogs of the colonial era. This was, therefore, the period of crisis of expectations because the new government simply could not find the support it needed to adequately meet the aspirations of the new citizens of Zimbabwe. The crisis arose partly due to the fact that the new government failed to undo the colonial legacy of inequality and underdevelopment.

The crisis of expectations, land reform and conflict

The domestic market was such that it was inadequate to keep up with high State expenditure. The economy was not growing fast enough, growing at an average of 4%. As early as 1982, the economy started overheating, with the gradual rise of inflation, the fall of the Zimbabwe Dollar exchange rate, the increase in the current and capital accounts deficits.[6] Money promised by donors did not come and this put the State in an invidious position.

The economic meltdown coincided with a period of severe drought, from 1982 to 1984, which crippled the crucial agricultural sector, robbing the economy of much-needed income. Then there were cross-border incursions by apartheid South Africa looking for African National Congress (ANC) operatives that took refuge in Zimbabwe. This was followed by a trade blockade designed to strangle the Zimbabwean economy in order to force it to collaborate with South Africa in its mission to clamp down on liberation movements. Mugabe's government was forced to deploy its military along major trade routes at great unplanned cost.[7]

With inadequate domestic sources of capital, the government turned to external creditors, mainly private banks and international financiers, for loans. The penchant for non-concessionary commercial sources of credit were particularly damaging because of short maturity periods and high interest rates. The public debt increased considerably from an inherited US$786 million in 1980 to US$2.304 billion in 1983. In the same period, the debt service ratio increased from 1.3% of export incomes to 25%.[8] The State responded by adopting a self-imposed stabilisation programme in 1982, which included the devaluation of the Zimbabwe Dollar, restrictions on new non-concessionary foreign borrowing, balance of payment controls, controls on price, a wage freeze, and export incentives. This was followed by the IMF and WB's Economic Structural Adjustment Programme (ESAP) in 1983. However, the IMF programme lasted only 18 months because the government refused to budge on trade liberalisation and price controls, which the IMF required as part of its financial support programme.[9]

All these conditions helped deepen the economic and political problems in Zimbabwe. Nepotism and kleptocracy worsened, with the political elite plundering State resources through patronage and corruption. This radicalised civil society, already disillusioned by increased unemployment, poverty and the failure of the land reform process. In this context, trade unions, students' organisations and social movements became even more militant. Even before Zimbabwe agreed to the IMF–WB austerity programme in 1991, the government was involved in street fights with radical civil society, led by the militant Zimbabwe Congress of Trade Unions (ZCTU).[10]

By 1995, the economy was in trouble. There was a high budget deficit of over 8% compared to the ESAP target of 5% of Gross Domestic Product (GDP). At the same time, instead of the target 5% GDP growth, the actual average growth rate under ESAP from 1991 to 1995 was 0.8%.[11]

Social costs increased in the form rising unemployment, deepening poverty, and food shortages, and, along with poor service delivery and corruption, contributed to public disillusionment and the growth of militant social movements. Evidence of deepened poverty, increased inequality and unemployment could be seen in the streets of major cities like Harare and Bulawayo in the mid-1990s. The number of strikes and protests over socio-economic conditions increased dramatically between 1990 and 1998.[12]

A major thrust of post-colonial agricultural policy was to achieve redress of inherited inequalities through reallocation of land, the development of marketing infrastructure, and extension services. However, there was very little land redistribution in the first decade of independence. By 1990, the land-reform process had only yielded three million hectares of land, almost 40% cent of which was not conducive to farming.[13] The LHA had restricted the land-reform process to the willing-buyer-willing seller principle for ten years.[14]

Although there was very limited land redistribution in the first decade, the government became complacent in the pursuit of land reform. Government was fooled by the relatively significant progress achieved in the first five years, before the pace of land redistribution slowed down. Only 14% of the total land targeted for resettlement was acquired between 1986 and 1990. Some 27% of households were resettled compared to 70% during the preceding five-year period. The communal land reorganisation programme slowed down. Between 1986 and 1991, plans had been drawn up for only four out of 90 villages in the Uzumba-Maramba-Pfungwe (UMP) district.[15]

In the meantime, the expected migration of households to towns and cities had not materialised. Rather than the communal areas being decongested to their target population of 325 000 households, the number increased to about one million by 1990. The limits of intensifying smallholder agricultural production had also been felt. Smallholder maize production levels, which had peaked in 1985 at 1.7 million tons, declined during the four following years to below 1.35 million tons. Generous pricing policies had, by 1986, created an oversupply of maize, while marketing support and subsidies saw large and unsustainable budget deficits develop.

Owing to poor loan repayment rates, smallholder credit tailed off considerably. The number of small farmers who received loans during the 1989/1990 cropping season dropped by over 40% from its peak in 1985.[16]

A confluence of problems: The crisis since 1997

Economic meltdown combined with the crisis of expectations to worsen the alienation of the State from citizens for whom independence had yielded limited dividends. The ruling party became increasingly unpopular in the 1990s. It became the target of a radical social movement campaigning for economic and political changes in Zimbabwe, which became visible in the mid-

1990s. In 1996/1997, in particular, there began a serious political fall-out between government and critical civil society in the country. It was at this time that Zimbabwe witnessed the longest public-sector strike. This was followed by many strikes where unionised workers were joined by students, unemployed youth, the urban poor and other disgruntled organs of civil society. This culminated in the formation of the National Consultative Assembly (NCA) in 1997, whose central mission was to build national consensus through a process of constitutional reform for a new, democratic State.

Thus, in the first two decades, ZANU-PF, the party that had led the liberation struggle acquired a paradoxical image. One face of ZANU-PF was positive; having won independence, it made visible strides towards national reconciliation by appointing former political enemies from the white community and from ZAPU into its government. However, the same party began building a one-party State – one that was willing to use the hard power of the security forces against its nemeses from the onset. Leaders of the sister liberation movement, ZAPU, under Joshua Nkomo, were pushed out of government and ostracised for dissenting about the one-party State project. Thousands of their followers, mainly in Matabeleland, were killed by the notorious North Korean-trained Fifth Brigade in a ruthless security crackdown on political dissent between 1983 and 1987. This transformed the regime into a monster for many ordinary Zimbabweans. Then, in 1987, Nkomo and Mugabe smoked a peace pipe and merged their parties, but the one-party ambition of the ZANU element continued.

By 1997, many in the ruling party's constituency expected land allocations as compensation for their past loyalty. They were unhappy that only a few were benefiting. They organised themselves into the Zimbabwe National Liberation War Veterans Association (ZNLWVA) and other pressure groups centred on black empowerment and affirmative action. When the war veterans disrupted Mugabe's speech at a rally in August 1997, the government panicked. Intent on avoiding fighting a two-pronged challenge from two separate civil society fronts, it agreed to pay each of the 50 000 ex-combatants a once-off gratuity of Z$50 000 by December 1997, an amount that was not budgeted for.[17] Then, in 1999, the government joined a SADC military expedition in the Democratic Republic of the Congo (DRC) in support of Laurent Kabila, sending some 11 000 soldiers and several helicopters and attack aircrafts at huge costs to the State coffers. This caused a major budget deficit as millions of US Dollars were spent outside of budget.[18]

The emergence of the MDC in 1999 created a political vehicle for the growing agenda for political change. This was a major watershed in domestic politics in general. Unlike the Zimbabwe Unity Movement (ZUM) before it, the MDC was founded on existing and entrenched institutions of civil society and mass-based politics. It had a charismatic leader and a leadership skilled in mass mobilisation given his almost leadership of the ZCTU. It also enjoyed generous donor support – a matter that would become a liability for the movement in domestic political circles.

In response to the NCA-MDC push for a comprehensive constitutional reform process in 1999/2000, the ZANU-PF government introduced a closely controlled constitutional reform process. It took advantage of the growing demand for a "home grown" constitution to replace one written with the participation of the UK government at independence. The NCA came to represent this public need for change, which forced the ZANU-PF government to establish, on 21 May 1999, a Constitutional Commission of 400 persons to draft a new constitution. After 5 000 public meetings held throughout the country, the Commission submitted a Draft Constitution to President Mugabe on 29 November 1999. It made provisions for a Bill of Rights, a new institutional framework of government, and obliged Zimbabwe to respect international law and conventions, including foreign policy.

However, the draft submitted to Mugabe had watered down changes to the power of the executive. The NCA boycotted the meetings because it feared that the process had been hijacked by ZANU-PF leaders to legitimise their one-party regime agenda. As the contestations grew ahead of the constitutional referendum, the ZANU-PF regime made further changes to the Draft Constitution, with special reference to land acquisition and absolving government from the need to compensate landlords for confiscated land.[19] This failed to win over the poor and, instead, bolstered the "No" campaign.

Indeed, the proposed constitution was defeated in the referendum with 45% of eligible citizens voting "Yes" against 55% who said "No" to the new draft. The government was shocked. Fearing that this was a bad precedent for the impending presidential elections billed for 2002, it began a crackdown on the young opposition and the radical civil-society movement. It used State security to annihilate the party's political opponents and secure, by means of intimidation and suppression, votes for Mugabe and ZANU-PF in subsequent elections. One security chief after another declared their commitment to keep ZANU-PF in power, beginning with the then Commissioner of Police, Augustine Chihuri. On 9 January 2002, chiefs of armed forces issued a joint statement ahead of presidential elections declaring that they would not submit to a Commander-in-Chief who lacked "liberation credentials".[20]

Having paid war veterans their dues, the ZANU-PF regime turned them into instruments of ruthless oppression of dissenting voices, beginning with the violent confiscation of farmland held by white farmers accused of being sponsors of the MDC. Government incorporated war veterans into the armed forces as a reserve force, to the chagrin of many. The harassment of commercial farmers impacted the economy badly. Total output of the agricultural industry in Zimbabwe declined from 4.3 million tons of agricultural products worth US$3.347 billion in 2000 to 1.3 million tons of products or US$1 billion in 2009. This was a decline of 69% in volume and 70% in value. The productivity of smallholder farming also declined by about 74% in the same period.[21]

The war veterans and ZANU-PF youth militia intensified their terror campaign in the run-up to the 2000 parliamentary and the 2002 presidential elections, both of which took place under conditions of suppression and violence. The militia were said to have received clandestine training by the military and intelligence institutions. Thus, ZANU-PF averted the defeat and forced its way back into power. It was a narrow and contested victory, though, with ZANU-PF garnering 48.6% of the vote in the parliamentary elections to the MDC's 47%. In 2002, Mugabe received 56% of the vote and Tsvangarai 42%.[22]

The run-up to the 2005 parliamentary elections was marred with violence and other forms of State brutality against the opposition, including the clampdown on independent media, strict control over donor funding, and arbitrary arrest of critics. Opposition activists and even critical journalists did not escape the brutal hand of State security offices as they endured harassment of various forms, including abduction, arbitrary arrest, beatings and torture. In 2005, pre-election violence was orchestrated to intimidate two major constituencies of the opposition: the urban middle class and the restless peri-urban poor.[23]

As part of ZANU-PF's strategy of controlled constitutional tinkering, it established just before the elections a lower house of parliament to be stuffed with chiefs and a number of senators appointed by their president. Through Constitutional Amendment no. 17, the government introduced the Senate with powers to review, decline or accept legislation proposed by the National Assembly. Ostensibly, the Amendment was meant to enhance legislative oversight and to make it difficult for any arm of the State to abruptly introduce new policies and laws without consulting with all key constituencies, including chiefs, lower classes and ethnic groups.

The Amendment only helped to precipitate acrimonious debate within the MDC over whether the party should support and endorse this move. When the party rejected the idea, a number of its senior leaders broke away to form another MDC faction under Arthur Mutambara, a former student-activist living in the USA.

With the MDC divided and voters largely apathetic to yet another managed election, ZANU-PF won 59.6% of the vote and the MDC 39.5%. In the newly created Senate, ZANU-PF won a whopping 73% of the vote and the MDC 20%.[24] Both MDC factions suffered electoral losses; they squandered a chance to mount a strong resistance to the ZANU-PF push for re-election, thus losing credibility in a large section of their constituency.

ZANU-PF used the opportunity to further consolidate its one-party State project. Mugabe returned to cabinet his most trusted lieutenants, and installed local military leaders in strategic State agencies. The reign of terror against the opposition was sustained, notwithstanding ZANU-PF's electoral victory. Arbitrary arrests and harassment continued. Then the government launched "Operation *Murambatsvina*", whereby State security forces demolished informal settlements, ostensibly because they harboured filth, crime and other social ills. However, observers suspected that this was political retribution against the urban poor for voting for the opposition.[25]

African responses to ZANU-PF brutality

The police attacks on Tsvangarai and other leaders of the opposition and critical civil society in March 2007, which precipitated the SADC intervention, were part of the deepening authoritarianism and an attempt to annihilate the MDC before the 2008 elections. Knowing that it had failed to meet the popular aspirations of the liberation struggle, the ruling party sought to annihilate the alternative political platform for disgruntled citizens. It signalled the refusal by the regime to listen to the citizens' demand for policy space. The State used crude power to resolve what was essentially a crisis of governance. The pictures of protesters and their leaders in local and international media in March 2007, with scars from a brutal encounter with the Zimbabwe police, further embellished the image of Zimbabwe.[26] This was preceded by the installation of senior security officers in leadership positions of parastatals and at the helm of public administration. Retired General Nyambuya was appointed Minister of Energy and Power Development; Retired Brigadier-General Chiwenza is on the board of Zimbabwe Electricity Supply Commission; Brigadier-General Nyikayaramba is chairman of the National Railways of Zimbabwe; the late Air Commodore Karakadzai was general manager of the National Railways of Zimbabwe; Retired Colonel Muvhuti is general manager of the Grain Marketing Board; Retired Major-General Mbewe heads Zimbabwe Parks and Wildlife Authority; Major-General Rugeje directs Zimbabwe Broadcasting radio programmes; and Colonel Mutize headed "Operation *Maguta/Inala*", the military supervision of agriculture.[27]

ZANU-PF seemed to have been taken over by a security cabal by 2007, with the Joint Operations Command (JOC) and the party's Politburo staffed with increasing numbers of senior security officials such as Defence Forces Commander, General Chiwenga; Army Commander, Lieutenant-General Sibanda; Air Force Commander, Air-Marshal Shiri; Central Intelligence Organisation (CIO) Director-General, Retired Brigadier Bonyongwe; Commissioner of Prisons, Retired Brigadier Zimondi; Police Commissioner, Augustine Chihuri; and Deputy Police Commissioner, Godwin Matanga.[28] This group became central to strategic decisions ascribed to Mugabe. No wonder then that the ruling party increasingly use military-style tactics to deal with its political nemeses. The problem threatened to destabilise the region as droves of ordinary people fled Zimbabwe to neighbouring countries as the economy nosedived.

This new phase of securitisation of State and society caused a lot of discomfort and swayed even cautious regional states like Namibia, South Africa and Angola in favour of some form of intervention to prevent a complete meltdown in Zimbabwe. It raised fears that, come 2010, the crisis would have so deepened that it would overshadow the FIFA World Cup showpiece. The worsening crisis was hurting the region already, not only in terms of image and international pressure, but also undermining the region's bold development agenda embodied in the SADC's Regional Indicative Strategic Development Plan (RISDP).[29] Because of the deliberate internationalisation of the crisis, it was also used to undermine the New Partnership for Africa's Development (NEPAD) and the African Union (AU). The combative State response further isolated Zimbabwe in the region. As Nkomo later found, leaders of the region who themselves had led liberation struggles were puzzled that "… a nation can win freedom without its people becoming free".[30] No defence or explanation of the deepening crisis could make sense anymore. It is at this point that some leaders in the region, especially Thabo Mbeki, sensed that the conflict was ripe for concerted diplomatic intervention, in search of an amicable and negotiated political settlement and an economic recovery programme.

However, many analysts have taken their cue from the UK and USA, believing the Zimbabwe government alone was to blame for the problems gripping the country. They overlooked the impact of the inherited structural constraints to land reform and transformation. For them, the LHA is in the past and has no bearing on developments of the past decade. They even ignored the resistance of white commercial farmers and land owners to land reform. They also overlooked the failure of donors to honour their pledges of financial support, both to land reform and economic recovery, in 1981 and 1998 donor conferences. Some US$5 billion was firmly committed by multilateral and bilateral donors, but, as is generally the case with these kinds of pledges, they did not act on them. For instance, the UK government's then International Development Secretary, Baroness Clair Short, reportedly wrote a letter to the Zimbabwean government repudiating the UK's legal obligation for compensation of land expropriated at the inception of the 1997 fast-track reforms.[31] They underestimated the impact that the donor penchant for using advocacy non-governmental organisations (NGOs) and political opposition to force their agenda and cause regime change had on the intransigence of the ZANU-PF government.[32]

There was a sizeable group of voices ranging from disgruntled Zimbabweans living in neighbouring countries to regional patriots committed to seeing genuine change in Zimbabwe. An estimated two million Zimbabweans live in South Africa, while a million live in Botswana and several hundreds of thousands live in Mozambique. They did not care who was in power, but how those who were in power exercised it. They expected the region to help Zimbabwe find consensus on change needed. These voices were often clouded out by the first group composed of powerful interests in society. The governments of the region, and the continent, painstakingly distanced themselves from "Zimbabwe bashing". This is mainly because African interstate politics detests name-calling and promotes negotiation and deal-making as a way of resolving political problems. Some of the countries were worried that the problems in Zimbabwe could arise in their own countries due to the existence of similar structural distortions. Instead, they chose to engage the Zimbabwean government on its commitment to the region's codes of good governance, democracy, human rights and sense of humanity.

From the onset of the current Zimbabwean crisis, the SADC troikas met and appointed prominent envoys, tabled the matter in SADC and AU summits, and individually chastised Zimbabwe behind closed doors. Many observers dismissed these measures as worthless, but failed to acknowledge that megaphone diplomacy and targeted sanctions also failed to yield positive outcomes. Instead, these strategies helped entrench the "us-against-the world" syndrome, and allowed Harare to use anti-imperial rhetoric to appeal to deep-seated anti-colonial and Pan-Africanist sentiments in Africa.

African leaders saw that the situation in Zimbabwe was ripe for a concerted SADC-AU mediation of inter-party negotiations towards a political settlement. It was clear to the region that the Zimbabwean economy had been badly battered by the political stalemate of seven years. The Zimbabwean government had lost international credibility, its "Look-East" policy was failing to yield results, and its services were collapsing fast. The MDC resistance had achieved many things, but the prospects of it catalysing the political settlement needed were dim. The resistance took its toll on the MDC leadership, with violent suppression by government, internal fissures and donor fatigue. Former South African president, Thabo Mbeki, calculated that the "time was now", referring to the propitious conditions for a negotiated settlement.[33] The time was ripe for a negotiated resolution.

SADC mediation

The SADC-mandated mediation under Mbeki, and the power-sharing deal signed on 15 September 2008 represented what was arguably the best opportunity for Zimbabweans to construct a new dispensation for millions of Zimbabweans. The establishment early in 2009 of an inclusive government provided an institutional vehicle for the process of shaping this new future. This is because mediation was discussed with Zimbabwe's parties in March 2007, rather than imposed. The SADC Double Troika Summit held in Dar es Salaam in early April 2007 appointed South Africa as a mediator. This was preceded by a visit to Harare by Tanzanian president, Jakaya Kikwete, in his capacity as chair of the troika of the SADC Organ on Politics, Defence and Security.[34] There were many behind-the-door engagements among members of the Double Troika – that is, the troikas of the SADC and the Organ combined (six Heads of State in total). In the weeks preceding, Kikwete had held discussions with leaders of the European Union (EU) to brief them on SADC diplomatic efforts to arrest the Zimbabwe crisis. Even earlier, Zambian president, Levy Mwanawasa, gave a hint that some backroom shuttle diplomacy was taking place by saying that "willing" neighbours were talking about constructive engagement with the Zimbabwean leadership.

There are strong indications that the initiative has the full backing from key states in the region and the powerful SADC Double Troika, whose integrity and authority is at stake in the process. Mbeki brought a wealth of experience in peace diplomacy, having been involved in brokering peace in Burundi, Cote d'Ivoire, the DRC and Lesotho. South Africa brought the diplomatic prestige that it enjoys throughout the world to help manage the international dimension of the Zimbabwean conflict, constantly assuring the international community of its commitment to bring finality to the mayhem in Zimbabwe. On one occasion, in the middle of 2008, the Mbeki administration sought to neutralise international powers bent on interfering with the SADC mediation process by insisting that it was Zimbabweans only that could pull the country out of the quagmire. It rejected the USA and UK push for a critical UN Security Council resolution on Zimbabwe, fearing that it could harden positions on the negotiation table.

While SADC mediation enjoys tacit support from key global players, clearly these actors are waiting in the wings, ready to drive a more forceful international intervention should the SADC initiative fail. The fear that this could happen every time the parties deadlocked has been used by the mediation skilfully to bring parties back to the negotiation table. The mediator understands that both parties realise that the best chance for securing their interests and coming out with a mutually satisfying resolution is through the SADC initiative. He has told them that the failure of the SADC mediation and the onset of an international process would almost certainly leave the parties very limited space to stake their claim on the outcomes of a peace process, as seen in cases such as Cote d'Ivoire and Sudan. This has helped force Harare to play the game by SADC rules, although on a few occasions, such as the presidential run-off elections and the continued maltreatment of Tsvangirai, the Mugabe government has breached the SADC's word. However, the government of Zimbabwe understands that it has a better chance of protecting its interests under this initiative than under an international process.

Indeed, the SADC mediation began in May 2007, with the mediator allowing both sides to table their proposals on the agenda and framework of the mediation, both in terms of substance and process. The harmonised agenda was finally adopted on 19 June 2007. The party positions put on the agenda at the onset showed that both ZANU-PF and MDC factions were narrowly focused on creating conditions for the next round of elections, which were a few months away. This meant that, for a moment, the aspirations of Zimbabweans for freedom from fear, want and oppression were neglected, as the competition for State power became the main focus of the negotiations. While the matter of the future political, constitutional and developmental dispensation was raised by the MDC-T, it was not at the centre of discussions. From the onset, parties tended to see the facilitation as an end in itself, rather than as a mini-dialogue that could culminate in a fully inclusive national dialogue on the creation of a new Zimbabwe.

First milestone: Constitutional Amendment no. 18

It did not take long before positive outcomes were registered. The first was Constitutional Amendment no. 18, which sought to clear the way for harmonised elections (i.e. simultaneous presidential, legislative and senatorial elections) in March 2008.[35] It was adopted in October 2007, barely five months after the beginning of talks. The Amendment altered the presidential term of office from six to five years, making it coterminous with the term of national parliament. While it kept Mugabe's term to 2008 intact, the parliamentary term was cut short by two years. The Amendment also changed the method of election of a new president in the event of death, resignation or removal from office, by allowing a joint sitting of both houses of parliament to elect a new president.[36] This was designed to allow Mugabe to resign and let a ZANU-PF-controlled parliament appoint his successor. The dilemma for the former ruling party was that it did not have a strong alternative candidate to lead it to an election win, and had to hold on to Mugabe and then choose a successor. But this plan did not anticipate that ZANU-PF would lose the March 2008 elections by getting 99 parliamentary seats compared to the MDC-T's 100 seats.[37]

The Amendment also altered the composition of the House of Assembly, the higher house with full powers to make laws and policies, and the Senate, the new lower chamber with a mandate to scrutinise laws and policies referred to it by the Assembly. The size of the Senate was changed from 66 to 93 members. Six were to be elected from each of the ten provinces, ten provincial governors, two to be president and deputy president of the Council of Chiefs, 16 chiefs, and five to be appointed by the president.[38] Some 200 would be elected by voters in 200 parliamentary constituencies and 10 would be appointed by the president. The Amendment also empowered the Zimbabwe Electoral Commission (ZEC) to re-delineate the boundaries of the 200 National Assembly constituencies and 60 senatorial constituencies. It made it mandatory for the Commission to produce and submit to parliament for approval a preliminary report containing the list and maps of wards and constituencies before elections can take place.[39]

The Amendment also established the Zimbabwe Human Rights Commission (ZHRC), to be chaired by a lawyer with at least five years' experience, and comprising eight other commissioners, five of whom had to be women. The eight commissioners and the chairperson would be appointed by the president from a list of 16 put together by the Standing Rules and Orders Committee (SROC). The Amendment made provision for the president to consult with the Judicial Service Commission before making these appointments. Among the responsibilities of the Commission is to promote awareness, protection and development of human rights, monitor the observance of human rights and investigate breaches by any authority or persons, and advise the president on the promotion of human rights. The Amendment also created the position of a Deputy Chief Justice and changed the titles of Commissioner of Police and Ombudsman to Commissioner-General and Public Protector respectively.[40]

Constitutional Amendment no. 18 received unusual bipartisan support in parliament and was thus approved without any hiccups. This was unusual for a parliament accustomed to fractures and inter-party conflict. The inter-party harmony and the Amendment were hailed as a beginning of a new chapter in the party politics of Zimbabwe, one built on mutual respect and ability to form cross-party alliances for the greater good of the country. This was seen as a good sign that facilitated negotiations were making progress in building inter-party trust and destroying the walls of hatred and acrimony that had characterised the relationship between ZANU-PF and the MDC since 2001.[41]

Second milestone: Harmonised elections in March 2008

As a result of the headways made during facilitated talks between ZANU-PF and the two factions of the MDC, the run-up to the 29 March elections was generally smooth. The beginning of these talks, in May 2007, resulted in a decline in political violence and the toning down of inflammatory political rhetoric by both sides. By the time Constitutional Amendment no. 18 was passed by parliament in October 2007, MDC factions were able to hold huge rallies without much intimidation.[42] Somehow, unruly youth and war veterans vacated the streets and stopped harassing peri-urban and rural villages thought to be pro-MDC. [43]

The electioneering period saw robust but relatively non-violent competition for voters between ZANU-PF and the MDC-T especially. ZANU-PF went full swing with its election campaign in January 2008, holding mass rallies mainly in its traditional rural powerbases, but later turned to the MDC-dominated urban centres of Bulawayo and Harare, as well as Mutare. The party used the personal aura and eloquence of Mugabe to sway voters. Mugabe upped his anti-Western rhetoric and, in the process, lumped the MDC-T with the colonial agenda to subvert the hard-won independence of Zimbabwe. However, in a massive show of strength, the MDC-T held huge rallies in rural constituencies in a calculated strategy to take advantage of the suspension of State brutality to expand its powerbase from urban to rural. Tsvangirai's public-speaking skills were combined with innovative campaign methods, including the use of a campaign bus that wooed the media to follow the MDC in its election trips across the country. Conditions were such that even the MDC could conduct door-to-door campaigns openly and relatively freely.[44] The watchful eye of the AU and SADC, and mediation, helped guarantee the much improved election conditions.

Under these circumstances, ZANU-PF reformist and former Minister of Finance, Dr Simbarashe Makoni, entered the elections in February 2008, standing as an independent candidate for the presidency. Makoni sought to take advantage of grave divisions within ZANU-PF over the results of primary elections to launch a reformist front from outside the party, although he had hoped to run without losing his membership of ZANU-PF. However, the party expelled him and he was forced to stand as an independent. This irked the ZANU-PF leadership, careful to hide internal divisions, and fearing that Makoni could play to ZANU-PF's deep weaknesses, which he knew too well. Mugabe called him a political prostitute, a sell-out and a political adventurer driven by ambitions for personal gain.[45] While ZANU-PF energies were directed at Makoni, Tsvangirai was allowed space to push ahead with his campaigns for several weeks without much challenge.

Pre-election conditions and the peaceful elections day helped make it possible for the MDC to narrowly defeat ZANU-PF in the 29 March polls. The much-expected results of the elections started trickling out on 31 March, with dramatic news that two senior ZANU-PF ministers – Justice Minister Patrick Chinamasa, and Public Affairs Minister Chen Chimutengwende – had lost elections in their respective constituencies. Then results started coming in in dribs and drabs, raising suspicion that there were attempts to manipulate them in two ways: one was to choreograph the release of results such that the two parties were running neck and neck until the very last moment, when a surprise tie or win by ZANU-PF would be announced; and the second was to swing the votes in favour of ZANU-PF when the final tallies were made. Employing this strategy caused delays in the announcement of results. It was only on 15 April, more than two weeks after the elections, that the ZEC released the final House of Assembly results. These showed that the MDC-T had won the contest with 100 seats to ZANU-PF's 99, the MDC-M's 10 and one seat to an independent candidate. The Senate results showed that ZANU-PF and the MDC-T had 30 seats apiece.[46] The new president would still have to appoint 12 more senators, thus leaving room for either Mugabe or Tsvangirai to tilt the balance in their party's favour. For this reason, the defeated ZANU-PF was determined from that point, as signalled by the tone of statements after its hastily convened Politburo and executive meetings, to ensure that Mugabe retained the presidency at all costs.

For more than a month, the ZEC refused to release the final results of the presidential contest, without a real reason. It appeared to be under pressure from ZANU-PF not to allow its complete departure from power. It was made to wait for ZANU-PF to hold its leadership meetings on their post-election strategies before releasing the final results on 2 May 2008. The ZEC blamed technicalities and workload for the delay, but there was fear that, in fact, it had been completely subordinated to Mugabe's inner cabinet of security chiefs and party apparatchiks to manage this part of the electoral management process. The delay caused fear that Kenya-like post-electoral violence might erupt in Zimbabwe, with dire consequences for the region. The SADC held an emergency meeting on 12 April 2008 to consider its response to the looming crisis. The meeting concluded with a commitment to finding political solutions to Zimbabwe's problems, urged the ZEC to verify and release all outstanding results without further delay, and called upon all parties to accept the results as the express will of the people.[47]

The confusion over the release of results was not the only controversy gripping Zimbabwe during the elections. The news of a Chinese ship, *An Yue Jiang*, carrying a load of all sorts of weapons destined for Zimbabwe caused alarm in the southern African region and elsewhere. It raised fears that the arrival of the weapons would enable the regime to intimidate and suppress opposition parties in a bid to return ZANU-PF to power. The ship, originally scheduled to dock in Durban, South Africa, was unable to dock due to a courageous strike by dock workers opposed to the shipment of arms to Zimbabwe in the midst of hot political contest. It was also refused entry into Angola and Mozambique, forcing its owners to recall it to China at the end of April.[48] This was a massive victory for anti-war and human rights movements in southern Africa. They had managed to force governments in the region to adopt a non-indifference stance on the shipment of arms to Zimbabwe. This was in contrast to the old tendency to hide behind non-intervention principles of the Organisation of African Unity (OAU) to avoid taking a stance against one of its members.

The final results of the presidential race were eventually released in early May 2008. They showed that Tsvangirai had won the elections with 47.9% of the votes to Mugabe's 43.2%, while Makoni received 8%. The failure of Tsvangirai to gain more than 50% of the votes forced him into a run-off against Mugabe, hastily scheduled for 27 June. Indications were that ZANU-PF was forewarned of this and had started preparing the ground to deploy the State security apparatus that it controlled to limit the ability of Tsvangirai to mount a real challenge to Mugabe's re-election campaign. The run-up to the run-off was a complete contrast to the calm and tolerant political environment before the March elections. There was a sudden resurgence of violence, unleashed mainly by ZANU-PF youth militia, and the brutality of the State security forces against opposition members, leaders and supporters. MDC rallies were disrupted and its rolling campaigns were hindered by illegal roadblocks and arbitrary arrests. The brutality was so bad that it forced Tsvangarai to withdraw from the run-off in early June, leaving Mugabe to run as sole candidate in the election that both the AU and SADC advised should be cancelled to allow Tsvangarai to participate.

Indications were that the military cabal that had become influential in ZANU-PF politics had decided, even before the release of election results, to win the run-off through any means. It was obvious from the activities that followed the announcement of the run-off that a security plan had been put in place to make it difficult for Tsvangarai to campaign and force him to quit the polls. ZANU-PF strategists were not certain if Mugabe could win the elections in an environment free of violence and intimidation. They feared that his loss on 29 March could lose them even more support as their supporters start seeing Mugabe as vulnerable.

Third milestone: The power-sharing deal

The SADC expressed dismay and called for a political settlement through its mediator, Thabo Mbeki. The AU effectively refused to recognise the results of the 27 June elections when the AU Summit in Egypt on 1 July called for a GNU.[49] Several African leaders spoke openly and loudly about the shenanigans caused by ZANU-PF's hunger for power. This included the presidents of Botswana and Zambia, the prime minister of Kenya, and various other prominent Africans.

The MDC victory in the parliamentary elections, narrow as it was, ushered in a new era in the legislature, with the election of its MP as the first opposition Speaker. However, the controversies surrounding the presidential elections have dominated Zimbabwean politics ever since. On 10 July 2008, the parties were back to the proverbial square one as they started negotiations towards a GNU. The three party principals met on 21 July to officially launch negotiations by agreeing to the framework for the talks. They signed a Memorandum of Understanding (MOU) in which they committed their respective parties to "… dialogue with each other with a view to creating a genuine, viable, permanent and sustainable solution to the Zimbabwean situation".[50] But the real work had begun as early as March of the same year in Kariba, where mediated talks between the two parties led to the Kariba Draft, which is believed to have informed Constitutional Amendment no. 18.

> The Memorandum of Understanding between ZANU-PF, MDC-T and MDC-M set out the framework agenda as follows:
>
> Economic stability:
> - Economic stabilisation
> - Sanctions
> - Land questions
>
> Political:
> - New constitution
> - Promotion of equality, national healing and cohesion, and unity
> - External interference
> - Free political activity
> - Rule of law
> - State organs and institutions
> - Legislative agenda priorities
> - Security of persons and prevention of violence
>
> Communication:
> - Media
> - External radio stations

The MoU further committed the parties to produce an implementation framework and guidelines, and a GPA at the conclusion of talks. They also committed to talk until they agreed, under the facilitation of SADC mediator Thabo Mbeki. The MoU also contained interim measures, namely: all parties would issue official statements condemning political violence and ensure that the institutions and people each party controlled refrained from acts of violence; ensured equal application of the law; assisted the return of displaced people; and refrained from talk that inflamed violence. The MoU was very significant as it established the basis for negotiating and sealing a political deal later.

It would take another painstaking six weeks of intensive talks in secret locations in South Africa for the parties to produce a GPA. The hostile relationship between ZANU-PF and MDC-T surfaced many times in the course of talks. Several times, Tsvangarai threatened to pull out of the talks because of continued harassment of members and activists. It also cited continued bully tactics by ZANU-PF and an uneven handling of the heated dialogue by the mediator. The MDC called for a change of mediator several times, but to no avail, as the AU and SADC stood steadfast by Mbeki.

The GPA was formally launched with much ceremony on 15 September 2008. It was similar to other power-sharing agreements in Africa, notably the Kenyan, Ivorian, and Sudanese deals, in that it was first and foremost about the sharing of executive power, despite making provisions for political and economic reforms on a grand scale. The agreement provided for a two-tier executive: one being a cabinet of ministers responsible for the overall strategic direction of government chaired by Mugabe as president; and the Council of Ministers charged with overseeing the implementation of policies and programmes of government under the chairpersonship of Tsvangirai as executive prime minister. Mugabe would be assisted by two vice-presidents, while Tsvangirai would also have two deputies, one of whom would be Mutambara, the leader of the smaller faction of the MDC. It was later agreed that the second deputy prime minister would be Thokozani Kuphe of the MDC-T.

The formula for the composition of both the cabinet and the Council of Ministers was similar, in that the 31 members would comprise of 15 ministers from ZANU-PF, 13 from the MDC-T, and three from the MDC-M. The detailed breakdown of the corresponding mandates of the two bodies demonstrated the will of the parties to ensure greater collaboration on the basis of a neat distinction of duties and clear lines of interface between institutions controlled by either party.[51]

The Agreement retained some powers of the president, including the power to chair the cabinet with the prime minister as a deputy chairperson; powers to approve laws brought to him by cabinet and sign treaties on behalf of Zimbabwe; the authority to declare war and conduct national ceremonies; and powers to appoint the cabinet and persons proposed for diplomatic posts. While the responsibility to direct the national effort to address the needs of the people through economic, social and political programmes were ceded to the prime minister, whose duty it was also to supervise the entire government and oversee coherent efforts by various departments and organs of State to achieve national goals. In a sense, therefore, the president lost significant powers that Mugabe had held on his own for three decades. The prime minister position was also given significant powers to run the government. In this way, Mugabe was to become Head of State, while Tsvangirai would become a head of government. This delicate balance was designed to ensure that power sharing in the new government would be serious. Further provisions on the functions of the various segments of the executive show an intention to force the president to consult and work with the prime minister in running the affairs of the State.

Although most of the analysis and public commentary on the Agreement tend to focus on the executive power arrangement, the deal was also significant in what it said about other matters significant for effective political change. Principal among these are provisions of the Agreement that set the framework for a more fundamental transformation of politics and society in Zimbabwe. This included the provision for a structured and inclusive process of constitutional reform.

The parties agreed that it was the fundamental right of the people of Zimbabwe to play an active part in the drafting of a constitution in a transparent and democratic process, so that they would own it. The expectation was that this would take a year to complete. The parties agreed to set up a Parliamentary Select Committee that would appoint multi-party sub-committees to draft various sections of the constitution for public comment. The Draft Constitution would be put through a referendum three months after the signing of the Agreement. The Agreement imposed no preconditions, except that it should give practical expression to the common values of national reconciliation, national unity, national sovereignty, human rights and the rule of law.

The Agreement also made provisions for a concerted effort led by the new government to bring about national healing and unity, cohesion and equality. The idea was that the new government would promote the equality of all Zimbabweans and equal development of all regions of Zimbabwe. Such a government was mandated to set up mechanisms to advise and assist it in promoting national healing, national unity and political tolerance after years of polarisation and violence. It would also put measures in place to attract Zimbabweans who had fled the country to come back and help rebuild its shattered economy and society in general.

The power-sharing agreement also pronounced in detail how the new government and society would be built on a human rights framework. Several articles of the agreement elaborated on how the new government would promote freedom of political activity, freedom of association, the rule of law, and respect for the constitution. Article 18 has a long list of measures to be taken to eradicate the culture and infrastructure of violence built over two decades of misrule. These include stopping the use of violence for political goals and promoting the culture of political tolerance, non-violence and dialogue. This was a significant move to shift the normative framework governing the conduct of politics and human behaviour in a new Zimbabwe away from authoritarianism, militarism and elitism.

The third major thrust of the Agreement is the transformation of economics and development. This has a number of elements. The first substantive article of the Agreement (Article 3) is actually about the restoration of economic stability and growth through the development and implementation of an economic recovery strategy and plan. This plan, which was to be developed by all parties working together, was meant to address urgent short-term problems of economic production, food security, inputs and seeds for the agricultural season of 2008/2009; and medium-term challenges of high inflation, interest rates and the exchange rate. The plan would also address long-term systemic challenges of the economy, such as deep poverty, high unemployment and disinvestment.

The Agreement provided for the establishment of a National Economic Council (NEC) comprising political parties and key economic sectors such as manufacturing, mining, agriculture, tourism, commerce, financial, labour and academia, to formulate economic plans and advise government in its management of economic recovery. It is not clear if this council will have a legal and formal standing like oversight structures. The parties also agreed to provide space for the implementation of SADC ideas on economic recovery, including support that SADC member states have committed to provide once a peace agreement is signed and a new government is established in Zimbabwe. Finally, the Agreement mandated the parties to re-engage the international community to stop sanctions and economic isolation of Zimbabwe. This has not happened yet, partly because the inclusive government is still setting its policies in place and consulting with the SADC on economic recovery. The hope was that, if this was made as a joint call by internal parties, with the support of guarantors of the agreement (SADC and the AU), it could assist the region begin an economic recovery support programme for Zimbabwe.

The question of land reform is also given special prominence, with a full article dedicated to this matter. The Agreement acknowledges that land question is part of the colonial legacy of Zimbabwe, with pre-independence patterns of land ownership having persisted into the post-independence period. It recognises that it was a major goal for which the liberation struggle was fought. It also expresses the desirability of comprehensive land reform, thus acknowledging that the ZANU-PF government's land expropriation programme was not comprehensive. However, the detail on how this reform programme would come about and how it could be implemented is not included in the Agreement. It is still a subject of further negotiations by the parties.

The stalemate over power sharing

At the outset, the Agreement was signed under protest. It was very clear that the parties had been rushed into an agreement so that the SADC could celebrate something at its scheduled Ordinary Summit in August 2008. The old problem of agreements for their own sake had, thus, somewhat resurfaced in this regard. During the launch of the Agreement, and in subsequent days, Tsvangirai was cautious about its prospects because, in his view, power-sharing arrangements are by nature undemocratic pacts by political elites for their own interests. He was also worried about being part of a growing trend on the African continent, where election losers use their control of the means of violence to force winners into an executive political power-sharing arrangement.

Political games and grandstanding aside, Tsvangirai knew about the general unease about the power-sharing arrangements. These long-held concerns had been heightened in the aftermath of the signing of a similar agreement in Kenya after terrible post-election violence. The Kenyan deal was mediated by former UN Secretary-General, Kofi Annan, following post-election violence in December 2007. There was a lot of media analysis pointing out the underlying weaknesses of power-sharing politics, which attracted a lot of public misgivings about the willingness of Africa to sacrifice the express will of the people to return unwanted rulers into power by some elite pact. Tsvangirai must have picked up on this sentiment and realised the negative bearing it would have on the MDC's high moral ground political stance in Zimbabwean politics.

On the other side, ZANU-PF was at pains to defend the power-sharing deal. Its discomfort was epitomised by ambiguity displayed by Mugabe in his speech during the formal signing ceremony in Harare; it too was less than willing to make it work strictly on its terms. Mugabe saw the accord as opening a new chapter in the history of Zimbabwe, one which ZANU-PF would not be in full control over, because it was to be governed by means it was not fully accustomed to. He pointed out that there were many provisions that he and his party were unhappy with, but praised Mbeki for his persistence and creativity. He suggested that they had been persuaded and forced by the skill of the mediator to agree to each term of the Agreement. Mugabe warned opposition parties not to act as if they were the governing party as ZANU-PF was still the ruling party despite losing the 29 March elections.[52] He committed ZANU-PF to a position where it would be senior party to the Agreement, suggesting that the party would mentor its MDC colleagues, whom they knew were inexperienced in the business of running a government. Again and again, this condescending attitude came out as ZANU-PF explained the stalemate over the allocation of ministerial portfolios where it suggested that the MDC were not ready to govern because they lacked experience and Tsvangirai had no tertiary education.[53]

Annoyed by constant reference to the fundamental weakness of the Kenya deal, ZANU-PF spokespersons were quick to point out that Zimbabwe would have its own unique approach to power sharing, different to that of the Kenyan model.[54] On closer examination of their statements and general conduct, ZANU-PF had a worse approach to power sharing than the parties in the much-vilified Kenyan model. It saw power sharing as a way of co-opting its nemesis into power as a junior party, to neutralise its links with its archenemy: the West. Its attitude was that it would take what it wanted from the new government and leave the rest to the MDC as a junior partner. ZANU-PF rhetoric shows that it views the Agreement as ceding elements of its power rather than about sharing power granted to it by the people of Zimbabwe. This is a fundamental problem in Zimbabwe at the moment.

Mugabe and ZANU-PF assumed that all they needed to do was make space for Tsvangirai, Mutambara and their party leaders to take junior posts in the cabinet. The three parties to the Agreement were scheduled to meet the day after its signing to finalise the appointment of the cabinet, but the meeting was called off because ZANU-PF had suddenly convened a meeting of its Politburo.[55] The MDC-T position was that the three parties should share the ministries equitably in each of the three clusters of government: security, administration/social cluster and economy. On this basis then, if ZANU-PF took control of the Defence ministry, the MDC-T would take the Home Affairs ministry, which controls the police, and the MDC-M would control Internal Security. The same would apply to the Industry and Commerce, Mines and Mining Development, and Finance ministries. The MDC-M kept an open mind, preferring to allow negotiations to find the best formula for the apportionment of ministries. This was calculated to give the MDC-M power to broker the impasse between the two senior partners. In turn, the party saw the Agreement as the easiest route to power sharing.

As the mediator made moves to avoid an impasse, ZANU-PF released to the media an apportionment of ministries in which it retained all key cabinet portfolios like Finance, Foreign Affairs, Defence, Home Affairs, Mines and Mining Development, and Internal Security; and allocated difficult and junior ministries like Labour and Social Welfare; Education, Sport and Culture; and Health and Child Welfare to the MDC factions. This precipitated a war of words between the MDC-T and ZANU-PF. With party negotiators around the table in October 2008, ZANU-PF went on to fill the ministries of Defence, Home Affairs, Justice and Legal Affairs, Information and Communications Technology, and Internal Security with its own leaders, without consultation.[56]

There are various perspectives on the stalemate from each of the three signatories to the September Agreement. The MDC-T contends that there has been no agreement on the allocation of cabinet portfolios and the appointment of ZANU-PF ministers was a unilateral move by the former ruling party and a direct onslaught on the Agreement. The proposal on the table is for the sharing of ministries by signatories in all sectors of government: security, political, social and economic. ZANU-PF wants the sharing of all but a few key ministries, which it argues should be run by its ministries because they have requisite experience and expertise, which the MDCs do not. These are the ministries of Defence, Home Affairs and Internal Security, and Foreign Affairs. In a further compromise brokered by the mediator, the MDC-T was forced to moderate its proposal, accepting ZANU-PF's right to security ministries on condition that the Home Affairs ministry is given to the MDC-T. ZANU-PF refused, leading to a proposal that was endorsed by the SADC that the two parties should share the portfolio of Home Affairs.[57] However, the MDC-T publicly condemned the SADC for forcing it to give endless concessions to ZANU-PF, without any compromises on its part. It expressed its disappointment in the mediator for allegedly failing to tell the truth about ZANU-PF obstinacy.

ZANU-PF ministers dismissed in January 2008:

- Samuel Mumbengegwi (Finance), appointed in February 2007
- Sikhanyiso Ndlovu (Information and Publicity)
- Oppah Muchinguri (Women's Affairs, Gender and Community Development)
- Munacho Mutezo (State Water Resources and Infrastructural Development)
- Michael Nyambuya (Energy and Power Development)
- Amos Midzi (Mines and Mining Development)
- Chen Chimutengwende (Public and Interactive Affairs)
- Sithembiso Nyoni (Small and Medium Enterprises Development)
- Rugare Gumbo (Agriculture), who lost in the Zanu-PF primaries.

Deputy Ministers who lost in the ZANU-PF primaries:

- Kenneth Mutiwekuziva (Small and Medium Enterprises Development)
- David Chapfika (Agriculture)
- Edwin Muguti (Health and Child Welfare)

Tsvangirai failed to get the government to issue him with a full passport to travel to an emergency SADC Summit in Swaziland in October 2008. He was, instead, issued with a temporary travel document that was valid for the duration of the meeting, a deliberate ploy to ensure that he did not have time to mobilise the region or Africa against ZANU-PF. Even this document was issued only after SADC leaders protested and postponed the meeting. After the meeting, Tsvangirai refused to return to Zimbabwe until he was issued with a full passport. While he waited for the passport, Tsvangirai mobilised support using South Africa's wide media platform and later relocated to Botswana, an outspoken critic of ZANU-PF.

To pile pressure and as part of an assertive element of its policy, the South African government withheld R300 million (US$30 million) meant to fund agriculture activities until an inclusive government was in place.[58] It used this figure as a carrot to get the Zimbabwean parties to resolve all remaining challenges on the table.

At the continental level, there was growing support for the SADC initiative and strong consensus on the need to provide high-level support to South Africa. The AU resolution of 1 July 2008 on the Zimbabwe crisis mediation led to the appointment of a reference group comprising the UN Secretary-General's representative, the SADC Executive Secretary, and AU Commission Chairman, Jean Ping.[59] This helped provide significant political support for the much-vilified mediator, Thabo Mbeki, at a time when he was under political pressure to concentrate on the domestic situation in South Africa. This was also the point when the MDC-T called for his replacement with Kofi Annan, in the hope that Annan would be able to replicate his quick success in a much more complex crisis in Zimbabwe.

In December 2008, Mugabe formally invited Tsvangirai and Mutambara to take up the positions of prime minister and deputy prime minister respectively. This followed an intense ZANU-PF National Congress that agreed the party strategy on power sharing. Indeed, subsequent to the meeting, the ZANU-PF-controlled administration finally issued Tsvangirai with a passport, bringing to an end several weeks of controversy over the decision to issue him with a temporary travel document to attend a SADC meeting in South Africa. Then, on 2 January 2009, Mugabe fired nine ministers and three deputy ministers who had failed to retain their parliamentary seats during the 29 March elections. Most of these ministers were considered lightweights in ZANU-PF's pecking order. In response, the MDC-controlled Speaker of Parliament decided to convene on 20 January 2009, to approve the formation of the new government and begin its part in the implementation of the Agreement, the clearest indication that some progress had been made in the inter-party dialogue. Tsvangirai returned to Zimbabwe in mid-January 2009 and had a one-on-one meeting with Mugabe to finalise some details about the dialogue.

The government was subsequently established with the swearing-in of MDC ministers and deputy ministers. But the MDC's treasurer, who was nominated for the position of Deputy Minister of Agriculture, could not be sworn-in because he was arrested for what some think were trumped-up charges by the ZANU-PF-controlled police. There was also tension over Mugabe's unilateral changes to the portfolios of Information and Communication, moving the powerful publicity and information (read propaganda) element to ZANU-PF's Webster Shamu, and leaving the MDC-T's Nelson Chamisa with the rest (*See* Appendix A).[60]

Perpetual movement from change to status quo: static dynamism in Zimbabwe's peace process

It remains to be seen whether the establishment of the inclusive government under the watchful eye of the SADC and the rest of the international community will translate to long-lasting peace and fundamental change in the culture of politics in Zimbabwe. The protracted peace process has, over the years, been characterised by many missed opportunities and a number of near-breakthroughs. There is mutual mistrust among the parties as shown by the speed with which they refer matters of difficulty to the mediator and guarantors.

There has been a tendency for the crisis to move from static to dynamic and back to static. This creates a sense of movement towards peace and democracy, but, in essence, the fundamental reality is that there is no movement. The developments that followed the signing of the Agreement in September 2008 suggest that a lot of progress is being achieved. In fact, the results of the March 2008 elections meant that the balance of power on the ground had swung in favour of the MDC factions at the expense of ZANU-PF. It is safe to read out of this that the latter was left with no choice but to follow the advice of the SADC regarding a negotiated settlement. The very fact that Mugabe shares his seat with Tsvangarai at SADC and AU summits is indicative of this shift.

It is not unlikely that ZANU-PF is buying time by making half-hearted concessions in order to avoid losing the support of the southern African region, without actually making progress towards peace. Superficial changes and peace rhetoric are part of the calculated strategy of the party to deceive its domestic opponents, external critics and the region into false hopes. It announced certain changes, even before the new government was formed, to suggest that it was capable of transformation on its own. But it also did so in order to pre-empt the changes that MDC ministers were bound to make, thus robbing them of the credit. For instance, it was the ZANU-PF cabinet that dropped price and exchange controls, and began the dollarisation of the economy in late 2008 when it was clear that the MDC-T would get the Finance portfolio in cabinet. This was also an attempt to minimise the amount of power that this and other portfolios would have in the name of deregulation. It seems that the former ruling party is intent on maintaining the status quo, allowing variations it can live with and resisting fundamental changes that would alter the balance of power and the political culture in Zimbabwe.

The disputes over the allocation of ministries in December 2008, the allocation of provincial governors until February 2009, and subsequent conflict over the appointment of the Attorney-General and Reserve Bank Governor suggest deep-seated mistrust between ZANU-PF and the MDC factions. It is also a sign of difficulties inherent in the shift of the balance of power away from ZANU-PF, as demonstrated in the 29 March elections. They also illustrate the difficulties that power sharing confronts when signed by two mutually suspicious parties.

Finally, government was formed with the swearing-in of members of the new cabinet from all three parties according to the formula agreed in the September Accord. The business of ruling in co-operation began in earnest. Keen to demonstrate that they were ready to run Zimbabwe, MDC ministers moved quickly to outline their plans, especially on economic rejuvenation, international relations and public services, including the payment of salaries to disgruntled public servants. Prime Minister Tsvangirai and Deputy Prime Minister Mutambara also stepped out from the word go to demonstrate visible leadership, visiting hotspots of political conflict and social disintegration. They spoke firmly against the continued invasion of farms and harassment of farmworkers by ZANU-PF aligned groups. They travelled the region assuring neighbouring states of their intention to make this government work at any costs. They moved quickly also to avoid internal rebellion within their own parties because of differences over how enthusiastically the MDCs should participate in the inclusive government.

The willingness of Mugabe to give this inclusive government the benefit of the doubt, at least, but more so its political leadership, also helped isolate ZANU-PF hardliners who wanted the power-sharing agreement undermined from the word go. Mugabe toned down on his anti-Western and anti-MDC rhetoric, allowing for a new kind of language to emerge in Zimbabwe's political platforms: a discourse of reconstruction and reconciliation. While he did not help resolve the ongoing dispute over the Reserve Bank Governor and Attorney-General positions, even Tsvangirai publicly declared that Mugabe had become a positive influence in the implementation of the power-sharing agreement. However, the inclusive government has had to refer matters time and again to the mediator because of ZANU-PF's reluctance to give in on anything without putting up a fight.

Mugabe's soft touch may have been motivated by his eagerness to leave a positive legacy after a decade of misrule, but ZANU-PF as an institution is still geared to undermining its political opponents in the hope of returning to a one-party regime scenario. This means that, until the crisis seriously hurts ZANU-PF, the process of change will be slowed down by frequent stumbling blocks placed mainly by this party. For as long as ZANU-PF see other ways of achieving its interests, the power-sharing deal will either be manipulated or ignored. It still believes that it can use the transitional power-sharing arrangement to weaken MDC power on the ground. ZANU-PF is constantly sending messages, domestically and externally, that the MDC factions have failed to help Zimbabwe get rid of Western sanctions, suggesting that the MDC had no political influence on their sponsors.

Until the MDC factions manage to galvanise all key internal and external role players in support of a thorough implementation of the agreement, the stalemate will persist. By stakeholders we mean active civil society, organised business and youth formations, as well as regional states, continental organisations and global institutions. As long as the perception persists in the region that the MDC is fighting to protect its narrow sectional interests and an external political agenda, its struggle will remain weakened in the region.

Conclusion

Another long meeting of the SADC Heads of State was held in Tshwane, South Africa, on 27 January 2009, produced a firm undertaking by ZANU-PF and the MDC to forge ahead with implementation of the September Accord. This led to the establishment of a three-apiece Joint Monitoring and Implementation Committee (JMIC) to oversee the implementation of the Agreement, receive and process progress reports, resolve disputes, and promote continuous dialogue among the parties.

Members of the Joint Monitoring and Implementation Committee

MDC-M	MDC-T	ZANU PF
Professor Welshman Ncube (co-chairperson) Mr Frank Chamunorwa Mr Edward Mkhosi Ms Priscilla Misihairabwi-Mushonga	Mr Elton Mangoma (co-chairperson), Mr Elias Mudzuri, Ms Tabitha Khumalo Mr Innocent Changonda	Mr Nicholas Goche (co-chairperson) Mr Patrick Chinamasa Mr Emmerson Mnangagwa Ms Oppah Muchinguri

The new cabinet was sworn in on 13 February 2009, after last-minute horse-trading under the guidance of SADC mediator, President Kgalema Motlanthe of South Africa, Minister Dos Anjos of Angolam and SADC Executive Secretary, Tomaz Salamão.

This illustrates the ability of the parties to make major strides with the assistance of SADC mediation. This was a major milestone, built on several other milestones littered between several deadlocks and collapses of the mediated peace process. It was built over a long period of patient persuasion and guidance by the mediation team, comprising senior officials from the SADC and AU under the leadership of Thabo Mbeki. It was also made possible by the ripeness of the Zimbabwe situation for resolution, made even more apparent by the high expectations that ordinary Zimbabweans had of the peace process, including a dire humanitarian situation due to the collapse of State services, a drought, and the outbreak of a cholera epidemic.

Making the agreement work will, however, be difficult because of a history of political acrimony between the ZANU-PF and the MDC-T, deep mutual suspicion and entrenched political cultures. While it is still at the crossroads with an inclusive government in place, Zimbabwe looks set to turn the corner towards an enduring democracy, provided the parties succeed in making peace and democratisation attractive, isolate spoilers, and create an inclusive national process of nation building and change. The role of the SADC and other regional organisations in support of this process will be so critical that it will be the defining factor between dynamism and statism in this process.

[1]   The agreement bound parties to a ceasefire accord, constitutionalism and inaugural elections. With regard to land reform, a clause in the agreement stipulated: "… the development or utilisation of that or other property in such a manner as to promote the public benefit or, in the case of under-utilised land, settlement of land for agricultural purposes. When property is wanted for one of these purposes, its acquisition will be lawful only on condition that the law provides for the prompt payment of adequate compensation and, where the acquisition is contested, that a court order is obtained". *See* Lancaster House Agreement at http://*www.zwnews.com/Lancasterhouse.doc*. *Accessed 6 September 2001. See also* Harold-Barry (2004:48).

[2]   UNDP (2008:149).

[3]   Kanyenze, in Harold-Barry (2004:112).

[4]   Originally, this appeared in *The Chronicle*, 18 April 1980. It is quoted by Bizos (2007:556).

[5]   Deve & Goncalves (1994:3–9).

[6]   Robertson (2007).

[7]   Harold-Barry (2004:123).

[8]   Kanyenze, in Harold-Barry (2004:112–113).

[9]   Ibid.

[10] Sachikonye (n.d.:102–104).

[11] Ndlela, in Lee & Colvard (n.d.:133 –158).

[12] Robertson (2007).

[13] Moyo (2000:5–28).

[14] Comments made at Southern African Liaison Office (SALO) meeting, Johannesburg, 1 March 2008.

[15] Moyo (2000:12).

[16] Ibid.

[17] In 2000, US$1 equalled Z$50.

[18] *See* "Mugabe's costly Congo venture" at http://news.bbc.co.uk/2/hi/africa/611898.stm. Accessed 4 May 2007.

[19] Author's interviews with constitutional expert, Harare, 20-26 May 2007. *See also* "Zimbabwe: Constitutional Reform – an opportunity to strengthen human rights" at http://www.amnesty.org/en/library/info/AFR46/001/2000. Accessed 2 September 2008.

[20] Maroleng (2005:5).

[21] Cross (2009:1–6).

[22] *See* "Zimbabwe: 2002 Presidential Election Results" at http://www.eisa.org.za/WEP/zimresults2002.htm. Accessed 23 September 2002.

[23] Chiroro (2005).

[24] Ibid.

[25] Maroleng (2005:3–5).

[26] "Zimbabwe: SA Government holds on the line" in *Business Day*, 22 March 2007.

[27] Many of these appointments were widely reported in the State press, *The Herald*, and debated in independent media.

[28] Muzondidya (2007).

[29] The RISDP was developed as part of SADC reforms that began in 1999 and ended in 2003/2004. It is a comprehensive developmental agenda for SADC integration incorporating all sectoral policies/plans. *See* Zondi (2007:47–53).

[30] Quoted in Masunungure, in Harold-Barry (2004:147).

[31] Quoted in *The Herald*, 4 March 2000.

[32] This point is made by various analysts, including Issa Shivji.

[33] *See* "Solve Zimbabwe or risk blight on World Cup" at http://www.monstersandcritics.com/news/africa/news/article_1285840.php/Tsvangirai_warns_Mbeki_Solve_Zimbabwe_or_risk_blight_on_World_Cup. Accessed 8 November 2008.

[34] This is the security arm of the SADC responsible for managing conflicts and wars in the region.

[35] *See* party responses to this amendment at http://www.newzimbabwe.com/pages/parly30.16937.html. Accessed February 2008.

[36] See comments on the amendment by MDC deputy head, Thokozani Khuphe, at http://www.newzimbabwe.com/pages/parly30.16937.html. Accessed 25 May 2008.

[37] "Zimbabwe Senate and Assembly Results", Reuters, 22 August 2008.

[38] Ibid.

[39] Ibid.

[40] *See* comments by Thokozani Khuphe on the amendment at http://www.newzimbabwe.com/pages/parly30.16937.html. Accessed 25 May 2008.

[41] The author was one of those who saw a silver lining, thereby raising public expectations of the SADC-mediated talks held in South Africa.

[42] This was the view of most observer mission reports, including the very critical Pan African Parliament and SADC Observer Missions.

[43] Ibid.

[44] Author's observations.

[45] *See* http://www.mg.co.za/article/2008-02-22-mugabe-says-challenger-makoni-is-a-prostitute. Accessed 23 February 2008.

[46] "Zimbabwe Senate and Assembly results", Reuters, 22 August 2008.

[47] "Summit delivers no quick fix to Zimbabwe deadlock", AFP (IOL), 13 April 2008.

[48] "Arms ship not docking" at http://www.thetimes.co.za/News/Article.aspx?id=752876.

[49] *See* http://news.bbc.co.uk/2/hi/africa/7484165.stm. Accessed 12 August 2008.

[50] *See* "Memorandum of Understanding" at http://www.issafrica.org. Accessed 3 October 2008.

[51] *See* the GPA.

[52] *See* http://www.mirror.co.uk/news-old/top-stories/2008/09/16/robert-mugabe-signs-historic-powersharing-deal-with-bitter-political-enemy-115875-20738423/. Accessed 17 October 2008.

[53] Ibid.

[54] *See* http://www.thezimbabwetimes.com/?p=4501. *Accessed 16 October 2008.*

[55] "Meeting to finalise cabinet line-up postponed" at http://allafrica.com/stories/200809161237.html. Accessed 16 September 2008.

[56] "Tsvangirai threatens to quit Zimbabwe deal after Mugabe seizes cabinet posts" at http://www.guardian.co.uk/world/2008/oct/12/zimbabwe1. Accessed 13 October 2008.

[57] "SADC Summit divided" in *Business Day*, 23 January 2009.

[58] "South Africa withholds aid" in *Business Day*, 27 November 2008.

[59] *See* transcripts of SABC interviews with Thabo Mbeki at http://www.dfa.gov.za.

[60] "The new cabinet" in *Zimbabwean Independent*, 26 February 2009.

Appendix A

Zimbabwe's Cabinet: February 2009	
Minister	**Deputy Minister/Ministers of State**
Minister of Defence, Hon. Emmerson Dambudzo Mnangagwa (Zanu-PF)	
Ministers of Home Affairs, Hon. Kembo Dugish Campbell Mohadi (Zanu PF) & Hon. Giles Mutsekwa (MDC-T)	

Minister of State for National Security in the President's Office, Hon. Dr Sydney Tigere Sekeramayi (Zanu-PF)	
Minister of Foreign Affairs, Hon. Simbarashe Simbanenduku Mumbengegwi (Zanu-PF)	Deputy Minister, Hon. Moses Mzila Ndlovu (MDC-M)
Minister of Justice and Legal Affairs, Hon. Patrick Anthony Chinamasa (Zanu-PF)	Deputy Minster, Hon. Jessie Fungai Majome (MDC-T)
Minister of Finance, Hon. Tendai Biti (MDC-T)	
Minister of Land and Rural Resettlement, Hon. Herbert Murerwa (Zanu-PF)	
Minister of Agriculture Mechanisation and Irrigation Development, Hon. Joseph Mtekwese Made (Zanu-PF)	
Minister of Industry and Commerce, Professor Welshman Ncube (MDC-M)	Deputy Minister, Hon. Michael Chakanaka Bimha (Zanu-PF)
Minister of Mines and Mining Development, Hon. Obert Moses Mpofu (Zanu-PF)	Deputy Minister, Hon. Murisi Zwizwai (MDC-T)
Minister of Energy and Power Development, Hon. Engineer Elias Mudzuri (MDC-T)	Deputy Minister, Hon. Hubert Nyanhongo (Zanu-PF)
Minister of Local Government, Urban and Rural Development, Hon. Ignatius Morgan Chiminya Chombo (Zanu-PF)	Deputy Minister, Hon. Sesel Zvidzai (MDC-T)
Minister of Public Works, Hon. Theresa Makone (MDC-T)	Deputy Minister, Hon. Aguy Georgias (Zanu-PF)
Minister of Water Resources and Development, Hon. Samuel Sipepa Nkomo (MDC-T)	
Minister of Environment and Natural Resource Management, Hon. Francis Dunstun Chenayimoyo Nhema (Zanu-PF)	
Minister of Education, Sport, Art and Culture, Hon. David Coltart (MDC-M)	Deputy Minister, Hon. Lazarus Dokora (Zanu-PF)
Minister of Higher and Tertiary Education, Hon. Stan Gorerazvo Mudenge (Zanu-PF)	Deputy Minister, Hon. Lutho Addington Tapela (MDC-M)
Minister of Health and Child Welfare, Hon. Dr Henry Madzorera (MDC-T)	Deputy Minister, Hon. Dr Tendai Douglas Mombeshora (Zanu PF)
Minister of Public Service, Hon. Professor Eliphas Mukonoweshuro (MDC-T)	Deputy Minister, Hon. Andrew Langa (Zanu-PF)

Minister of Transport and Infrastructural Development, Hon. Nicholas Tasunungurwa Goche (Zanu-PF)	Deputy Minister, Hon. Dr Tichaona Mudzingwa (MDC-T)
Minister of Information and Publicity, Hon. Webster Kotiwa Shamu (Zanu-PF)	Deputy Minister, Hon. Jameson Zvidzai Timba (MDC-T)
Minister of Youth Development, Indigenisation and Empowerment, Hon. Saviour Kasukuwere (Zanu-PF)	Deputy Minister, Hon. Thamsanqa Mahlangu (MDC-T)
Minister of Women's Affairs Gender and Community Development, Hon. Olivia Muchena (Zanu-PF)	Deputy Minister, Hon. Evelyn Pfugamayi Masaiti (MDC-T)
Minister of Small and Medium Enterprises and Co-operative Development, Hon. Sithembiso Nyoni (Zanu-PF)	
Minister of Economic Planning and Development, Hon. Elton Mangoma (MDC-T)	Deputy Minister, Hon. Samuel Undenge (Zanu-PF)
Minister of Science and Technology, Hon. Professor Henry Dzinotyiwei (MDC-T)	
Minister of Housing and Social Amenities, Hon. Fidelis Mhashu (MDC-T)	
Minister of Constitutional and Parliamentary Affairs, Hon. Advocate Eric Matinenga (MDC-T)	
Minister of Regional Integration and International Cooperation, Hon. Priscilla Misihairabwi-Mushonga (MDC-M)	Deputy Minister, Hon. Reuben Marumahoko (Zanu-PF)
Minister of Information Communication Technology, Hon. Nelson Chamisa (MDC-T)	
Minister of State Enterprises and Parastatals, Hon. Gabbuza J. Gabuzza (MDC-T)	Deputy Minister, Hon. Walter Kufakunesu Chidhakwa (Zanu-PF)
Minister of Tourism and Hospitality Industry, Hon. Walter Mzembi (Zanu-PF)	
Minister of Labour and Social Welfare, Hon. Paurina Gwanyanya (MDC-T)	Deputy Minister, Hon. Tracy Mutinhiri (Zanu-PF)
Minister of State for Presidential Affairs, Hon. Didymus Noel Edwin Mutasa (Zanu-PF)	
Minister of State in the Prime Minister's Office, Hon. Gordon Moyo (MDC-T)	

Minister of State in the Prime Minister's Office, Hon. Sekai Masikana Holland (MDC-T)	
Minister of State in the President's Office, Hon. John Landa Nkomo (Zanu-PF)	
Minister of State in Vice President 1's Office, Hon. Flora Bhuka (Zanu-PF)	
Minister of State in Vice President 2's Office, Hon. Sylvester Robert Nguni (Zanu-PF)	
Minister of State in Deputy Prime Minister Mutambara's Office, Hon. Gibson Jama Sibanda (MDC-M)	

6

Challenges of foreign policy and international dimensions

Ulf Engel[1]

The complex multilevel and interlocked political, economic and social conflict in Zimbabwe, which has unfolded since the end of the 1990s, has domestic origins, but has been tightened by external interventions of various kinds. Currently, another round of radicalisation and militarisation of the situation seems possible. It is premised here that any sustainable solution to the Zimbabwean conflict has to be based on a home-grown solution, which calls for shared responsibilities of internal and external actors.

Over the last 15 years, the country has seen a contraction of political space, which, in academic and political discourse, mainly has been attributed to issues of governance and what has been labelled the "liberation movement in power syndrome".[2] Robert Mugabe's government came under domestic and international pressure when, in a situation of fading legitimacy, it implemented the so-called fast-track land reform.[3] At the end of the 1990s, while acknowledging that the Zimbabwean government increasingly lacked legitimacy, some authors have suggested that the country, from 1997 onwards and in particular during the years 2000 to 2003, in fact has experienced a "revolutionary situation" in terms of the land question and a radicalising State (Moyo & Paris, 2007).

For a variety of reasons, major international actors – first and foremost the governments of the United Kingdom (UK) and the United States of America (USA) – actively opposed the regime led by the Zimbabwe African National Union Patriotic Front (ZANU-PF) and its land policy, which was radically accelerated after the party lost the 2000 referendum on the Constitution. Violent farm occupations started on 12 March 2000 across the country. In part, he USA and the UK acted through the World Bank (WB), which, on 1 October 2000, put Zimbabwe on non-accrual status, allegedly for failing to make any payment on its debt to the WB for the last six months, thus effectively cutting the country off from International Bank for Reconstruction and Development (IBRD) loans.[4] This triggered a spiral of radicalisations on both sides. In order to consolidate its power, Mugabe's government introduced repressive legislation and increasingly embarked on exclusionary and violent strategies, while an international anti-Mugabe alliance came together and, ultimately, pushed for regime change through a comprehensive sanctions regime.

The situation has since escalated due to a combination of dialectic internal and external reasons. From the point of view of a UK-led international anti-Mugabe alliance, four closely interrelated dynamics have exacerbated the conflict: vigilantism by so-called war veterans and youth militias;[5] systematic human rights abuses in the run-up to elections;[6] electoral engineering and the displacement of people through "Operation *Murambatsvina*" in mid-2005;[7] and the general decline in quality of the presidential and parliamentary elections held in 2000, 2005 and 2008.[8]

The 2008 elections resulted in a deadlock. According to the chief electoral officer, in the first round of the presidential elections held on 29 March 2008, Robert Mugabe scored 43.24% of the valid votes cast (with a turnout of 42.75%), whereas the main opposition candidate Morgan Tsvangirai of the Movement for Democratic Change (MDC) scored 47.84% of the vote. Independent candidates Herbert S. Makoni and Langton Towungana received 8.31% and 0.58% cent of the votes respectively.[9] Since none of the four presidential candidates won an absolute majority, a run-off was held between Mugabe and Tsvangirai on 27 June 2008. However, on 22 June, Tsvangirai pulled out of the second round of presidential elections, arguing that free and fair elections could not be expected in the climate of State-sponsored violence. Mugabe achieved 90% of the valid votes cast. Some 9.78% of the electorate voted for Tsvangirai although he was no longer a candidate.[10] Elections for the House of Assembly, the lower chamber of parliament, were held on 29 March, with by-elections in three constituencies held on 22 June. Including these by-elections, MDC-Tsvangirai (MDC-T) won 47.62% of the valid votes cast, which translated into 100 out of the 210 seats, ZANU-PF got 47.14% and 99 seats, and the break-away MDC faction of Arthur G. Mutambara (MDC-M) 4.78% and 10 seats.[11]

On 15 September 2008, due to international pressure and as a result various mediation efforts, the contesting political parties approved the Global Political Agreement (GPA), which provided for a power-sharing Government of National Unity (GNU), which took effect on 11 February 2009.[12] Continued rivalry between the disputing parties, and factionalism within both ZANU-PF and the MDC, made for an uneasy and cumbersome implementation process. Critical issues included the adoption of amendments to the Constitution, security sector reform, the independence of the Zimbabwe Electoral Commission (ZEC), national reconciliation, etc.

It is in this context that, on the eve of the Second Stakeholders Conference on the Draft Constitution, scheduled for 21–23 October 2012, increased levels of involvement of the security forces in keeping the Mugabe regime in power were reported.[13] On 11 October 2012, the Minister of Justice, Patrick Chinamasa, issued the following threat of a *coup d'état*:

> *He [Tsvangirai] cannot win. He has been campaigning and mobilising against the interests of Zimbabweans on many issues, whether talking about land, seeking to reverse the gains of the liberation struggle. And this is where the military comes in … Now if anyone is going to say "When I come into power I'm going to reverse that," they [the military] have every right to say "Please – you are asking for trouble. You will be asking for trouble." He [Tsvangirai] will be asking for trouble to seek to reverse the land reform programme. There is no-one who is going to accept any enslavement.*[14]

Chinamasa continued:

> *I know he [Tsvangirai] is the front of [sic] the countries that impose sanctions. And if those countries impose for him to win, that result will not be acceptable. We will not accept it. We will just not accept it. Isn't that clear?*

At an earlier occasion, the chief of staff of the Zimbabwe National Army (ZNA), Major-General Trust Mugoba, expressed that the military would not allow a presidential candidate to assume office if he did not share the "ideals" of Mugabe and his ruling party.[15] These and other statements to the same end constitute the problem of the veto power of parts of the security establishment over a possible electoral defeat of Mugabe and ZANU-PF.

International interventions in the Zimbabwean conflict

In principle, analysis of international interventions in Zimbabwe could be structured according to sequence, actors, guiding theories or some systematic considerations. Here, the latter is given preference. Conceptually speaking, different international interventions in the Zimbabwe conflict can be discussed in terms of "preventive diplomacy", though, for some in the Zimbabwean case, the term may a have a connotation that is too positive. With a view to the later identification of policy options, it seems feasible to structure the following analysis along the activities that are usually subsumed under this rubric. Going back to the "Agenda for Peace"[16] preventive diplomacy is at the heart of United Nations' (UN) efforts to support peace in the world; it is also a key domain of the African Union (AU) and its dual agenda of firmly establishing a continental peace and security, as well as a democracy agenda.[17] According to Gomes Porto (2012), preventive diplomacy comes in different non-public and public ways, including indirect and ad hoc contacts (informal high-level consultations, diplomatic demarches); direct and ad hoc missions to dispute/conflict areas (issuing of statements, fact-finding missions, appointment of special envoys, facilitation); and direct and structured mediation and good offices to prevent the collapse or re-establish a stable political process (appointment of special representatives, dialogue-building through proximity talks and pre-negotiation, support to political dialogue, adjudication of discreet areas in dispute or problem-solving workshops).

Different international actors have influenced and are still influencing the ongoing conflict in Zimbabwe through at least six forms of activities:

- by trying to establish facts about what actually is happening within Zimbabwe through fact-finding missions, which, in turn, allows one to frame the problem (e.g. Is the conflict over "land" or over "governance"?)

- by expressing concern over dynamics in Zimbabwe, thus identifying, but certainly also framing the problems at stake, and bringing (and keeping) the issue on the international agenda

- by condemning one or more of the conflict parties, thus defining the scope for further action and the nature of problem-solving solutions

- by bestowing or withholding legitimacy of electoral outcomes through election observer missions and their reporting

- by putting pressure on the Mugabe regime through imposing comprehensive targeted sanctions, though the aims of applying sanctions vary: from allowing mediation to actively advocating regime change, and

- by offering good offices and mediating – in different constellations and with varying interests, strategies, intensity and success – between the conflict parties.

The remainder of this chapter will look at these six interwoven strategies in greater detail, before discussing very briefly the responses to these strategies by the Zimbabwean government, and concluding with some observations and policy recommendations. The focus will be on four decisive moments in the country's recent history, as seen from the external environment:

- the period between the 24–25 June 2000 parliamentary elections and the 10–11 March 2002 presidential elections, which, firstly, resulted in a considerable increase of parliamentary seats (57 from 120) for the newly established MDC; secondly, was followed by repressive responses from the Mugabe regime; and, thirdly, flawed presidential elections that finally led to the introduction of targeted international sanctions

international responses to "Operation *Murambatsvina*", which, on 17 May 2005, started to clear informal business and residential development in Harare, and later in other towns (demolishing 92 460 housing structures and affecting 133 534 households), and was seen to have a gerrymandering or election engineering dimension[18]

- the aftermath of the violent 2008 presidential and parliamentary elections, which ultimately led to the establishment of the GPA and the GNU, and

- following the adoption of an implementation roadmap for the GPA in April 2011, the current run-up to general elections scheduled for not later than June 2013.

Fact-finding missions

In the case of Zimbabwe in the 2000s, diplomatic fact-finding missions rarely occurred because the country was already facing a situation where most actors had made up their minds and simply responded to what they perceived as aggravating circumstances. The few exceptions relate to the UN and, in particular, the UN Secretary-General, who, for instance, held talks after the first round of presidential elections with MDC-leader Tsvangirai on 24 April 2008 in Accra, Ghana.

Another example of a fact-finding mission is related to a situation that emerged between elections and includes the appointment on 20 June 2005 by the Secretary-General, acting in agreement with Mugabe, of Anna Kajumulo Tibaijuka, the Tanzanian-born executive director of the UN Human Settlements Programme (UN-Habitat), as a special envoy to investigate "Operation *Murambatsvina*" and the extent and impact of the evictions. The findings of this mission (26 June to 8 July) on "the failure of the government of Zimbabwe to protect its people", published on 25 July, were taken up by the Commonwealth governments of Australia, Canada and New Zealand, who, on 26 July, in a letter to the president of the UN Security Council (UNSC), tried to establish a "linkage between humanitarian and human rights crises and peace and security" and called for the Security Council "to be seized of the situation as a matter of urgency and to engage actively with the government of Zimbabwe to bring an end to this situation". This was support in separate letters to the president of the UNSC by the permanent representative of the UK. Under Rule 48 of the UNSC's Provisional Rules of Procedure, the Council convened a private meeting on Zimbabwe the following day.

Concern

Public forms of preventive diplomacy often set the agenda by making a particular conflict an issue for an international audience. This is usually done through the expression of concern over a political situation (though this concern rarely is free from political interest).

Thus, in June 2001, European Union (EU) foreign ministers set the tone by issuing a statement deploring the "lack of progress" in improving the situation in Zimbabwe, and spelling out a number of priority areas for political dialogue that "should yield rapid and tangible results" on the following:

- an end to political violence and, in particular, an end to all official encouragement or acceptance of such violence
- an invitation to the EU to support and observe pending elections, with full access to this end
- concrete action to protect the freedom of mass media
- independence of the judiciary and respect of its decisions, and
- an end to illegal occupation of properties.[19]

Under the Cotonou Convention of 23 June 2000, the EU has a specific diplomatic set of instruments to link concern and condemnation with further action, by invoking a so-called policy dialogue under Article 96 of the Convention. On 26 October 2001, the Commission communicated that, in recent years, Zimbabwe:

> ... has not lived up to its previously good reputation regarding the essential elements [of the Convention]. The human rights record has deteriorated with growing violence and insecurity. There are problems with respect for democratic principles, such as freedom of expression. Zimbabwe has enacted a law limiting the freedom of broadcasting, there have been arrests of journalists, and accreditation procedures for foreign journalists are becoming increasingly difficult. Violence and intimidation took place prior to recent by-elections. The rule of law has been undermined by illegal occupation of farm-land with tacit support from the government, and by strong political pressure on the judiciary, including the forced resignation of the chief justice. There are reports of police inaction following court decisions. This serious erosion of the quality of governance has contributed to Zimbabwe's dramatic economic decline. The EU and EC co-operation programmes have been progressively reduced and adapted to this situation.[20]

The EU Commission vowed that the following elements should be discussed with the Zimbabwean government: an end to political violence; an invitation to the EU "to support and observe coming elections and full access to that end"; concrete action to protect the freedom of mass media; independence of the judiciary; and the rapid implementation of the Abuja Accord with respect to land reform. Political dialogue started on 11 January 2002, on the eve of the presidential elections. While most of the EU member states aligned themselves with the British position, the French government not only continued its cooperation with the Mugabe regime, but also significantly increased its engagement (and was therefore criticised in a resolution passed by the European parliament[21]).

A delegation of leaders from the Southern African Development Community (SADC) visited Zimbabwe 10-11 October and found strong words.[22] The leader of the delegation, SADC chairperson President Bakili Muluzi of Malawi, was quoted as saying: "We are very concerned about the worsening economy, the decline in the rule of law, and the spread of violence and political instability in Zimbabwe," and added: "Of great concern to all of us is that, if the land issue is not urgently resolved amicably and peacefully, the economic and political problems Zimbabwe is facing now could easily snowball across the entire southern Africa region".[23] The delegation included then president of South Africa, Thabo Mbeki; the presidents of Namibia, Botswana and Mozambique; and ministers from Angola, Nigeria and Tanzania. Later, a ministerial-level committee was appointed "to monitor the restoration of rule of law and effectively gave Mugabe one month within which to address the land crisis or face isolation".[24] Essentially, Mugabe was embarrassed by the two-day summit as the SADC, for the first time, demanded a meeting with the MDC, white farmers and others.

However, at the same time, a Commonwealth Committee delegation that was in Zimbabwe 25-27 October 2001 failed to issue a strong public statement and provide dominant discursive framing because it was divided over "whether the fundamental issue in Zimbabwe is land or rule of law".[25]

Other examples of this dimension of preventive diplomacy were the repeated call for "free and fair" elections and the release of the results of the presidential elections, issued on 16 April 2008 by eight members of the UNSC (Belgium, Costa Rica, Croatia, France, Italy, Panama, UK and USA) at a high-level meeting on peace and security in Africa, and the verbatim report by the UN Deputy Secretary-General to the UNSC on his participation in an AU summit.[26]

The most serious expression of concern, which some may have misread as almost bordering on diplomatic condemnation, came from the AU Assembly of Heads of States and Government issuing a clear warning to the Mugabe regime and urging for a negotiated solution. In a "Resolution on Zimbabwe" adopted at the 11th Ordinary Session held 30 June to 1 July 2008 in Sharm El-Sheikh, Egypt, the summit showed itself to be deeply concerned "with the prevailing situation in Zimbabwe" – in particular "the negative reports of SADC, the African Union and the Pan-African Parliament observers", as well as "the violence and loss of life that have occurred in Zimbabwe."[27] The Assembly stated that there was an "urgent need to prevent further worsening of the situation in order to avoid the spread of conflict with the consequential negative impact on the country and the sub-region", for the first time raising the potential threat Zimbabwe might constitute for regional security. This line of reasoning was, in fact, later taken up by the UK and others when they introduced a draft resolution to the UNSC calling for sanctions.

Condemnation

Strong words on the escalating Zimbabwean crisis also came from fellow African countries. At the opening session of the Commonwealth Abuja talks on 6-7 September 2001, Nigeria's foreign minister pointed out that Zimbabwe should stop creating the impression that it is "incapable of enforcing its own laws, thereby fostering the image of lawlessness and lack of respect for the rule of law".[28]

The 2008 elections constituted the next major political crisis that caught the attention of international stakeholders. In this respect, a strong signal was sent to the Mugabe government when, in response to the second round of the presidential elections, and following a request by Belgium, the UNSC held an open meeting on 23 June 2008, where it was briefed by the UN Under Secretary-General for Political Affairs on the situation in Zimbabwe. The Council then adopted a presidential statement in which it condemned in rather strong words "the campaign of violence against the opposition ahead of the second round of the presidential elections scheduled for 27 June, which has resulted in the killing of scores of opposition activists and other Zimbabweans, and the beating and displacement of thousands of people, including many women and children." The Council furthermore condemned "the actions of the government of Zimbabwe that have denied its political opponents the right to campaign freely, and calls upon the government of Zimbabwe to stop the violence, to cease political intimidation, to end the restrictions on the right of assembly, and to release the political leaders who have been detained". It called on the government of Zimbabwe to stop the violence, political intimidation and restrictions on the right of assembly, release detained political leaders, allow humanitarian organisations to resume their services, and cooperate with all efforts aimed at finding a peaceful solution. Finally, the UNSC noted that the results of the 29 March elections should be respected.

Election observer missions

Observer statements on the conduct of an election either attest to the legitimacy of the electoral process ("free and fair") or withhold this recognition. In 2008, they became a critical instrument to put further pressure on Mugabe's government. In the past, all elections in Zimbabwe had been monitored by international observer groups. Having allowed the EU to field an observer mission for the parliamentary elections held in 2000, the Mugabe government now decided to refuse the EU and the following institutions accreditation because it feared negative reports would taint the legitimacy of the poll:[29] the Commonwealth, the USA, the Electoral Institute for Sustainable Democracy in Africa (EISA), the Carter Center, the World Council of Churches and All Africa Conference of Churches, and – indicative of the emergence of different policy stances within the South African tripartite coalition over this country's role in the mediation – the Young Communist League of South Africa (YCLSA).

The SADC-Parliamentary Forum (SADC-PF) was told to send members under the SADC mission. Other invited bodies included representatives from the African and Caribbean Pacific (ACP), the AU, the Association of South East Asian Nations (ASEAN), the Common Market for Eastern and Southern Africa (COMESA), the Community of Lusophone countries, the East African Community (EAC), Economic Community of West African States (ECOWAS), the Economic Community of Central African States (ECCAS), Inter-Governmental Authority on Development (IGAD), the Arab Maghreb Union (AMU), the Non-Aligned Movement (NAM), the Pan-African Parliament (PAP), whose observers were included in the AU group), and the SADC.

While the SADC more or less rubber-stamped the elections, other observers were highly critical. In a communiqué issued at the First Extra-Ordinary SADC Summit of Heads of State and Government, held on 13 April 2008 in Lusaka, Zambia,[30] the summit noted that the report of the chairperson: "indicated that the electoral process was acceptable to all parties", commended "the people of Zimbabwe for the peaceful and orderly manner in which they conducted themselves", and "commended the government of Zimbabwe for ensuring that elections were conducted in a peaceful environment".[31] Earlier, the Botswana members of the SADC mission had disagreed and issued a separate statement.

Demonstrating its discontent with both the role of the South African government and the SADC, the Democratic Alliance (DA) issued a minority statement claiming that the SADC observers':

> … *preliminary report either ignores or downplays material defects in the conduct and organisation of the poll, which resulted in the transgression of 9 of the 10 SADC election guidelines.[32]*

The DA furthermore argued that the majority of the SADC principles guiding the conduct of elections were actually violated, "particularly with regard to the access to media, freedom of association, political tolerance and the impartiality of the Zimbabwe Electoral Commission". [33]

Equally critical on the conduct of the elections were the Carter Center and EISA, who in a joint statement issued on 23 May 2008 concluded:

> … *since the first round of the presidential election in Zimbabwe on March 29, police have harassed the legitimate, peaceful activities of staff and observers of the Zimbabwe Election Support Network (ZESN), a legally established and widely respected citizen rights group that conducted observation in compliance with the country's electoral laws, code of conduct, and international principles for election observation. ZESN members have been arbitrarily detained and interrogated by police and their offices have been searched. These actions are a violation of civil and political rights and run counter to the government's responsibility to ensure the freedom of movement and association of election observers throughout the country.[34]*

On the second round of the presidential elections, Zimbabwe's major African allies concluded that these elections were far from "free and fair". Withdrawing the diplomatic cover the SADC observers had provided the Mugabe regime in the first round of the presidential elections in March 2008, it now, on 29 June 2008, in no unclear words concluded:

> *The pre-election phase was characterised by politically motivated violence, intimidation, and displacements. The process leading up to the presidential run-off elections held on 27 June 2008 did not conform to SADC Principles and Guidelines Governing Democratic Elections. However, the election day was peaceful. Based on the abovementioned observations, the Mission is of the view that the prevailing environment impinged on the credibility of the electoral process. The elections did not represent the will of the people of Zimbabwe.[35]*

Partly this shift can be explained by increasing dissatisfaction of a number of SADC leaders with the situation in the country.[36] After calling for a special summit in 2007 to address the increasingly violent situation in Zimbabwe, Zambia's President Levy Mwanawasa was the first to speak out in favour of the "peoples' verdict" in April 2008. On 4 July, Botswana expressed that, for the time being, Zimbabwe should not be allowed to participate at SADC meetings, and, protesting Mugabe's attendance President Ian Khama boycotted the SADC summit. In November 2008, Botswana's foreign minister called to isolate Mugabe and close borders to Zimbabwe.[37]

PAP observers, part of the AU mission, concluded "that the atmosphere prevailing in the country, at the time, did not give rise to the conduct of free, fair and credible elections".[38]

Sanctions

The history of the imposition of sanctions on Zimbabwe by various international actors has been well documented by, among others, Gomes Porto (2012) and Alden (2010). Basically, the US and UK governments were at the forefront of states advocating the imposition of targeted sanctions against the Mugabe regime. In particular, the UK pushed its partners in the Commonwealth and the European Union hard to establish Zimbabwe as an international pariah. Right from the beginning this has been supported by the Brussels-based International Crisis Group (ICG), an international advocacy organisation that provides analysis and policy recommendations on political crisis and conflicts – and which, in terms of interpretation and framing, earned itself somewhat of a gatekeeper position on the Zimbabwe question. Yet it would be too simple to reduce the sanctions debate to a binary struggle between Zimbabwe and her former, though brief, colonial master. The number of actors involved is substantial, the alliances forged changed over time, as did the positions of some of the actors. In this chapter, the interest is on the interplay of preventive diplomacy instruments and alliance building, and space does not allow detailed analysis of the underlying rationales of the various stakeholders.

In March 2001, European foreign ministers initiated the enhanced "political dialogue" procedure under Article 8 of the Cotonou Agreement, which prepared the ground for future steps to be taken against the Mugabe government. In a report released on 13 July 2001, the ICG described the country as:

> ... in a state of free fall. It is embroiled in the worst political and economic crisis of its twenty-year history as an independent state ... [The crisis] has exacerbated racial and ethnic tensions, severely torn the country's social fabric, caused fundamental damage to its once-strong economy, dramatically increased the suffering of Zimbabwe's people, accelerated a damaging brain drain, and increased the use of State-sponsored violence, the perpetrators of which operate with impunity.[39]

Sole responsibility for this situation was seen to lie with Mugabe's government, "which has mismanaged the economy, institutionalised State violence, and moved further toward autocratic rule".[40] Provided the conditions for free and fair elections were not met, the ICG called for the imposition of UNSC-authorised targeted sanctions, including freezing the assets in places where ZANU-PF officials and their families had important holdings, and imposing travel restrictions "on the most senior and responsible Zimbabwean government officials and their families". In addition, it was recommended the Commonwealth "should move to suspend Zimbabwe's membership".[41]

In a briefing paper released on 12 October 2001, the ICG concluded that, because of the non-implementation of the Abuja Accord, electoral violence and manipulation, pressure on the independent media, the undermining of the independent judiciary and the intensifying humanitarian crisis, it was:

> ... *time for the international community to raise its pressure to the next level by instituting "smart" sanctions against Mugabe and the ZANU-PF leadership, and providing direct aid to the opposition and civil society organisations. The purpose of these measures is to encourage positive policy changes in Zimbabwe while time remains, and to give encouragement to the people of that country who are working for such change.*[42]

A few weeks later, on 29 October, the EU warned Mugabe that, political dialogue having in effect been exhausted, "Zimbabwe faced possible sanctions under the Cotonou Agreement unless specific steps were taken to restore the rule of law and create conditions for free and fair elections".[43] This was echoed in late December 2001 by the Australian Foreign Minister, Alexander Downer, who indicated that another Commonwealth body, the Ministerial Action Group (which was established in 1995 and comprised Australia, Bangladesh, Barbados, Botswana, Canada, Malaysia, Nigeria and the UK), would consider suspending Zimbabwe at its next meeting on 30 January 2002 "if nothing changes for the better". Along the same line, British Foreign Secretary, Jack Straw, also threatened suspension if the situation "continues to deteriorate".[44] Meanwhile, on 11 January 2002, after a meeting was held with a Zimbabwean delegation led by the foreign minister in Brussels, the EU issued a stiff warning of possible action to be taken at the next session of EU foreign ministers on 28-29 January.[45] So, by the end of 2001, and driven by the British government, the EU and the Commonwealth had synchronised their rhetoric and plans of action. For the first time, on 21 December 2001, the USA put sanctions in place, through the Zimbabwe Democracy and Economic Recovery Act (ZIDERA). The related Executive Order 13288 was issued by President George W. Bush (Sr) on 7 March 2003, and was later superseded by a wider set of sanctions on 23 November 2005, and renewed in March 2007. On 18 February 2002, the EU Commission called off the Cotonou dialogue and threatened to implement targeted sanctions, including an arms ban, travel restrictions for a group of 20 core regime representatives, and a freeze on assets "if the government of Zimbabwe prevents the deployment of an EU election observation mission [which it did], or if it later prevents the mission from operating effectively"; if international media was prevented from having free access to cover the election, or there is "a serious deterioration on the ground, in terms of a worsening of the human rights situation or attacks on the opposition"; or "the election is assessed as not being free or fair".[46]

Expectedly, developments culminated with the presidential elections held on 9-10 March 2002. Several election observer missions, including the Commonwealth, declared this election as not "free and fair"; the EU was hindered to deploy its observers; and the head of the mission was deported from the country. The ICG reasoned that the Mugabe regime had introduced a *de facto* State of Emergency, that State violence and intimidation was escalating, and that a humanitarian and economic crisis was looming. At the same time, the ICG criticised previous international responses as just "hand wringing, rhetorical posturing, and ultimatums".[47] Thus, the doors were wide open to finally introduce sanctions. Largely in response to the 2002 elections, the EU imposed targeted sanctions or "restrictive measures", including travel bans on 72 ZANU-PF leaders, including Mugabe, the vice presidents, the cabinet, and the leaders of the security services.[48] Following the UK, New Zealand (April) and Australia (August 2002) adopted sanctions, Canada joined the club in April 2008.[49]

A Commonwealth troika, comprising the leaders of Australia, South Africa and Nigeria, announced the suspension of Zimbabwe from membership in the Commonwealth for a year, with the full support of all African member states. According to the Australian Prime Minister, John Howard, chairman of the troika, the observers had concluded that the elections were "marred by a high level of politically motivated violence" and conditions did not allow adequately for a free expression of will by the electorate.50 This basically left Zimbabwe with diplomatic support of different quality and persistence in the region, while it faced a consolidated alliance made up of the EU, US and the Commonwealth.

In contrast, at an SADC extra-ordinary summit held on 28-29 March 2007 in Dar es Salaam, Tanzania maintained that the 2002 presidential elections were "free and fair".[51] The SADC clearly favoured a continuation of the Mbeki mediation. It was concerned about the economic situation in Zimbabwe (and, one can assume, the region as a whole), and "reiterated the appeal to Britain to honour its compensation obligations with regards to land reform made at the Lancaster House [of 1979]." Finally, the extra-ordinary summit "appealed for the lifting of all forms of sanctions against Zimbabwe" – a position that was reiterated at regular intervals.[52]

Against the background of an aggravating crisis following the 2008 March and June elections, Zimbabwe's diplomacy and the levels of international support it still enjoyed were put to a severe test when the Western coalition pushed for an intensification of the sanctions regime through a draft UNSC resolution. On 18 June 2008, Belgium and other members of the Council expressed their concern about the deterioration of the situation in Zimbabwe.[53] The following day, the US Secretary of State convened a closed meeting of diplomats and humanitarian groups, and urged the Council to take stronger action against the violence in Zimbabwe. From 12 to 18 June, the Council held consultations on the situation of the presidential elections. On 23 June it met and condemned the Mugabe regime for its campaign of violence, and declared that the Friday run-off election would be a travesty and unrecognised by the international community.[54] However, the USA, UK and France failed to insert the statement "by declaring Mugabe's rule illegitimate in light of the March election, and recognising Morgan Tsvangirai as the elected president of Zimbabwe".[55] China and Russia resisted this move, and South Africa opposed stronger measures.

After Mugabe stood as the only candidate in the presidential elections of 27 June 2008, the group of states that now constituted the anti-Mugabe alliance pushed ahead. At the G8 Summit in Hokkaido Tokyo, Japan, on 8 July, the group of eight industrialised States, including Russia, heavily criticised the situation and called for the appointment of a special envoy of the UN Secretary-General to report on the political, humanitarian, human rights and security situation, and to support regional efforts to take forward mediation between political parties. The G8 openly threatened that it would "take further steps, *inter alia* introducing financial and other measures against those individuals responsible for violence".[56]

On 11 July 2008, the USA and others tabled a resolution in the UNSC aimed at tightening existing measures taken against the Mugabe regime.[57] Apparently the process was coordinated by the US State Department.[58] The draft resolution concerning the situation in Zimbabwe was co-sponsored by Australia, Belgium, Canada, Croatia, France, Italy, Liberia, New Zealand, The Netherlands, Sierra Leone, the UK and the USA. Recalling the AU resolution on Zimbabwe (1 July) and the SADC statement (29 June), and furthermore referring to the concerns about the conduct of the elections and the exacerbating human rights situation in the country, the draft resolution seized the opportunity to buy into the previous AU analysis of the implications of the Zimbabwean conflict to regional stability and the AU Deputy Chairperson's statement "that Zimbabwe was the 'single greatest challenge to regional stability in southern Africa'".[59] Going a decisive step further, the draft resolution determined "that the situation in Zimbabwe poses a threat to international peace and security in the region", thus allowing for action under Chapter VII of the Charter of the United Nations.

Following a series of demands addressed to the Mugabe government ("cease attacks against and intimidation of opposition members"; "begin without delay a substantive and inclusive political dialogue between the parties with the aim of arriving at a peaceful solution that reflects the will of the Zimbabwean people and respects the results of the 29 March elections"; "accept the good offices offered by various international organisations and their representatives"; "cooperate fully with investigations of the political violence experienced by the country between March and June 2008, and hold accountable those who have carried out abuses of human rights"; and "end immediately all restrictions on international humanitarian assistance and support international aid organisations' access to all parts of the country for distribution of food, medical assistance, and other humanitarian aid"), the UN Secretary-General was requested to appoint "as soon as possible" a special representative on the situation in Zimbabwe.

Then the sanctions regime was extended, in particular with regard to monitoring and mapping compliance. Apart from a detailed arms ban and measures against a list of annexed people who had "engaged in or provided support for actions or policies to subvert democratic processes or institutions in Zimbabwe since May 2005" (travel bans, freezing of funds), the draft resolution called for the establishment of a UNSC sub-committee to serve as a compliance and monitoring mechanism, plus the establishment of a separate reporting mechanism.

Nine Council members voted in favour (Belgium, Burkina Faso, Costa Rica, Croatia, France, Italy, Panama, UK, USA), five against (China, Libya, Russian Federation, South Africa, Vietnam), with Indonesia abstaining.

The positions have not changed much in the run-up to the 2013 elections. While the various sanctions have been renewed every year, at the beginning of 2012, the SADC reportedly maintained "that sanctions exacerbate already difficult conditions; do not contribute to constructive solutions; and their removal would recognise progress made and be an important confidence-building measure".[60] In the more than 340 meetings of the AU Peace and Security Council (PSC) held since 2004, the Zimbabwe conflict has never been brought up as a challenge to peace and security.

Mediation

Technically speaking, mediation is also part of the wide field of preventive diplomacy. It ranges from offering good offices[61] to firmly facilitating, for instance, a power-sharing arrangement and the establishment of a GNU. As the case of Zimbabwe clearly demonstrates, mediators are neither neutral, nor without interests. Summarising an argument developed by Jabri (1990:17–23), Gomes Porto (2012:34) highlights that "the factors which influence a third party's decision to take up the role of intermediary" include the following four determinants: "(1) third party's conflict-related interests (issues, parties, environment); (2) third party's set of preferred outcomes (the value attached to perceived possible outcomes to the conflict); (3) third party's influence potential (the likelihood that the third party could influence the outcome to the conflict); (4) third party's process-related interests (the likelihood that the third party could influence the outcome best by taking up one role as compared with other strategies available to it)".

A major first-mediation effort was undertaken on 6–7 September 2001, when a special Commonwealth delegation consisting of the foreign ministers of the UK, Canada, Kenya, Jamaica, Nigeria, South Africa and a senior representative of Australia met with Zimbabwe's foreign minister to facilitate an agreement with Zimbabwe that aimed to set standards for land reform.[62] The Abuja Accord attempted to create a *quid pro quo* between Zimbabwe and the UK. Zimbabwe agreed to end farm invasions and violence on occupied farms, and restore rule of law. The government committed itself to take firm action and to implement land reform "in a gradual, fair, and transparent manner. In turn, Britain agreed to make substantial funds available to Zimbabwe to compensate displaced farmers, and finance infrastructure in the resettled areas, provided Zimbabwe met its commitments".[63]

Other than that, mediation was delegated to African sub-regional bodies and their appointed mediators.[64] The AU deferred the question to the SADC, which, in turn, appointed then South African President, Thabo Mbeki (August 2001 to November 2009), and current president, Jacob Zuma, as mediators. According to Cawthra (2011:24), Mbeki in fact "played a prominent part in making sure that Mugabe no longer continued as the chair of the OPDSC [Organ on Politics, Defence and Security] at the SADC Summit in August 2001". Beyond this, however, according to Cawthra, Mbeki and the SADC initially took little action, though they supported a split in the MDC. Observers and actors, including the Congress of South African Trade Unions (COSATU), often criticised what Mbeki sold as "quiet diplomacy" for its lack of real impact.[65]

Ndlovu-Gatsheni (2011) and others have repeatedly discussed the common history of most actors in the liberation struggle of southern Africa, and what the many personal entanglements mean for concrete mediation in Zimbabwe. Ndlovu-Gatsheni holds that only the leaders of Botswana and Zambia (Ian Khama and Levy Mwanawasa), and "to some extent Tanzania, have differed openly with Mugabe and condemned ZANU-PF's political conduct". This divide also reflects an ongoing debate within the SADC about competing notions of security – regime security, which is favoured by most liberation movements in power, or human security, which is underpinning the new African peace and security, as well as the African governance architectures.[66] In addition, initially the MDC, founded in 1999, was isolated in the region, both because of the scattered white-dominated history of opposition politics in Zimbabwe in the 1980s, and because the MDC in principal presents a change option many incumbents are not keen to have replicated in their own countries. However, the MDC made deliberate efforts to counter ZANU-PF propaganda in the region, as evidenced by the successful lobbying for the adoption of an electoral framework and the condemnation by the African Commission on Human and Peoples' Rights (ACHPR) of the Zimbabwean government for torturing opposition politicians.[67]

The lack of progress and mounting regional crisis in terms of economics and migration, slowly contributed to divisions in the SADC.[68] While the regional body was very positive about the first round of presidential elections held on 29 March 2008,[69] the second round held on 27 June 2008 changed this posture. Given the heavily flawed elections, intimidation and violence, the SADC saw the opportunity to "establish a mechanism on the ground in order to seize the momentum for a negotiated solution".[70] In cumbersome negotiations, the SADC-backed mediator, Thabo Mbeki, managed to bring ZANU-PF, the MDC-T and the MDC-M to the table on 15 September 2008, to sign a GPA that provided for the creation of a GNU, a conflict-resolving formula that has strong roots in South Africa's experience and many of the conflict-resolution attempts on the continent ever since.[71] After months of dragging, Tsvangirai was sworn-in as prime minister on 11 January 2009.[72]

In view of the slow implementation of the GPA, the SADC troika held an emergency summit in Maputo, Mozambique, on 5 November 2009. Recording some "notable achievements" in terms of "peace and stability in the country" and "positive progress on economic recovery", the summit also urged the parties to "fully comply with the spirit and letter of the GPA and SADC Summit decisions of 27 January 2009" and "should not allow the situation to deteriorate any further". In deviating from previous practice the summit issued a deadline to achieve compliance by giving signatory parties to the GPA "fifteen (15) days not beyond thirty (30) days" to start dialogue with "immediate effect". Cawthra (2011:26) regards the emergency SADC summit "as a turning-point". Mugabe was apparently privately told in Maputo that he had to make the inclusive government work, and move towards free and fair elections. However, the deadline expired without significant progress.

Ultimately, South Africa and the SADC are interested in the restoration of stability rather than the introduction of democracy and 'regime change'. According to Ndlovu-Gatsheni (2011:15–17):

> SADC states do not have a common policy towards Zimbabwe. [While] Botswana or South Africa share a concern about the possibility of a total economic and political implosion in Zimbabwe, not least because of the domestic fallout of a flood of Zimbabwean refugees pouring over the border … Zambia, Kenya and, to some extent, Tanzania have indicated they may accommodate the MDC-T as a legitimate political formation that must be allowed to assume power if it wins elections[73]

Comparing the mediation styles of the two South African presidents, Ndlovu-Gatsheni (2011:12)[74] observes that four issues influenced Mbeki's approach:

> *Firstly, Mbeki was determined to avoid the pitfalls of unilateralism that South Africa had encountered in its dealings with Nigeria, Lesotho and the Democratic Republic of Congo (DRC). Secondly, Mbeki wished to avoid repeating the bullying strategy that was associated with the apartheid regime in the SADC region. Thirdly, Mbeki consistently avoided being seen in Harare as pushing a Western agenda of regime change. Finally, Mbeki had his own ambitions of positioning South Africa as a concerned African State that was taking a leading role in stabilising the continent politically and economically, fighting for a dignified space for Africa within the global order and projecting the philosophy of "African renaissance".*

In contrast, Zuma and his team – international advisor Lindiwe Zulu, Charles Nqakula (a former Minister of Defence) and Mac Maharaj (another Umkhonto we Sizwe operative and former cabinet minister who worked with Zuma in exile in Maputo when the former was head of ANC intelligence) – so far have been given the benefit of the doubt. On the basis of a report by Zuma, which frankness was appreciated, the SADC Troika on 31 March 2011 "expressed its impatience in the delay of the implementation of the GPA" and "noted with grave concern the polarisation of the political environment as characterised by, inter alia, resurgence of violence, arrests and intimidation in Zimbabwe". It therefore resolved that:

a. there must be an immediate end of violence, intimidation, hate speech, harassment, and any other form of action that contradicts the letter and spirit of the GPA

b. all stakeholders to the GPA should implement all the provisions of the GPA and create a conducive environment for peace, security, and free political activity

c. the inclusive government in Zimbabwe should complete all the steps necessary for the holding of the election, including the finalisation of the constitutional amendment and the referendum

d. the SADC should assist Zimbabwe to formulate guidelines that will assist in holding an election that will be peaceful, free and fair, in accordance with the SADC Principles and Guidelines Governing Democratic Elections.[75]

In order to expedite this process, the SADC Troika decided to appoint a team of officials to join the facilitation team and work with the Joint Monitoring and Implementation Committee (JOMIC) to ensure monitoring, evaluation and implementation of the GPA. Progress would be reviewed by the next summit. On 22 April 2011, Zimbabwe's parties – ZANU-PF, the MDC-T and the MCD-N, headed by the Minister for Industry and Trade, Trevor Ncube[76] – despite considerable disagreement, signed a GPA implementation roadmap. However, the SADC did not enforce clear timelines for implementation and, four years after signing the GPA, Zimbabwean democracy and human rights activists drew very mixed conclusions on the achievements and perspectives of both the mediation and the political process in Zimbabwe.[77]

How to explain Zimbabwe's enduring international standing?

Some observers seem surprised that the Western alliance is not succeeding in bringing about regime change in Zimbabwe. Others blame this failure solely on the Chinese-Russian veto power exercised in the UNSC. For several reasons, such as perspective would be misguided. Despite all objectionable domestic politics – from the way party unity between ZANU and ZAPU was brought about, to the horrendous Matabeleland campaign, to corruption and nepotism, to infringements of human rights, etc. – since independence on 18 April 1980, Zimbabwe has earned and enjoyed an incredible amount of diplomatic goodwill.[78] This can be attributed to a number of reasons, but mainly to the way in which Zimbabwe took the lead in organising regional, continental and Global South diplomacy on the apartheid issue and sanctions. Zimbabwe actively tried to protect the region's transport corridors against South African destabilisation. This led to various forms of recognition and responsibility, including becoming a member of the UNSC twice (1983–1984, 1991–1992), leading the NAM (1986–1989), hosting the Commonwealth Heads of States and Government Summit (1991), and being elected a member of the AUPSC (2010–2013). Admittedly, the end of apartheid and the rise of a democratic South Africa to the international stage changed Zimbabwe's international role considerably.[79] What also needs to be noted in the context of this chapter is that, in its international relations, three centres of gravity dominated decision making, depending on the issue area: foreign policy, economic and finance, and security. All centred around Mugabe and, in cases of conflict of interest, the securocrats dominated.[80]

Against this backdrop, the brief analysis of four lines of reasoning (or discursive *epistimés à la* Foucault) help to understand how the Mugabe regime managed to maintain considerable levels of diplomatic support from neighbouring countries and other external allies after 1993/1994. All examples below are drawn from the debate at the UNSC held on 11 July 2008.81

Firstly, Mugabe and his government increasingly reverted to a general anti-imperialist (the Third Chimurenga theme), anti-Western and, at times, anti-white or even anti-homosexual rhetoric.[82] For instance, in the 11 July 2008 debate on the draft UNSC resolution tabled by the USA, the UK, France and others, Zimbabwe's permanent representative responded: "The current sanctions are basically an expression of imperialist conquest and no amount of propaganda or denial can ever wish this away." Although it is not part of diplomatic debate, some of the other abovementioned underlying post-colonial experiences, images and stereotypes are shared far beyond Zimbabwe, and may also resonate extremely well in public debate outside Zimbabwe.

In more concrete terms, the regime utilised its past track record as a custodian of the legacy of liberation politics and sound, rule-guided international diplomacy. It insisted, as Zimbabwe's permanent representative to the UN did, on proper adherence to international rules, accusing the USA and others of abusing UN Chapter VII and imposing sanctions under the pretext that Zimbabwe constituted a threat to international peace and security. In this context, Zimbabwe could be sure that the argument would resonate with most fellow SADC and African governments, but also other regimes in the Global South, which took issue with the ambitions and behaviour of the allies in the "War on Terror" as it unfolded in Iraq and Afghanistan. In Africa in particular, what is sometimes felt as a disregard by the West of African institutions and solutions in a situation like this, clearly plays into the hands of Mugabe.[83] The argument about this misuse of the international system by the US administration was immediately supported by the permanent representative of the Russian Federation, and, ultimately, by Vietnam. In a slightly similar vein, and speaking in his capacity as chair of the SADC Organ on Politics, the permanent representative of Angola emphasised the role of regional and sub-regional organisations, as well as the importance of dialogue between the UNSC and the AUPSC.

Thirdly, the regime repeatedly made reference to ongoing mediation efforts that, from its perspective, had yielded positive results. At the same meeting of the UNSC, the Zimbabwean permanent representative stated that political dialogue was ongoing between the contending parties; Mugabe had reached out to the opposition and called for all political parties to enter into a comprehensive inter-party dialogue sooner rather than later. It was also stated that reconciliation was not a new concept to Zimbabwe, which fully welcomed the recent AU resolution (1 July 2008). The South African permanent representative to the UN, Dumisani Kumalo, reiterated this line of reasoning when he stated that the AU, in its resolution on Zimbabwe, had indeed not called for sanctions against Zimbabwe, but instead "appealed to States and all parties concerned to refrain from any action that may negatively impact on the climate for dialogue". It also encouraged Mugabe and Tsvangirai "to honour their commitments to initiate dialogue, with a view to promoting peace, stability, democracy and reconciliation of the Zimbabwean people". Because of the ongoing efforts by the SADC and its OPDSC, as well as the activities of the facilitators of the intra-Zimbabwe dialogue (Thabo Mbeki and Jean Ping), South Africa, as a member of both SADC and the AU, felt obliged to follow the decision of the regional bodies. According to the Russian Federation's permanent representative, the draft resolution was not only an attempt to interfere in the internal affairs of a country, but also ignored the dialogue launched between the parties and the various mediations. Speaking to the concerns of the AU and the SADC, he continued that the draft's co-sponsors had not considered the position of regional States. This position was strongly supported by the People's Republic of China. In addition, the permanent representative of Angola stressed that the SADC had spared no effort in encouraging the parties to initiate dialogue to promote democracy and reconciliation, and that he had great hopes for South Africa's mediation. This view was supported by the SADC permanent representative from Tanzania, the permanent observer of the AU to the UN, and the permanent representative of Libya. Indonesia, the only country on the Council that abstained, also emphasised the need for continued mediation, stressing that any action by the Council should serve to promote dialogue and reconciliation in Zimbabwe.

And, finally, Zimbabwe argued that sanctions would contribute to a deterioration of the economic and social situation in the country that would, first and foremost, affect the ordinary citizen. Inflation figures hit a new high in June 2008, growing at 231 million per cent. After the EU, the USA and the Commonwealth introduced sanctions against Zimbabwe in 2002, the SADC leaders at summit held in Dar es Salaam, Tanzania, committed themselves on 26 August 2003 "to continue opposing" these sanctions "as they hurt not only ordinary Zimbabweans but also have profound social and economic implications on the region as a whole".[84] In the UNSC debate of 11 July 2008, this point was directly challenged by the permanent representative of Croatia.

Only one African country did not support Zimbabwe's position in the UNSC – Burkina Faso – whose permanent representative bought into the argument that Zimbabwe constituted a threat to international peace and security. This position was shared by Costa Rica and Panama, both countries that one could assume were acting not totally free of the influence of their specific relations with France and the USA respectively.

What follows from this brief overview is that the Western powers apparently believed that it was sufficient to recall critical African positions on the developments in Zimbabwe, but failed to reflect on how a very common perception of their own politics might work against it. Leaked cables clearly demonstrate the USA had detailed access to the views of the governments of, for instance, China and South Africa, and it was even reported that "South Africa also believes strongly that Africans should solve African problems. The international community should only become involved when requested by the AU or other African leaders." But this did not filter down into strategising the imposition of sanctions by the USA and others.[85]

Summary

International efforts to address the Zimbabwe conflict since the beginning of the last decade have focused on different strategies, which for systematic reasons can be summarised under the rubric of preventive diplomacy (see Table 1). As such, actors' interest and coalitions have changed. Nevertheless, it became clear that certain actors were driving the agenda on Zimbabwe from the beginning, ahead of everyone the UK and the USA, backed up by the work of international advocacy organisations such as ICG and Human Rights Watch (HRW). They managed to rally the support of the EU and the Commonwealth; initially the old domino bloc of Australia, New Zealand and Canada; and later the African member states.

As the conflict progressed, activities moved from concern/condemn to sanctions and mediation, in particular in response to the different reports of election observer missions. With regard to sanctions, the Western bloc failed to build up a broad-based international alliance. The effects of sanctions on mediation and the preparedness of different Zimbabwean actors to compromise may be a different question.[86] Mediation was mainly advocated by the African actors – the AU and the SADC. Here, the West, but also critical actors within Africa, were rather impatient, to the point were serious frictions showed within the SADC.

Table 1: Strategies and coalitions in addressing the Zimbabwe conflict

	Fact finding	Expressing concern	Condemn	Observation and monitoring	Sanctions	Mediation
2001/2002	Common-wealth, SADC	European Parliament, EU Commission, SADC, Nigeria, Common-wealth		Common-wealth, SADC (EU barred)	UK, ICG, Australia, Common-wealth, EU, USA	SADC, South Africa
2005	UN Secretary-General special envoy	Australia, Canada, New Zealand, UK				South Africa
2008			UNSC	SADC, PAP, AU, Common-wealth (EU barred)	UK, EU, USA	South Africa
2012					Contra: SADC	

Source: Compiled by the author.

The subsequent analysis of mediation roles is based on the innovative work of Jabri (1990) and Kleiboer (1998), as well as a critical reading of the different academic debates on mediation by Gomes Porto (2012). Drawing on an analysis of international relations theory paradigms, Kleiboer (1998) develops four different models of mediation analysis: the "mediation as power-brokerage" (realism/neorealism); "mediation as political problem-solving" (political psychological theories of international conflict); "mediation as restructuring relationships" (critical theory/human needs approach); and "mediation as domination" (structuralist theories of international relations).[87] Three important questions arise: Who has tried to impose a solution to the Zimbabwe conflict? Who has aimed at true conflict transformation? And who has not only addressed the current conflict constellation, but also the root causes of conflict in Zimbabwe with a view to a sustainable solution?

Table 2: Roles

	Agenda setting	Urging for reforms	Advocating regime change	Preventing regime change	Benign third-party intervention
2001/2002	UK, France, EP, ICG	Commonwealth, SADC, South Africa	Not yet firmly on the agenda		SADC, Commonwealth
2003		Botswana, Malawi, South Africa, Kenya, Nigeria			
2005	UNSG				
2008	EISA, Carter Center, Belgium, Costa Rica, Croatia, France, Italy, Panama, UK, USA	SADC, AU	UK, USA, France, etc.	PR China, Russia, South Africa, Libya, Vietnam	AU, SADC, South Africa
2011/12	ICG, HRW		ICG		SADC, South Africa

Source: Compiled by the author.

Some rather general observations follow from this:

- It has become evident that some of the preventive diplomacy strategies employed by actors have not primarily or always been used to prevent conflict, but rather to turn an unbeloved regime into an international pariah and, more or less openly, push for regime change.

- This strategy was weakly coordinated and implemented – no stable, broad-based Western coalition emerged that managed to engage both the SADC and the non-Western permanent members of the UNSC (in particular, the USA administration of George Bush (Jr) was inconsistent in its policy).

- The set of preventive diplomacy tools has yielded different, very contingent results, mainly because of poor coordination among actors and the ability of the Mugabe regime to maintain important regional and other international support.

- In 2008, election observer reports proved to be a strong preventive diplomacy tool.

- Actors' interests and their collective identities have been inconsistent, especially SADC and South African sanctions and mediation.

- In July 2008, the Russian Federation sent mixed signals (G8 Summit statement on Zimbabwe vs UNSC vote on draft resolution).

- Throughout the 2000s, Western powers demonstrated little understanding for or appreciation of African diplomacy in general, and Zimbabwe's role in particular; historic legacies and African personal networks were underestimated.

- Most actors showed very little interest in real preventive diplomacy, which reflects disagreement on what the root causes of conflict in Zimbabwe really are: the land issue, or bad governance, a combination of these, or something else?

Recommendations

General

- Define the aim of intervention: stability or regime change.
- Contract the conflict parties: offer incentives in the form of clear contributions to a stable economic environment, including access to predictable flows of foreign currency, development assistance and post-conflict reconstruction development, and assist the region in migration control, etc.
- Define a compliance mechanism and a fall-back position, including a clearly communicated gradual escalation of punitive measures, and an alternative policy scenario for the EU and the USA (exit option).
- Develop a regional/international strategy to deal with spoilers (especially in the security forces and among youth militias) in this context: assist security sector reform in Zimbabwe with independent civilian oversight bodies.
- Define and invest in structural prevention (i.e. take the land issue seriously and address it systematically); make binding commitments with regards to land reform; organise a buy-in for a process of redistributive justice and reconciliation, and security sector reform.

European Union, etc.

- Define the aim of intervention: stability or regime change? This may call for compromise. (What could be the difference between a British and a European position?)
- Be realistic about sanctions as an instrument of leverage in the absence of international consensus shared by the SADC, the AU and the UNSC.
- Base contract on lead mediation role under the auspices of the AU and the SADC.
- Develop consensus among all permanent UNSC member states about the division of labour and responsibilities of the AU/SADC mediator, and, if to be appointed, a possible UN Special Envoy.
- Develop a coherent and integrated sanctions strategy.
- Secure deployment of long-term election observer mission.

AU, SADC, South Africa

- Define the aim of intervention: stability or regime change? This may call for compromise. (Regional stability or democratic change?)
- Define measurable and timed benchmarks of mediation.
- Link mediation to an AU/SADC monitoring mechanism.
- Develop a compliance mechanism.

Epilogue

In view of the referendum on a new Constitution held on 16 March 2013, which had an approval rate of almost 95%, some international actors have loosened the sanctions regime imposed on Zimbabwe. In response to the announcement of the referendum, Australia lifted sanctions against 55 individuals in Zimbabwe on 11 March 2013; and in response to the successful referendum the EU, on 25 March 2013, suspended its sanctions against 81 officials and eight companies in Zimbabwe.[88] Sanctions remained in place against 10 people, including President Mugabe and two companies.

[1]   The author would like to thank David Moore and João Gomes Porto for valuable comments and critique.

[2]   *See* Melber (2009), Saunders (2011).

[3]   On the land question, see Moore (2001), Shaw (2003), Moyo (2011).

[4]   *See* "World Bank in Zimbabwe" at http://web.worldbank.org/WBSITE/EXTERNAL/COUNTRIES/AFRICAEXT/ ZIMBABWEEXTN/0,,menuPK:375745~pagePK:141132~piPK:141129~theSitePK:375736,00.html. Accessed 12 November 2012.

[5]   *See* McGregor (2002), Rupiya (2005).

[6]   On the violent 2008 elections campaign, *see* Bratton (2011), Masunungure (2009), Bratton & Masunungure (2008). On the 2005 elections, *see* Andrews & Morgan (2005). On the 2002 elections, *see* Raftopoulos (2002). On continuity *vis-à-vis* previous elections, *see* Kriger (2005).

[7]   *See* Tibaijuka (2005), Bratton & Masunungure (2007), Musoni (2010).

[8]   *See* Commonwealth Secretariat (2000), EISA (2008) and, in particular, HRW (2008a, 2008b, 2009, 2011).

[9]   All figures according to EISA at http://www.eisa.org.za/WEP/zim2008results5.htm. Accessed 12 November 2012.

[10] *See* http://www.eisa.org.za/WEP/zim2008results6.htm. Accessed 12 November 2012.

[11] *See* http://www.eisa.org.za/WEP/zim2008results1.htm. Accessed 12 November 2012. According to the Constitution, only 60 out of the 93 seats of the Zimbabwean Senate are elected by universal adult franchise from single member plurality constituencies, six from each of ten provinces. In addition, 28 people become ex-officio members of the Senate, and five are appointed by the incoming president. Out of the elected 60 seats, ZANU-PF got 30, MDC-T 24 and MDC-M 6. *See* http://www.eisa.org.za/WEP/zim2008results4.htm. Accessed 12 November 2012.

[12] *See* GoZ MFA (2008), Cheeseman & Tendi (2010), Mehler (2009).

[13] *The Independent* of 12 October 2012 reported: "In a desperate bid to reverse the tide in Masvingo and Manicaland, the military is organising clandestine meetings with chiefs and other traditional leaders to mobilise their subjects to support Zanu-PF ahead of elections". *See* http://allafrica.com/stories/201210161137.html. Accessed 12 November 2012.

[14] Here and in the following verbatim from the BBC, Andrew Harding, 11 October 2012 at http://www.bbc.co.uk/news/world-africa-19912593>. *See also Financial Gazette*, 17 October 2012 at http://allafrica.com/stories/201210181219.html and *Zimbabwe Standard*, 14 October 2012 at http://allafrica.com/stories/201210140353.html. All accessed 12 November 2012.

[15] *See* John Campbell, "Military Saber-Rattling in Zimbabwe", Council on Foreign Relations Blog, 11 June 2012 at http://blogs.cfr.org/campbell/2012/06/11/military-saber-rattling-in-zimbabwe/. Accessed 12 November 2012.

[16] UNSG (1992).

[17] *See* African Union (2002), AU Assembly (2007).

[18] *See* Tibaijuka (2005).

[19] ICG (2002b:14f).

[20] EU Commission (2001).

[21] *See* ICG (2002b:15).

[22] ICG (2001b:1).

[23] Ibid, p. 4.

[24] Ibid.

[25] ICG (2002b:17).

[26] *See* UNSC 5929th meeting, 8 July 2008, S/PV. 5929.

[27] AU Assembly (2008)

[28] ICG (2001b:3).

[29] *See* http://www.eisa.org.za/WEP/zim2008eom.htm. Accessed 15 November 2012.

[30] SADC (2008).

[31] Strange as it seems, this was also the gist of a statement issued by the EU and South Africa after a ministerial troika meeting held on 3 June: "Both parties discussed the situation in Zimbabwe and commended the people of Zimbabwe for the peaceful manner in which the elections were conducted." *See* EU Council (2008).

[32] Democratic Alliance, "Minority Report on the 2008 Zimbabwe Elections", April 2008. *See* http://www.eisa.org.za/PDF/zim2008da.pdf. Accessed 15 November 2012.

[33] Democratic Alliance (2008:2).

[34] Carter Center and EISA. *See* http://www.eisa.org.za/EISA/pr20080523.htm. Accessed 15 November 2012.

[35] SEOM (2008:6).

[36] *See* Ploch (2010:20f).

[37] *See* US Cable, Embassy Gaborone, 4 July 2008 at http://www.insiderzim.com/stories/4741-botswana-said-it-did-not-recognise-mugabes-victory.html; SW Radio Africa (London), 4 August 2008 at http://allafrica.com/stories/200808041628.html; and *Botswana Gazette*, 27 November 2008, at http://palapye.wordpress.com/2008/11/27/. All accessed 16 November 2012).

[38] PAP (2008:21).

[39] ICG (2001a:i).

[40] Ibid.

[41] Ibid.

[42] ICG (2001b:2).

[43] ICG (2002b:14f).

[44] ICG (2002b:17).

[45] ICG (2002b:15).

[46] EU Council (2002).For an update on the full range of sanctions imposed (and the list of legal instruments) *see* "Delegation of the European Union to the Republic of Zimbabwe. Restrictive Measures" at http://eeas.europa.eu/delegations/zimbabwe/eu_zimbabwe/political_relations/restrictive_measures/index_en.htm. Accessed 15 November 2012.

[47] ICG (2002b:2).

[48] ICG (2004:17).

[49] Gomes Porto (2012:191).

[50] *The Telegraph*, 19 March 2003, at http://www.telegraph.co.uk/news/1388188/Zimbabwe-suspended-from-Commonwealth.html. *See also The Guardian*, 20 March 2002, at http://www.guardian.co.uk/world/2002/mar/20/qanda.zimbabwe. Both accessed 15 November 2012.

[51] SADC (2007).

[52] *See*, for instance, SADC (2009).

[53] Letter dated 18 June 2008 from the Permanent Representative of Belgium to the United Nations addressed to the President of the Security Council, S/2008/407.

[54] Statement by the President of the Security Council, S/PRST/2008/23, 23 June 2008. *See also* UNSC, 5919th meeting, 23 June 2008, S/PV. 5919.

[55] Here and in the following UNSC, 5933rd meeting, (PM)/SC/9396, 11 July 2008. http://www.un.org/News/Press/docs/2008/sc9396.doc.htm. Accessed 12 November 2012.

[56] *See* G8 Hokkaido Tokyo Summit, G8 Leaders Statement on Zimbabwe, 8 July 2008. http://www.g8.utoronto.ca/summit/2008hokkaido/2008-zim.html. Accessed 12 November 2012.

[57] UNSC Draft Resolution on Zimbabwe, S/2008/447, 11 July 2008.

[58] US cable by Secretary of State, Urgent request for demarche on USNC Chapter VII, 2 July 2008. http://www.insiderzim.com/stories/2682-us-pushes-for-military-intervention-in-zimbabwe.html. Accessed 12 November 2012.

[59] Ibid. The deputy chairperson was actually referred to as the "Deputy Secretary-General", a position that only existed in the OAU, which was transformed into the AU in 2000.

[60] ICG (2012:1).

[61] Such as the UN good offices mission of the UN Secretary-General, led by Assistant Secretary-General, Haile Menkerios, around the June 2008 elections.

[62] ICG (2001b:1, 2).

[63] ICG (2001b:3).

[64] See Engel (2012).

[65] *See* Maudeni (2004), McKinley (2004), Freeman (2005), Sachikonye (2005b), Lipton (2009), Soko & Balchin (2009).

[66] Engel (2013).

[67] *See* http://allafrica.com/stories/201303260173.html. Accessed 6 April 2013). The author would like to thank David Moore for drawing his attention to this.

[68] *See also* Matlosa (2009).

[69] These elections were held in conjunction with elections to both houses of parliament and municipal elections.

[70] SEOM (2008:6.f)

[71] GoZ MFA (2008).

[72] For a detailed account of the politics of the GPA government, *see* Ploch (2010).

[73] Ndlovu-Gatsheni (2011:15–17).

[74] *See also* Kagwanja (2006):

[75] SADC (2011).

[76] Mediation also involves decisions about which parties are recognised by the mediators. In this case, the SADC resolved after its 2012 summit in held Maputo, Mozambique, that the mediator would talk to Ncube's MDC, rather than that of Deputy Prime Minister Mutambara.

[77] ZEN et al. (2012).

[78] Engel (1994).

[79] For a few recent accounts *see* Nkiwane (1999); Adar, Ajulu & Onyango (2002); Chigora (2007).

[80] Engel (1994). This has implications for bilateral relations in the context of mediation, as demonstrated with reference to South Africa by Kagwanja & Rupiya (2009).

[81] UN Security Council, 5933rd Meeting, (PM)/SC/9396, 11 July 2008. http://www.un.org/News/Press/docs/2008/sc9396.doc.htm. Accessed 12 November 2012.

[82] With reference to Mugabeism as a specific constellation, *see* Ndlovu-Gatsheni (2009).

[83] In order to understand this deep-rooted position, one could refer to the way AU member states and institutions responded to the NATO-led intervention in Libya in 2011, when their efforts for an African solution were side-lined.

[84] SADC (2003:§25).

[85] US Embassy Pretoria, Report on a press conference by South African Deputy Foreign Minister Aziz Pahad, 4 July 2008. http://www.cablegatesearch.net/cable.php?id=08PRETORIA1467; and US Embassy Beijing, Report on a talk with the Ministry of Foreign Affairs' International Organisations and Conferences Department, UN Division Deputy Director Sun Xiaobo, 9 July 2008. http://www.leakoverflow.com/questions/510226/08beijing2675-china-will-not-support-unsc-zimbabwe-resolution. Both accessed 14 November 2012. See also Lyman (2006). For a discussion of policy options for the USA *see* Todd & Patrick (2005), Gavin (2007), and Rotberg (2011). *See also* US Senate, Subcommittee on African Affairs of the Committee on Foreign Relations (2008, 2009, 2010).

[86] *See* Grebe (2010).

[87] *See also* Gomes Porto (2012:36).

[88] *See* http://foreignminister.gov.au/releases/2013/bc_mr_130311.html, http://www.europeanvoice.com/article/2013/march/eu-eases-zimbabwe-sanctions-again/76831.aspx. Both accessed 6 April 2013.

7

The "sanctions debate" and the political role of the security sector

João Gomes Porto [1]

Political developments in Zimbabwe over the last decade have exposed the limits of the targeted sanctions' regime imposed by the European Union (EU), the USA and others on the country's top leadership. Eleven years have passed since the imposition of restrictive measures and, although some progress has been made as regards economic stability as well as a reduction in human rights violations, and the majority of individuals subject to sanctions have been removed from the list, there is little evidence to suggest that the fundamental conditions underlying the imposition of targeted sanctions were met. As the country heads for elections this year, Robert Mugabe and the Zimbabwe African National Union Patriotic Front (ZANU-PF) remain firmly in control of the fragile unity government set up under the Global Political Agreement (GPA), and continue to hold a tight rein over the prospects for democratic transition in Zimbabwe. While the imposition of restrictive measures may have been partly the result of misguided assumptions about their leverage potential over Mugabe and ZANU-PF, issues of timing, gradualism and strategic coordination with other dimensions of EU interventions are particularly poignant – in part, as the EU was and remains the primary donor in the country. From a procedural point of view, and within the context and rationality supporting the imposition of restrictive measures (or sanctions in EU parlance), several issues are worth reflecting on. These include timing, gradualism and, critically, strategic coordination and policy coherence with all other relevant EU/European Community (EC) interventions. Timing is indeed critical in the

106

application of a set of tools that, in the arsenal of diplomatic leverage – and precisely as a result of the inappropriateness of general trade and economic sanctions, and the then inconceivable and unjustifiable scenario of military intervention – should be seen, when used in their entirety, as a last resort. The absence of a process of gradual escalation of punitive measures marked by the imposition of comprehensive targeted sanctions and the suspension of development assistance on the same day in February 2002, following an unusually brief period of Article 96 consultations, left the EU with a severely restricted set of policy options in the event of non-compliance. In fact, faced with the exponential growth in the ability of Mugabe and ZANU-PF to contravene, there was little the EU could do but publicly condemn the regime, enlarging the list of persons and organisations it deemed responsible for the situation at the annual renewal of the sanctions regime. Indeed, would a gradual build-up of the sanctions regime (in both scope and participation) have been more prudent and ultimately yield more results? For the author, the Zimbabwe case ultimately reveals the inadequacy of autonomous targeted sanctions as an instrument of leverage in the absence of an international consensus, particularly a United Nations Security Council (UNSC) mandate. If the most powerful effect of targeted sanctions is said to be a function of their symbolism, Mugabe's masterly transmutation of the intended "stigmatization" into "victimization" (as part of his pan-Africanist, anti-colonial and anti-West discourse around a   in Zimbabwe) dealt a severe blow to the symbolic power of targeted sanctions.

Developments in Zimbabwe since the formation of the GNU in February 2009, seem to indicate a relative if painfully slow halting of the macro-economic decline of the country. The country has experienced 4.7% GDP growth in 2009 and 9.3% in 2011. Schools and hospitals have begun to operate, civil servants are being paid and there is a visible reduction in human rights violations in the country.[2] Yet, Mugabe and the top leadership of ZANU-PF continue to hold a tight rein on political and military power in the country, having delayed key provisions of the power-sharing agreement signed with the Movement for Democratic Change (MDC). As the country heads for elections this year (2013), the prospects of renewed instability and election-related violence may compromise the democratic transition in the country.

Overcoming a decade of socio-economic decline will not be easy. Coupled with the climate of widespread violence and intimidation that characterised life in this southern African country for at least a decade, the consequences of the humanitarian crisis that unfolded from 2000 onwards are still very much present. At its height, more than four million Zimbabweans required emergency food and medical assistance in a country where unemployment rates reached 80%, the annual inflation rate reached a staggering 200 million percent in January 2009, the health and education sectors collapsed, and basic foodstuffs and fuel were extremely difficult to find. It is estimated that more than three million Zimbabweans remain as refugees in neighbouring countries (mostly in South Africa and Botswana) and further afield, in a movement that has seen hundreds of thousands of professional cadres flee the country. If there is a statistic that more than any other demonstrates the crisis that beset Zimbabwe, it is that of average life expectancy. The contrast between 1990 (when average life expectancy was 61 years) and 2007 (when average life expectancy was 34 years for women and 37 years for men) couldn't be starker.[3] Moreover, the 2007/08 Human Development Report gives a comprehensive picture of socio-economic decline in the country; suffice to say that Zimbabwe is ranked 151th out of 177 countries, occupying the 89th position out of 103 in terms of levels of poverty.[4]

The political dimensions of the crisis have dominated international policy towards Zimbabwe for at least a decade, particularly that of the EU and the US, in an effort to pressure Mugabe's ZANU-PF regime to negotiate with the MDC, to respect human rights and fundamental liberties, to repeal draconian legislation and, finally, to implement transparent and free and fair elections. The instrument chosen to accomplish these aims was that of "targeted sanctions", first suggested by the USA in December 2001 in the Zimbabwe Democracy and Economic Recovery Act (ZIDERA).[5] In February 2002, the EU – the largest donor to Zimbabwe since independence – followed suit and imposed "restrictive measures" on Mugabe and ZANU-PF's top leadership. New Zealand and Australia adopted similar measures respectively in April and September of the same year, while the US adopted targeted sanctions in March 2003. Following the presidential run-off election of 2008, Canada adopted similar sanctions.

By imposing restrictive measures on the country's top leadership, the EU hoped that Zimbabwe would alter its behaviour, believing that the approach had sufficient leverage to push Mugabe in the direction of respecting human rights and fundamental freedoms, the rule of law and good governance. Within the framework of the EU's Common Foreign and Security Policy (CFSP), restrictive measures are regarded as instruments of a diplomatic and/or economic nature "imposed by the EU to bring about a change in policy or activity by the target country, part of a country, government, entities or individuals".[6] Moreover, the EU Council has emphasised that "sanctions should be targeted in such a way as to have maximum impact on those whose behaviour they are intended to influence; in so doing, accurate targeting should reduce to the absolute minimum any adverse humanitarian effects, the risk of unintended consequences for persons not targeted or possible adverse effects on neighbouring countries".[7]

The evaluation of the efficacy of targeted sanctions must therefore be based on whether such change has indeed occurred. In light of developments in the country since 2002, it is clear that the EU restrictive measures have not achieved their fundamental objectives; the fact that sanctions remain in place for Mugabe, his family and some of his closest allies within ZANU-PF, leaves no room for ambiguity. In fact, that the EU based its decision earlier in March 2013 of lifting the sanctions on 81 individuals and eight businesses in Zimbabwe on the basis of a "peaceful, successful and credible" referendum on a new constitution held the same month, is evidence not of a carefully thought through process, but an attempt at finding an exit strategy for a policy that had become, and perhaps always was, incongruent. Indeed, the sanctions regime has become ZANU-PF's weapon of choice in its efforts to block the implementation of key provisions of the GPA, outmanoeuvring the MDC factions to whom the sanctions regime represent what little leverage it may have.

Yet, the risk of renewed election-related violence is real and ever present as the country embarks on the first election post GPA. One must only remember the events of March 2007, when hundreds of opposition supporters and members of civil society organisations were arrested and beaten, including the president of the MDC, Morgan Tsvangirai. These events provoked widespread international and regional condemnation, leading South Africa to break with its traditional "silent diplomacy" and appeal to Harare to abide by the law and respect human rights; and a rather angry Levy Mwanawasa, President of Zambia, to compare Zimbabwe to "the sinking of the Titanic".[8] Nevertheless, no one quite anticipated the carnage that would characterise the farcical elections of March 2008. In fact, strong international condemnation and the renewed effort by the Southern African Development Community (SADC) to give institutional support to South African President Thabo Mbeki's meditation process would notably fail in their efforts to reduce the levels of arbitrary detention, violence and intimidation perpetrated by Mugabe's regime throughout 2007.[9] That the March 2008 elections occurred in the way they did should not come as a surprise.

The trend towards an increasingly authoritarian and militarised approach to government by Mugabe and ZANU-PF had been there for some time, hardening during the period between the referendum of 2000 and the presidential elections of 2002. For some authors, the origins of this authoritarian tendency can be found in the way ZANU-PF conducted the struggle for independence and consolidated power in the immediate post-independence period in Zimbabwe – as David Blair, Steve Kibble, Lloyd Sachikonye, Brian Kagoro and Timothy Scarnecchia have so aptly demonstrated.[10] Throughout the first decade of the century, the regime displayed a proclivity to act through a combination of legislation enacted to assure total political, economic and social control, coupled with military-style operations in areas as distinct as elections, the economy and the private sector, land reform, informal trade and housing. Examples have included the Fast-Track Land Reform programme, the Public Order and Security Act (POSA), the Access to Information and Protection of Privacy Act (AIPPA), and the Private Voluntary Organisations Act (PVOA). Military-style operations as a way of implementing policy may be found in operations "*Murambatsvina*", "*Dzikisa Mitengo*" and "Taguta", among many others.[11] In these operations, the use of the armed forces, the intelligence services, the police, and so-called "war veterans" and militias has been widespread. In addition, the gradual militarisation of the regime was pursued through the increasing executive power of the Joint Operational Command (JOC) in the political, social and economic affairs of the State – in practice, replacing the Council of Ministers as decision-making body.[12] Excluding the period of the 2008 elections, the Zimbabwe Human Rights NGO Forum had registered more than 25 000 human rights violations, in their vast majority perpetrated by forces of the State.[13]

Eleven years since the imposition of restrictive measures, and as events unfold leading to the first elections post GPA, a reflection on EU policy towards Zimbabwe seems appropriate. While the imposition of restrictive measures may have been partly the result of misguided assumptions about Mugabe and ZANU-PF, issues of timing, gradualism and strategic coordination with other dimensions of EU interventions are particularly poignant. One needs to explore the limits and, perhaps unexpectedly, the counter-productive nature of the targeted sanctions applied by the EU on Zimbabwe by raising a number of critical and interrelated issues. The first and perhaps most important question relates to the extent to which the policy was based on a fundamental misreading of the situation in Zimbabwe. Broad economic sanctions (such as an export/import ban) were not an option for the EU, as this type of sanction would directly affect ordinary Zimbabweans and be in contravention of the EU's humanitarian norms.[14] Accordingly, the EU decided to target those it deemed directly responsible for the situation in the country, and used a basket of measures (comprising an arms embargo, a visa ban, and freezing of funds and economic assets) in the belief that these types of restrictive measures have "maximum impact on those whose behaviour we want to influence".[15] Underlying the imposition of targeted sanctions was the assumption that the international stigma attached to being the subject of sanctions, coupled with the costs of non-compliance which would result from the specific type of "restrictive measures" chosen (coupled, of course, with the suspension of budgetary support through development cooperation), would persuade Mugabe to change course. With hindsight, these were fundamental miscalculations, particularly as regards the level of costs Mugabe and ZANU-PF's top leadership were, and still are, prepared to incur. And, if the most powerful effect of targeted sanctions is said to be a function of their symbolism, Mugabe's masterly transmutation of the intended "stigmatisation" into a profoundly counter-productive "victimisation" (as part of his pan-Africanist, anti-colonial and anti-western discourse around a *Third Chimurenga* in Zimbabwe) dealt a severe blow to the symbolic power of targeted sanctions.

Faced with the ability of Mugabe and ZANU-PF to contravene, the severance of political relations and the suspension of the Cotonou Agreement, the EU was left with a restricted set of options. These included public condemnation and the inclusion of ever more persons and organisations on the sanctions' list at best. At worst, there was no other option but to accept Mugabe's conditions on the GPA, thereby adding legitimacy to an election (2008) fraught with manipulation and violence. On the ground, the EC delegation threaded a very difficult balancing act in its efforts to continue to provide assistance to the most vulnerable in Zimbabwe in the context of the suspension of development assistance. To what extent was there appropriate reflection on the impact of targeted sanctions on other areas of EU-Zimbabwe relations, in particular development cooperation and humanitarian assistance? Would a gradual build-up of the sanctions regime have been more prudent and ultimately yield more results? To what extent was there consideration of the possible downside of a sanctions regime that lacked international consensus and was, therefore, instrumentalised by Mugabe, negatively affecting relations between the EU and its African partners?

The context: a deep, protracted and multifaceted crisis

For many international observers, the crisis in Zimbabwe has been eminently political, with Mugabe's unwillingness to stand down providing the context within which Zimbabwe's spiralling collapse must be understood. In Zimbabwe's downward trajectory, the defeat of ZANU-PF in the constitutional referendum held in 2000 and the results of the 2000 parliamentary elections are often regarded as watershed moments, signalling a turning point in the political destinies of the country.[16] For David Blair, from the moment Mugabe, "the last standard-bearer of a famous generation", lost the 2000 referendum, he began "fighting like a tiger to hold power against an opposition born from the spiralling economic collapse of his country".[17]

The 2000 elections, considered by many international observers as having been neither free nor fair, for Sachikonye represent a "cataclysmic shift" in the political environment of the country, while Chris Maroleng notes that their historical significance relates to the fact that they transformed the MDC into the best performing opposition party in Zimbabwe's independent history.[18] As poignantly noted by David Blair (2003:164), "the MDC, a party just nine months old, had given ZANU-PF an electoral pounding without precedent in Zimbabwean history" (gaining 47.02% of the popular vote against ZANU-PF's 48.40 %). In fact, the radicalisation of Mugabe's discourse around themes that have now become all too familiar – around "nationalist credentials" (participation in the liberation struggle as the fundamental factor of participation in the political life of the country), his increasingly "anti-West" rhetoric (Who is behind the creation of the MDC?) and around the land issue – can be traced to the period between 2000 and 2002.[19]

While a thorough understanding of Mugabe's and ZANU-PF's trajectory over the last 11 years must necessarily address the series of motivations and political and economic dimensions of a proximate nature, the watershed period referred to above points to a longer historical trend in which structural dimensions and entrenched political behaviour are evident. In this regard, authors have highlighted the peculiarities of Zimbabwe's liberation struggle and the way it produced a leadership with an authoritarian outlook unwilling to transform colonial structures into truly democratic institutions; the gradual entrenchment of neopatrimonialist and clientelistic relations within ZANU-PF leading to nepotism and corruption; the negative effects of structural adjustment programmes; and the effects of poverty, particularly socio-economic inequality, as forming the background conditions (necessary but not sufficient) to the present crisis.[20]

Mugabe's personal trajectory has also been a fertile locus of reflection and speculation in the search for clues to his authoritarian stance and the gradual militarisation of the regime he controls.[21] For some authors, there is a clear continuum linking current authoritarian patterns of government to that of Ian Smith's regime, including the maintenance post-1980 of the security apparatus that supported the Rhodesian regime. For others, such as Sachikonye, the way in which ZANU-PF consolidated its power in the immediate post-independence period, including the civil war that opposed it to Joshua Nkomo's Zimbabwe African People's Union (ZAPU), and that led to the death of 20 000 people in Matabeleland between 1982 and 1987, constitute but the preamble to the current situation. Sachikonye (2002:15) points to an authoritarian trend, which be traced back to the Unity Accord and the resulting fusion ("absorption" would be a better term) of the two parties in 1989, noting in an earlier article (1990:92–99) that already during the 28–30 March 1990 elections, a substantial proportion of the candidates supported the creation of a single-party regime in Zimbabwe. Kagoro (2003) shares this view, adding that, following the signature of the Unity Accord, ZANU-PF would intensify the pressure towards the creation of a single-party regime under the pretext that only then could national unity and development be assured.

As noted by Sarah Bracking (2005:343):

> *Zimbabwe now exhibits a form of authoritarianism that can be traced from the social transformation catalysed by the Economic Structural Adjustment Programme (ESAP) of 1991–95, the economic crisis after 1997, and the more general economic and moral bankruptcy of the post-colonial nebula of hybrid liberal democracy.*

For Mary Ndlovu (2007):

Most objective observers would trace the economic problems back at least to the late 1980s. Certainly the introduction of structural adjustment at the beginning of the 90s can be seen as the process which eroded the living standards of Zimbabweans, and spawned the first broad-based opposition party ... Instead of taking the criticism and the pressure and sitting back to plan a coherent strategy of how to deal with the inter-related issues, ZANU-PF panicked, saw their ruling position threatened, and from 1997 on have responded piecemeal, reactively and irrationally, bringing us to the tragedy which unfolds before our eyes.

A few words on the political economy antecedents of the current crisis are therefore needed. As noted above, the current economic collapse has been marked by hyperinflation; soaring unemployment; rapid economic contraction in the agriculture, industry and service sectors; and severe lack of food, fuel and other basic commodities. These factors have pushed millions of Zimbabweans below the poverty line and created an unprecedented humanitarian catastrophe. In fact, the government of Zimbabwe has itself admitted to the seriousness of an economic situation where living standards dropped by more than 150% over the ten-year period between 1996 and 2005, and it was estimated that more than 63% of rural populations were unable to simultaneously afford basic food and non-food items.[22]

In the 1980s, the government pursued a cautious economic policy, largely independent of the influence and pressure of donors, and with positive results in various areas.[23] At that time, although the land question (in pair with claims to the deepening of the democratic process and economic development) dominated the strongly afro-Marxist discourse of Mugabe, and although the Matabeleland caused a degree of discomfort in international circles, the ZANU-PF government was often referred to as an example of good economic and political governance in a southern African region ravaged by internationalised civil wars in Angola and Mozambique, and the struggle against apartheid in South Africa. To all effects, Zimbabwe had an efficient (albeit bloated) civil service, a diversified economy, a solid human resource base, an enviable education sector, and urban populations enjoyed access to electricity and water in ways unparalleled in the region.

The introduction of the first structural adjustment programme in 1991, titled "Zimbabwe: A Framework for Economic Reform 1991–1995"[24] saw the adoption, timidly at first, of liberalisation policies designed to deregulate the economy and reduce the apparatus of the State as part of an ambitious agenda predicated on export-led growth to sustain a 5% annual GDP growth. Although largely home grown, this programme enjoyed the support of the World Bank (WB) and the International Monetary Fund (IMF).[25] While relations between Harare and international financial institutions were difficult from the beginning, they deteriorated markedly in light of the pressure exerted on the government to accelerate liberalisation in a context where unemployment had soared from 30% in 1991 to 50% by 1995, the country's industry had lost competitiveness and the budget deficit was out of control. Potts (2006) considers that the irreparable damage inflicted on Zimbabwe's economy during this period, and the resulting impact on the standard of living of urban populations in particular, led to the appearance, for the first time in Zimbabwe's history of extreme poverty in the cities, the unparalleled growth of shanty towns in peri-urban areas and the "explosion" of the informal economy.

In June 1995, three years into the programme, the IMF suspended the programme – a suspension that became indefinite when, in 1998, Harare decided to send troops to the Democratic Republic of the Congo (DRC).[26] From that point onwards, the economic situation in Zimbabwe declines rapidly, as the analysis of Sachikonye makes clear. The collapse of the economy accelerated in 1997 and 1998 when Mugabe authorised non-budgeted payments of around Z$5 billion to "war veterans" and sending troops to the DRC in 1998. In an already difficult economic context, these two decisions considerably increased the budget deficit, causing a devaluation of the currency by more than 50%.[27] Indeed, it is in this period that hyperinflation and economic contraction take the dramatic contours they have today. By 1999, it was estimated that 75% of people already lived below the poverty line and, for a great proportion of Zimbabweans, food security had become a survival issue. Indeed, in January 2001, already half a million people needed emergency food assistance, while in 2003 in the urban areas, 75% of homes were classified as poor and 51% as "very poor".[28]

While in the late 1990s the context was already one of economic depression, a very specific group of top ZANU-PF officials (including Mugabe himself) would benefit from the structural adjustment programmes through indigenisation and empowerment policies. In fact, the control of key government and administration positions would enable a small group within ZANU-PF to benefit from economic liberalisation, to the extent that the funds available for the financing of projects allowed for the creation of a new financial class composed of key individuals of the ruling party, which over time positioned itself in marked opposition to the "pre-structural adjustment" entrepreneurial class. As noted by Bracking (2005), although nominally independent, these "party capitalists" depended on the ruling party-State in crucial aspects of their activities such as the purchase of businesses (below market price), to obtain economic licenses or to have access to foreign exchange. In fact, Bracking notes that, since 1997:

> Businesses run by people identified as "outside" the ruling party have increasingly been run out of the market, their operating conditions made hopelessly impossible by targeted failures to the power supply, invasion by Chinotimba's "war veterans", or simply bureaucratic obstacle and revoked licences. The election slogans in 2005 even included an overt ideological endorsement of the "Industrial Chimurenga", the forcible takeover of profitable businesses by the ruling "party-State" in the "empowerment though takeovers" policy.

As economic conditions deteriorated, a more critical, oppositional stance was taken by Zimbabwe's labour movement, human rights organisations, student associations and the media.[29] As noted by Kagoro (2003), the government reacted by adopting the first two in a series of laws to prevent protest and increase its grip on Zimbabwean civil society: the Labour Relations Amendment Bill and the University of Zimbabwe Amendment Act. The Zimbabwe Congress of Trade Unions (ZCTU) reacted by severing relations with ZANU-PF.

The emergence of the pro-democracy movement at the beginning of the 1990s was, in fact, as much a result of widespread dissatisfaction with the negative consequences of economic liberalisation as it was a reaction to Zimbabwe's *de facto* single-party State.[30] The first organised political articulation of opposition to the regime came with the creation of the National Constitution Association (NCA) by several non-governmental organisations, with the expressed aim of exerting pressure on the government to allow for wider participation in the constitutional revision process (entirely dominated by ZANU-PF). A tacit alliance between the ZCTU and the NCA would lead to the creation of the MDC following a joint conference held during February 1999 – an alliance, one should add, that albeit based on quite different social movements that shared little in ideological terms, had its rationale strongly rooted in a visceral opposition to Mugabe and ZANU-PF. That the MDC has since been characterised as a very "broad church" should not come as a surprise. For Maroleng (2004:2–3), the MDC's roots in the ZCTU – which had for several years been in direct confrontation with a regime bent on implementing a disastrous economic policy – coupled with its diffuse and somewhat opportunistic membership and international linkages, made it into an ideal target for accusations by the government-controlled media of being a vehicle for foreign interests. Kagoro, on the other hand, notes that it is this very past that allows us to understand that one of the main challenges to the MDC is cohesion. Indeed, this weakness was most recently demonstrated when, at a crucial phase of the current process, the MDC split into two factions.[31]

It is in this context that the political significance of ZANU-PF's defeat in the referendum of 2000 and the results of the 2000 legislative elections should be understood. Deepening a trend that had become increasingly evident in the preceding decade, that the regime's reaction was the enacting of repressive legislation coupled with the gradual securitisation and militarisation of life in the country (political, economic, social) should not come as a surprise. The period between the 2000 legislative elections and the 2002 presidential elections is particularly important, as this was when POSA and AIPPA were adopted. If POSA gave the regime the instruments required to control the opposition, restricting freedom of association and giving the national police discretionary powers (effectively placing it outside of the law), AIPPA severely limited freedom of expression, opening the way to the banning of all independent media in the country. It is also in this period that one witnesses the forced relocation of more than 70 000 people (between January and March 2002) with a markedly political objective (the redrawing of electoral boundaries), to the creation of 150 militia bases across the country, and the nomination of senior military officers to the Electoral Supervisory Commission.

Later, the government's adoption of an amnesty for all political acts of violence perpetrated between January and July 2000, and the adoption of the PVOA, confirmed, if any doubts remained, the lengths the regime would go to to remain in power, to assure its complete dominance of the State (key government and public service positions) and the private sector.[32] Of note was the strategy pursued in efforts to control the judiciary, in clear violation of the principle of separation of powers; the regime did and continues not to shy away from replacing and intimidating judges it sees as not sharing its agenda.[33] Blair (2003:247) considers that "taken together, the effect of these laws was to plunge Zimbabwe into a permanent State of Emergency".

The instrumentalisation of the land issue has also been a critical weapon in Mugabe's survival strategy. In Zimbabwe, as in many other southern African countries where colonial regimes depended on white settlement achieved through forced expropriation of land, land redistribution remains an important policy priority of black majority governments. Indeed, the patterns of inequality in the extreme that characterised land ownership at the time of independence, required land redistribution if social justice and true economic independence were to be achieved.[34] For a more exact picture of the situation in Zimbabwe in the immediate post-independence period, it suffices to say that approximately 5 000 white owned commercial farms occupied 15.5 million hectares of the very best agricultural land in the country. While the average size of these properties was 3 000 hectares, the average size of communal plots was a mere 20 hectares. It is not surprising, therefore, that during the liberation struggle (the *Second Chimurenga*) both ZANU and ZAPU adopted, as their *leitmotif*, the radical redistribution of land and promised to carry it out once they assumed power.[35] This is precisely the reason why the Lancaster House Agreement (LHA) contained a series of provisions on land redistribution, giving the British government some responsibility for the financing of a programme initially based on the principle of "willing buyer, willing seller".[36]

In its first incarnation between 1980 and 1989, the Land Reform and Resettlement Programme (LRRP) redistributed a mere 2.6 million hectares, benefiting only 52 000 families out of a total of 162 000. One of the consequences of the economic recession of the 1990s was that the land redistribution programme was, for all practical purposes, paralysed.[37] Although the government restructured the programme and in 1997 launched the LRRP2, which now allowed for compulsory occupation in certain cases, the redistribution process remained painfully slow. By 2000, Zimbabwe's economy was still controlled by 4 500 white commercial farmers whose interests extended to other key sectors such as tourism, forestry, the agro-industrial sector and exports.[38] When the first violent land seizures by "war veterans" occurred in February 2000, only 90 000 hectares had been redistributed under the new programme.

Developments took a turn for the worse when, having lost the 2000 referendum, Mugabe announced the "*Third Chimurenga*", unleashing the violent occupation of commercial farms across the country. By 12 March 2000, 450 large commercial farms had been occupied in what the government regarded as a spontaneous expression of "popular will". That the war veterans were directly paid by the government through the War Veterans' Association, seemed not to be of relevance. During July of the same year, the government announced the Fast Track Land Reform Programme, and by so doing gave its support to the occupations that were taking place throughout the country. In that year alone, and according to data from the Commercial Farmers' Union, a combined total of 1 600 commercial farms had been forcefully and violently occupied.[39] In the context of an already dire economic situation, the disruption caused by the speed of the uncontrolled and violent Fast Track Land Programme, devoid of the financial, technical and human means to carry out true agrarian reform, contributed to precipitating economic and financial meltdown. From an economic point of view, the immediate consequence of this policy was a drastic reduction in agricultural production (21% in 2001 and 40% in 2002).

Moving towards "restrictive measures" or the anatomy of a hasty policy decision

The EU's relations with an independent Zimbabwe date back to November 1980 when the country acceded to the Lomé II Convention. Since then, development aid and trade between the two parties have been regulated by a series of Lomé Conventions (II, III and IV) and subsequently by the ACP-EU Partnership Agreement (signed in Cotonou on 23 June 2000, and henceforth referred to as the Cotonou Agreement). Prior to the imposition of restrictive measures in February 2002, EU development assistance had focused on a number of key areas defined in Zimbabwe's National Indicative Programme (NIP), including budgetary support, agriculture and resources' management, education and health, humanitarian assistance, and support for structural adjustment.

In a rather intriguing brochure published in 2004, more than two years after restrictive measures had been imposed and at the height of what could be described at best as an acrimonious relationship at the highest political levels, the European Commission (EC) delegation to Zimbabwe described "a solid 23 years of cooperation" noting that EU support to the country had amounted to €327 million since 1982. The EC delegation goes on to emphasise that "the European Union (EU) is currently Zimbabwe's major co-operating partner in the health sector"; explains how it "supports local communities to implement social and economic infrastructure projects in rural areas"; that its funds contribute to "a more efficient, equitable and sustainable education system in Zimbabwe"; and it has become one of Zimbabwe's biggest humanitarian aid donors.[40]

While for many readers this may come as a surprise, it testifies perhaps to the paradox resulting from the EU's policy of restrictive measures in Zimbabwe, which has required an extensive public relations exercise that, since 2002, aims at clarifying, indeed explaining, the EC's continuing commitment to the people of Zimbabwe in the context of the backlash experienced across Africa (and southern Africa in particular) against what became erroneously known as "sanctions on Zimbabwe/Zimbabweans", part of a propaganda discourse so masterfully orchestrated by Mugabe. To understand the predicament the EU has found itself in since, a discussion of the series of events and processes that led to the adoption of restrictive measures seems appropriate.

In the early months of 2001, the EU decided to use the umbrella provided by the Cotonou Agreement to exert pressure on the government of Zimbabwe in light of what it regarded was a serious disregard of democratic principles and the continued deterioration in the human rights situation in the country. The calculation, of course, was based on the assumption that the government of Zimbabwe would bow to pressure once it realised that the development assistance provided by the EU, which at that time accounted for roughly two-thirds of all aid to the country, could be at risk, in particular direct budgetary support.

In February 2001, the Council of the EU called for consultations under Article 8 of the Cotonou Agreement. The parties began a political dialogue one month later. By June of the same year, in its review of progress made, the Council (General Affairs) was unreserved in its pessimism. No visible movement on an end to political violence – in particular the official encouragement of it – had occurred, no concrete steps to restore the freedom of the media and the independence of the judiciary had been taken, and the EU had still not been invited to observe the presidential elections of 2002. This would prompt the Commission to increase pressure by invoking Zimbabwe's breach of the essential elements that underlined their partnership. The Council followed suit and called for Article 96 consultations during October 2001. The essential elements of the ACP-EU Partnership Agreement are defined in Article 9.2 paragraph 4 as "respect for human rights, democratic principles and the rule of law, which underpin the ACP-EU Partnership, shall underpin the domestic and international policies of the parties".[41]

On 26 October 2001, in perhaps its strongest communication to date, the Commission denounced the growing violence and intimidation observed in Zimbabwe's by-elections, the limiting of the freedom of expression and the independence of the judiciary, the illegal occupation of farm land, and the issues surrounding free and fair elections. In no uncertain terms it noted that "this serious erosion of the quality of governance has contributed to Zimbabwe's dramatic economic decline". It concluded that "it is hardly realistic to expect an early reversal of present policies, baring social upheavals, military intervention, strong pressure from countries with substantial leverage or other such dramatic change in the situation".[42]

Within the spirit of Article 96 consultations, the Commission recommended the scaling down of development cooperation.[43] Indeed, Article 96 specifies that "if the consultations do not lead to a solution acceptable to both Parties, if consultation is refused, or in cases of special urgency, appropriate measures may be taken". Focusing on assessing the efficacy of development aid cut-offs in the framework of the Cotonou Agreement, Portela (2007) posits that "in parallel to its CFSP sanctions, the EU continues to impose some measures whose characteristics approximate those of economic sanctions. The suspensions of development aid as part of the 'appropriate measures' foreseen in Article 96 of the Cotonou Agreement are measures of an economic nature taken on political grounds and with a coercive intention". More importantly, the author notes that the EU "does not label these measures 'sanctions', and keeps this practice legally separate from CFSP measures".

Yet sanctions – in the sense of "restrictive measures" under the CFSP – were, in fact, being considered right from the outset of Article 96 consultations. This is evidenced by the fact that some consideration of the possible consequences of "restrictive measures" was noted and limitations of the EU's leverage were acknowledged, albeit not fully explored. The downside of sanctions was rehearsed and two risks deemed important: "the issue of neo-colonialism and anti-white sentiment" which, because of sanctions, "could figure more prominently in the elections" and "the opening of consultations should be done in such a way as to not complicate co-operation with other key players (Commonwealth and SADC)".[44] In years to come, these two risks became quite serious liabilities, both in terms of Mugabe's use of the sanctions regime as part of his *Third Chimurenga* discourse, and in the way it has affected dialogue between the

EU and its African partners at regional and sub-regional levels, including the postponement of the EU-AU Lisbon summit several times.[45]

In addition, a certain degree of ambivalence characterises the initiation of Article 96 consultations. While it could be interpreted as an olive branch, to assure that all options remained open, in hindsight it hints at the difficult balance the EU would attempt to strike between applying the suspension of development aid and possibly "restrictive measures" under the CFSP, and remaining engaged in the country in a humanitarian and development capacity. Niceties of diplomatic language aside, this ambivalence is clearly evidenced in the following extract:

> [I]t is possible to interpret the deterioration regarding respect for the essential elements as the result of an authoritarian ruling party, which is becoming increasingly determined in its efforts to preserve power. But this would probably be an oversimplification [author emphasis]. The ruling party's perception appears to be that the political opposition in Zimbabwe is orchestrated and financed by the very forces the party fought against in the liberation struggle.[46]

Article 96 consultations would finally begin on 11 January 2002, on the eve of the 2002 presidential elections.[47] At the consultations, Stan Mudenge, Zimbabwe's Minister of Foreign Affairs, expressed his government's concerns about "what it saw as interference into the internal affairs of the country by some member States of the EU through alleged funding of the opposition, the broadcast of hostile propaganda from their territories, and selective condemnation of acts of political violence".[48] Although the minister pledged that concrete steps would be taken to address the human rights situation (including guaranteeing freedom of opinion and association), to investigate the causes of alleged political violence in 2001, to guarantee freedom of expression and independence of the judiciary, and timely invitation to and accreditation of international election observers, the Commission remained sceptical.[49] It concluded: "At this stage the EU is not satisfied that its concerns will be met; it needs more precision on these commitments. It also needs to see concrete actions".[50]

The context within which these consultations were held is critical in understanding the rapid deterioration of EU-Zimbabwe relations over the months of January and February 2002, leading to the crucial presidential elections of March 2002. The increase in political violence before the presidential elections, the continuation of the fast-track land "reform" programme and, perhaps as important, the obstacles to the deployment of the EU election observation team were sufficient proof of the unwillingness of Mugabe to abide by the commitments made by his foreign minister during January 2002. Blair 2003:43) poignantly notes that:

> ... everything that Mugabe had done since the loss of the referendum more than two years earlier, every attack on the rule of law, every outpouring of verbal venom, every invasion of farm and every act of violence, had been but a preparation for what was about to happen. The presidential elections would mark the climax of the long, agonising struggle for power in Zimbabwe.

At the end of January, the Council moved up a gear, threatening targeted sanctions in Council Decision of 28 January 2002.[51] The Council noted with concern that the assurances given by the government of Zimbabwe during Article 96 consultations notwithstanding, "serious violations of human rights continue to occur" and that "little progress has been made in allowing for international election observers". The promulgation of POSA and the General Laws Amendment Act, as well as the remarks by General Vitalis Zvinavashe, Chief of the Armed Forces in Zimbabwe – that the democratic process could be overturned if military commanders did not agree with the result of the presidential elections – were vehemently condemned.[52] On the same day, in an interview with BBC Radio 4, EU Commissioner for External Relations, Chris Patten, explained the EU position in some detail:

> …we've been extraordinarily patient with Mr Mugabe and his colleagues. But there comes a point when we have to determine whether or not he's serious and his colleagues are serious about holding fair elections and about honouring their obligations under our development agreement with them … [T]here is a slight sense of suspicion, I think, in the European Union that they [Mugabe and his colleagues] are inclined to string us along and say they'll be prepared to do things and then when you actually look at the not-so-fine print you discover that the promises aren't quite what you were led to expect.[53]

On 18 February, consultations with Zimbabwe under Article 96 of the Cotonou Agreement were brought to a halt and measures "within the meaning of Article 96(2)§c" imposed by EU Council Decision of the same date.[54] The Council called into question the prospects for a free and fair election on 9-10 March, noting with concern the refusal of Zimbabwean authorities to accredit the EU Chief Observer, Ambassador Pierre Schori, who was not allowed to stay in the country.[55]

On the same day that the Council suspended all relevant provisions of the Cotonou Agreement and announced the suspension of development aid, it moved towards the application of "restrictive measures", demonstrating that the suspension of development cooperation was not the entire gamut of punitive measures available at its disposal. On this occasion, the EU would indeed use all the available tools in its arsenal of punitive measures and move to targeted sanctions the same day. Portela (2007:48) notes:

> The case of Zimbabwe is exceptional in a number of respects: it is the only example in which a suspension of aid under article 96 has been complemented by CFSP sanctions … the EU moved very quickly from the political dialogue under article 8 of the Cotonou Agreement to article 96 consultations, and these were apparently exceptionally short … Immediately after the suspension, the EU imposed CFSP sanctions.

> … for as long as the violations occur, the Council deems it necessary to introduce restrictive measures against the government of Zimbabwe and those who bear a wide responsibility for such violations.

The EU approved the first 12-month renewal on 18 February 2003, in light of "further deterioration in the situation in Zimbabwe, where serious violations of human rights and freedom of opinion, association and peaceful assembly continue to occur".[64] Over time, and in addition to the renewal of the sanctions framework through Common Positions (and Regulations), EU presidencies have been instrumental in clarifying EU policies and denouncing the gradual deterioration of the situation in the country. When, on 18 and 19 March 2003, hundreds of opposition supporters were arrested, suffering unprecedented levels of violence by government forces, the EU presidency was quick to react: "We strongly condemn President Mugabe's recent appeals on 21 and 22 March to smash any democratic opposition".[65]

As expected, EU targeted sanctions were vehemently condemned by the government of Zimbabwe, with Mugabe demonstrating his ability to use them as further argument in his increasingly anti-imperialist, anti-West and anti-white discourse. Indeed, the declarations of SADC member states following the organisation's summit in Dar es Salaam on 19-26 August 2003, made it clear that Mugabe's rhetoric resonated in several southern African capitals. In their final communiqué, SADC member states affirmed their opposition to "the Commonwealth, the European Union and the United States of America sanctions as *they hurt not only ordinary Zimbabweans but also have profound social and economic implications on the region as a whole* [author emphasis]", reaffirming the indivisibility of the organisation and their "solidarity" with Zimbabwe.[66]

Mugabe's masterly use of propaganda within and outside Zimbabwe dealt a severe blow to the symbolic power of targeted sanctions. In fact, although outside the scope of this chapter, the implications of EU policy towards Zimbabwe on the broader area of EU-Africa relations is in and of itself a theme worth exploring.

It was patently clear that a stronger effort was needed by the EU to minimise the negative effects of Mugabe's propaganda on its relations with SADC countries. For those working for the EC on the ground, the irony was that their commitment to Zimbabwe remained unchanged, with the EU directly supporting Zimbabweans to the tune of several hundred million Euros under very difficult circumstances. The EC's delegation to Zimbabwe tried to put the record straight in a series of explanatory notes, explaining that "none of these measures could affect or cause any hardship to the Zimbabwean population" and that "humanitarian assistance given to the people of Zimbabwe by the EU and its member states has continued over the last two years and amounted to €300 million". For the delegation, "the main cause of the serious social and economic crisis … should be sought in inappropriate economic policies, the manner in which the land reform has been carried out, the drought and the HIV/AIDS pandemic".[67]

This perhaps explains a concern with thinking through more proactive approaches to Zimbabwe during 2003 and 2004. A process of scenario development was initiated to enable rapid response to a post-crisis situation, with special focus on a so-called "change scenario", on the basis of which short- and medium-term measures could be explored and implemented in the country under the 9th EDF. Although in hindsight highly unrealistic and perhaps too rigid (this "change scenario" implied a resolution of EU concerns on politically motivated violence, free and fair elections, freedom of the media and independence of the judiciary, etc.), a positive consequence of this approach was that the level of financial allocations to Zimbabwe was not reduced in the hope that "this would secure the capacity to mobilise a quick EC response to a changing scenario resulting from a positive political breakthrough, allowing for a lifting of the appropriate measures against Zimbabwe and the full resumption of full EC development cooperation".[68]

Throughout 2003, 2004 and 2005, an already precarious situation deteriorated even further. From the EU's perspective there was no other option but to renew the sanctions, which it did in February 2004 and February 2005.[69] The violent closure of the *Daily News*, the last of Zimbabwe's independent newspapers, during September 2003 received strong condemnation[70] as did the adoption of the NGO Bill on 9 December 2004 by the Zimbabwe Parliament, noting that "if the Bill is implemented immediately, the EU's ability to provide assistance to Zimbabwe will be significantly affected".[71]

By the 2004 renewal of sanctions, 95 names were included in the Annex of Council Regulation 314/2004. With no other points of leverage, the EU had no option but to keep increasing the list of named persons.[72] Further clarification of the rationale behind the sanctions was attempted: "The objective of these restrictive measures is to encourage the persons targeted to reject policies that lead to suppression of human rights, of the freedom of expression and of good governance".[73]

In 2005 a particular series of events would further deteriorate the relationship – the parliamentary elections in March, the Constitutional Amendment in August, the Senate elections in November, and especially "Operation *Murambatsvina*", which assured that "sharp differences between the EU and Zimbabwe remained".[74] It was increasingly clear that the "change scenario" hoped for by Brussels was not going to arrive any time soon.[75] More significantly, as far as the bilateral relationship was concerned, the EU would not be invited to observe the parliamentary elections of 31 March 2005, which it considered not free and fair.[76] On "Operation *Murambatsvina*", the presidency denounced "the brutal actions which have led to over 20 000 arrests and to the massive and arbitrary destruction of the dwellings and means of existence of the neediest urban populations are blatant proof of the Zimbabwean government's lack of concern of the well-being of the civilian population".[77]

The fact that there had been no tangible movement on any of the conditions required for a lifting of sanctions, led the European parliament to recognise that "the EU's targeted sanctions against both Zimbabwe and certain individuals in Zimbabwe have failed to have the desired impact on those directly responsible for the impoverishment of Zimbabwe and the hardships endured by its people". Yet, failing to offer an alternative, the parliament concluded by calling on the Council to "ensure that all member states rigorously apply existing restrictive measures, including the arms embargo and the travel ban, *erring on the side of exclusion rather than permissiveness* [author emphasis]".[78]

ZANU-PF's proclivity to act through a combination of legislation and military-style operations continued unabated, as evidenced by operations *Murambatsvina* and *Dzikisa Mitengo*.[79] In these operations, the use of the armed forces, the intelligence services, the police, and so-called "war veterans" and militias was widespread. Indeed, the increasing executive power given to the JOC in the political, social and economic affairs of the State meant that, in practice, it replaced the Council of Ministers as the decision-making body in the period leading to the 2008 elections.[80]

The delays in the release of the 29 March 2008 election results, and the unprecedented levels of violence that marked the process, led EU foreign ministers meeting at the 2865th External Relations Council to call for the immediate release of the results, which one would expect to be "a genuine reflection of the free and democratic will of the Zimbabwean people". Hinting at an acknowledgement of the lack of positive results, the Council "confirms its willingness to continue to make use of any opportunity provided to engage in the dialogue with a democratically elected government of Zimbabwe and, as soon as conditions allow, to begin working towards the resumption of full cooperation".[81] By July, the EU regrets "that the Zimbabwean people were unable to vote freely in the run-off presidential elections, which the UN Secretary General had asked to be differed".[82]

It is at this stage that EU support to a "government of national unity" seems to take hold – a support that puts into question the rationale supporting six years of "restrictive measures" against the ZANU-PF government and Mugabe. Does this signal a re-alignment of EU policy towards that of regional actors, in particular the AU's position defined at its 1 July 2008 Sharm-el-Sheikh summit? An attempt at clarifying what type of power-sharing formula it is ready to accept was made: "The European Union will only accept a formula which respects the will of the Zimbabwean people, as expressed in the elections of 29 March 2008, which saw the MDC and Mr Morgan Tsvangirai win." It adds that 'the objective of any solution must be to reconsult the Zimbabwean people on a free, democratic and transparent basis as quickly as possible".[83] Yet, by September 2008, the EU had no choice but to accept the GPA between the parties, noting that it "will study the details of the agreement and will be attentive to its implementation".[84]

Dilemmas of practice: consistency, politics and the restructuring of development assistance

While at a political level the relationship between the EU and Zimbabwe had profoundly deteriorated, it should be noted that the reorientation of development assistance resulting from the suspension of Cotonou was achieved in close cooperation with the National Authorising Officer (NAO) and other Zimbabwean authorities.[85] This is perhaps one of the more perplexing dimensions of this case study, potentially uncovering deep contradictions arising from the simultaneous application of development aid suspension (Cotonou) and restrictive measures (CFSP), and demonstrating some of the practical challenges of implementing a framework where foreign, development assistance and external relations' dimensions are to complement each other under a simplified chain of command.

The EC Delegation notes that:

> [While the] lack of dialogue has impacted negatively on the policy environment in which
> EC projects, particularly in the health and education sectors continue to be carried out …
> the good cooperation on the working level between the EC Delegation in Harare, the NAO

and officials in the Ministries of Health and Education have ensured that the problems of implementation have been overcome.[86]

Yet, this was possible partly because "analysis has been shared on the basis of common denominator on sensitive issues (political situation, economic and humanitarian crisis, nature of EU measures, mainly)", and dialogue and cooperation continued over the period.[87]

In fact, the EC did not simply put an end to development cooperation and tried to adapt its instruments under the political environment created by the targeted sanctions policy, engaging in what could only be termed "development cooperation" by another name. It remained engaged in health, education, micro-projects and decentralized cooperation, and in activities to promote democratisation, respect for human rights and the rule of law under the European Initiative on Democracy and Human Rights. At its disposal it had funds directly allocated through the Commission's budget and the so-called "B" envelopes of the various EDFs.[88]

In the health sector, for example, the EU continues to be the major donor to Zimbabwe, with an estimated €57.7 million committed to the sector between 2000 and 2006, and focusing on the supply of essential drugs, vaccines and supplies as well as the strengthening of district level health services.[89] In fact, if one takes the combined contributions from the EDF and the European Commission Budget, the contributions to Zimbabwe's health sector between 2005 and 2007 amount to €150 million.[90] Other long-term programmes have included the EU Zimbabwe Micro-Project Programme (between 1982 and 2004 estimated at €72.2 million); the Education Transition and Reform Programme (operational since 1999, with an estimated expenditure of €11.4 million).

The EU has also remained focused on emergency assistance programmes, which since 2001, with the establishment of an office of the Humanitarian Aid and Civil Protection Department of the European Commission (ECHO) in the country, have remained critical.[91] By 2003, total EU and member state contributions to emergency response amounted to over €138 million, the EU being the largest donor in the country as far as emergency response was concerned.[92] In 2005, with funding of approximately €70 million (from both EDF "B" envelopes and directly from the Commission's budget), the "EU remained the most important donor in Zimbabwe in terms of amounts provided for the support of the Zimbabweans".[93] Food aid and support for food security became particularly important over the period as the combined effect of drought and the decline of agricultural production, which resulted from the land reform programme, created a situation of high vulnerability for several million Zimbabweans, but particularly so for those affected by HIV/AIDS, orphans and other vulnerable groups. In this effort, EC funds were channelled through the WFP, which amounted to €22.5 million in 2005 and €26 million in 2006.[94]

Furthermore, one should note that, while ECHO has been an important vehicle for funding of classic humanitarian operations, it has also provided much-needed development assistance by another name. During 2004/2005, ECHO changed its strategy of an exclusive focus on classic relief operations to a "value-adding" package of instruments geared at addressing both short-term needs and the link to rehabilitation and development.[95] In the period under analysis, ECHO became an important actor in more traditional development aid, particularly in agricultural recovery assistance by supporting vulnerable groups "in a manner that rebuilds their food production capacity and regains their food self-sufficiency status". ECHO's rationale was based on the fact that, while transitory vulnerability had declined, the population in chronic vulnerability was increasing as a consequence of a series of structural factors, including the economy-wide impacts of land reform, HIV/AIDS, inappropriate economic policies, declining capacity for service provision in the public sector, and the consequences of "Operation Murambatsvina".[96] The results of this strategy were highly praised and the political implications explored:

> To some extent, clever use of relief assistance in the food security sector managed to jump-start the link to recovery by promoting nationwide introduction of improved seed and agricultural practices.[97]

This change in strategy is evidence of perhaps the hardest dilemma facing the EC in Zimbabwe: between choosing to expand relief through ECHO operations (ultimately unsustainable) or to begin to think through new long-term development programmes (politically impossible). This dilemma is highlighted in an evaluation of ECHO's activities in the following words:

> [T]his dilemma equally confronts the EC and its member states as it does other donors because of the political implications of funding such programmes in the context of the current impasse over governance issues in Zimbabwe. Hence renewed efforts are needed at taming the political stalemate between the Zimbabwean government and the international community.[98]

Conclusion

This chapter set out to reflect on a series of issues raised by the EU's restrictive measures policy in Zimbabwe. The first related to the set of assumptions that underlined the imposition of restrictive measures. As broad economic sanctions (such as an export/import ban) were not an option – this would directly affect ordinary Zimbabweans and be in contravention of the EU's humanitarian norms[99] – the EU decided to target those it deemed directly responsible for the situation in Zimbabwe. A basket of restrictive measures was adopted, comprising an arms embargo, a visa ban, and the freezing of funds and economic assets of persons and entities in Zimbabwe.

Underlying the imposition of these measures was the assumption that the international stigma attached to being the subject of sanctions, coupled with the costs of non-compliance (including, as noted above, the costs associated with the suspension of direct budgetary support), would persuade Mugabe to change course – the expectation here being that these measures would have "maximum impact on those whose behaviour we want to influence".[100] The evaluation of the efficacy of targeted sanctions must, therefore, be based on whether such change has indeed occurred. In light of developments in the country since 2002, it is clear that EU restrictive measures have not achieved their fundamental objectives. The fact that sanctions remain in place leaves no room for ambiguity. Ironically, the sanctions regime has become ZANU-PF's weapon of choice in its efforts to block the implementation of key provisions of the GPA.

With hindsight, these were fundamental miscalculations, particularly as regards the level of costs Mugabe and ZANU-PF's top leadership were, and still are, prepared to incur. Indeed, these assumptions reveal a fundamental misreading of Mugabe's own political trajectory, invariably leading to the belief that what was occurring in Zimbabwe at the time restrictive measures were imposed (2002) was an anomaly that could be corrected through the application of leverage. A close reading of Zimbabwe's post-independence political and economic history would have indicated the extent to which Mugabe has steered the country closer and closer towards a single-party regime, and perhaps more importantly, uncovered the logic behind the increasingly totalitarian and anti-democratic approach taken by ZANU-PF.

The radicalisation of Mugabe's discourse around themes that have now become all too familiar – "nationalist credentials", anti-West rhetoric and the land issue – can indeed be traced to the period between 2000 and 2002.[101] And yet, a slightly longer historical trend of entrenched despotic political behaviour is at work in Zimbabwe, evidenced in the peculiarities of Zimbabwe's liberation struggle and the way it produced a leadership with an authoritarian outlook, and the gradual entrenchment of neopatrimonialist and clientelistic relations within ZANU-PF, leading to nepotism and corruption.[102]

Mugabe's personal trajectory has also been a fertile locus of reflection and speculation in the search for clues to his authoritarian stance and the gradual militarisation of the regime he controls.[103] For some authors, there is a clear continuum linking current authoritarian patterns of government to that of Ian Smith's regime, including the maintenance post-1980 of the security apparatus that supported the Rhodesian regime. Sachikonye notes that already during the 28-30 March 1990 elections, a substantial proportion of the candidates supported the creation of a single-party regime in Zimbabwe.[104] Kagoro (2003) shares this view, adding that, following the signature of the Unity Accord, ZANU-PF would intensify the pressure towards the creation of a single-party regime under the pretext that only then could national unity and development be assured.

And, if the most powerful effect of targeted sanctions is said to be a function of their symbolism, Mugabe's masterly transmutation of the intended "stigmatisation" into "victimization" dealt this a severe blow.

From a procedural point of view, and within the context and rationality supporting the imposition of restrictive measures by the EU, several issues are worth reflecting on. These include timing, gradualism, and, critically, strategic coordination and policy coherence with all other relevant EU/EC interventions. Timing is indeed critical in the application of a set of tools that, in the arsenal of diplomatic leverage – and precisely as a result of the inappropriateness of general trade and economic sanctions and the then inconceivable and unjustifiable scenario of military intervention – should be seen, when used in their entirety, as a last resort. The absence of a process of gradual escalation of punitive measures, marked by the imposition of comprehensive targeted sanctions and the suspension of development assistance in the same day in February 2002 following an unusually brief period of Article 96 consultations, left the EU with a severely restricted set of policy options in the event of non-compliance. In fact, faced with the exponential growth in the ability of Mugabe and ZANU-PF to contravene, there has been little the EU can do but publicly condemn the regime and enlarge the list of persons and organisations it deems responsible. Indeed, would a gradual build-up of the sanctions regime (in both scope and participation) have been more prudent and ultimately yield more results? For the author, the Zimbabwe case ultimately reveals the inadequacy of autonomous targeted sanctions as an instrument of leverage in the absence of international consensus, particularly a UNSC mandate.[105] Having been at "the forefront of the promotion of targeted sanctions at the UN level",[106] the EU would ultimately be unable to build the necessary international and regional consensus once it had applied restrictive measures.

Finally, but no less important, to what extent was there appropriate reflection on the impact of targeted sanctions on short-, medium- and long-term priorities of other areas of EU-Zimbabwe relations, in particular EC development cooperation and humanitarian assistance? While in theory the EU may be committed to "using sanctions as part of an integrated, comprehensive policy approach, which should include political dialogue, incentives, conditionality and could even involve, as last resort, the use of coercive measures in accordance with the UN charter",[107] the lack of such coordinated and strategic reflection prior to the imposition of restrictive measures in February 2002 resulted in a situation where the EC has threaded a very difficult (and ultimately politically unrewarding) balancing act on the ground in its efforts to continue to provide humanitarian and development assistance to the most vulnerable in Zimbabwe.

From an EU perspective, at a time when it is undertaking a substantial transformation of its foreign, development and external relations' machinery under the Treaty of Lisbon and the new European External Action Service, the Zimbabwe case provides a set of key lessons on the practical challenges of implementing a framework where these dimensions complement each other under a simplified chain of command. Indeed, the Zimbabwe case clearly demonstrates in a very practical way the need for consistency across all areas of EU intervention, the imperative of an appropriate institutional framework capable of managing political and operational level tensions, and, finally, a better understanding of EU restrictive measures as an instrument of leverage.

---

[1] An earlier version of this paper was published as "Multipronged Strategies for a Multifaceted Crisis? A critical reflection on EU policy towards Zimbabwe" in Ganzle, Grimm & Makhan (2012). The author would like to thank Antonia Witt for her research support and valuable comments on earlier versions of this paper.

[2] *See* International Crisis Group (2010).

[3] *See* Progressio (2007).

[4] UNDP (2007).

[5] The main provision of ZIDERA comprised instructions to US representatives on international financial institutions, including the multilateral development banks, to vote against new loans, credits, guarantees or debt relief to the

government of Zimbabwe until the US president certified that the rule of law had been restored and other related requirements met. See Oxford Analytica report of 9 March 2010.

6   EU Council (2005:4). *See also* EU Council (2004).

7   European Parliament (2009).

8   International Crisis Group (2007).

9   Amnesty International, Zimbabwe Human Rights NGO Forum and Zimbabwe Lawyers for Human Rights, joint statement: "Human rights issues must be at the centre of any dialogue between the government of Zimbabwe and the opposition political parties", 29 June 2007.

10   *See* Blair (2003), Sachikonye (2002), Scarnecchia (2006), Kagoro (2003).

11   The example of "Operation *Murambatsvina*" between May and July 2005, when 700 000 people lost their homes, represents a paradigmatic case of this type of approach. Ostensibly designed to end illegal housing and informal economic activity in Harare, in practice this operation was deployed to punish peri-urban populations who were known to have supported the MDC. With "Operation *Dzikisa Mitengo*", the government forced all businesses to reduce the price of consumer goods by 50%, and in light of protest by traders and businessmen the government did not hesitate in imprisoning 8 500 people. See International Crisis Group (2007:3).

12   The JOC is formed by ministerial level and chiefs of staff level representatives of the Ministry of Defence, Ministry of State Security, Police Commissioner, Chief of Staff of the Zimbabwean National Defence Force, head of the Central Intelligence Organisation, and a war veterans' representative.

13   The systematic abuse of human rights in Zimbabwe has been documented in detail by organisations such as the Zimbabwe Human Rights NGOS Forum, Amnesty International or Human Rights Watch. *See* Human Rights Watch (2007), Zimbabwe Human Rights NGO Forum (2007), Amnesty International (2007).

14   As noted by Clara Portela (2007:2), "... this feature is not unique to EU sanctions: general trade embargoes have been replaced by targeted or 'smart' sanctions also in the practice of the UN and other international actors. The unpopularity provoked by the acute humanitarian consequences of trade embargoes, such as those imposed on Iraq brought about a preference for the use of targeted measures".

15   EU Council (2004). Furthermore, in deciding on restrictive measures the EU notes, "it is important to consider which measure or package of measures is most appropriate in order to promote the desired outcome". *See* EU External Relations, "Sanctions and Restrictive Measures" at http://ec.europa.eu/external_relations/cfsp/sanctions/index.htm.

16   As noted by Mary Ndlovu (2007): "In February 2000, ZANU PF discovered, in a rare moment of truth, that they were unpopular enough to be defeated at the polls, in spite of all the advantages they had in controlling most of the media, the electoral machinery and all the state security apparatus. They immediately began the process of ensuring that no matter what the people wanted, never again would ZANU PF lose a vote."

17   *See* Blair (2003). The 2000 referendum on a new constitution proposed by the ZANU-PF government called for the strengthening of presidential powers, would enable Mugabe to stand for election for a further two terms, and, in its famous clause 57, placed responsibility on compensations towards expropriated lands to the UK. Yet, more than a referendum on a new constitution it became, in the eyes of Zimbabweans, a referendum on the performance of the ZANU-PF government, and in particular Mugabe.

18   The author notes that merely a year after its creation, the MDC won 57 seats in the parliamentary elections of 2000, compared with 62 seats won by ZANU-PF. *See also* Maroleng (2004).

19   *See* Sachikonye (2002).

20   Kibble has noted that the emergence of neopatrimonialist and clientelistic structures side by side with the maintenance of a culture of intolerance and impunity is a direct function of the way ZANU-PF conducted the liberation struggle. *See also* Kagoro (2003).

21   Several authors have reflected on the psychological motivations that may explain Mugabe's political survival strategy. A good example of this is found in Blair (2003).

22   Integrated Regional Information Networks (IRIN), "Zimbabwe: Government reports 150% drop in living standards", Harare, 6 December 2006.

23   The reduction in the proportion of people living below the poverty line was outstanding; between 1980 and 1991 they were reduced from 60% to 25–30% respectively. *See* Potts (2006).

24   This programme would later became known as ESAP or Zimbabwe's Economic Structural Adjustment Programme.

25 From 1992 onwards, the IMF took direct control of the programme. *See* Brown (1999:75–91).

26 Brown (1999:75–91).

27 It should be noted that the intervention of Zimbabwe in the DRC was pursued at an estimated annual cost of US$360 million. *See* Sachikonye (2002:14).

28 Potts (2006).

29 Including the Zimbabwe Congress of Trade Union (ZCTU); Zimbabwe Human Rights Organisation, the Catholic Commission for Justice and Peace; the National Constitutional Assembly (NCA) and the Women's Rights Group. It should be noted that it was following the 1989 series of protests that Morgan Tsvangirai (then at the helm of the ZCTU) was arrested and, for the first time, accused of acting on behalf of foreign interests and being on the payroll of the South African intelligence services. *See* Kagoro (2003).

30 The adoption of Constitutional Amendment 7 contributed further evidence of this gradual move towards a single-party system by considerably strengthening presidential powers and creating a single-chamber parliament, but reserving 30 of the 150 seats for direct appointed by the president.

31 Kagoro (2003).

32 In addition to government and public service positions, Mugabe placed loyal ZANU-PF individuals in key private sector positions, including in the National Oil Company, the Zimbabwe Electricity Company, the Grain Marketing Board, the Rail Company of Zimbabwe, etc.

33 One of the best known cases regarded intimidation by war veterans and ZANU-PF members of the Supreme Court judges who judged the Fast Track Land Programme to be unconstitutional.

34 *See* Cliffe (2000).

35 Maroleng (2004:2).

36 *See* Sachikonye (1990:92–99).

37 *See* Thomas (2003:692).

38 Moyo (2000:6).

39 Maroleng (2004:5).

40 Furthermore, it states that "over and above this figure, Zimbabwe has been able to access regional cooperation funds made available to SADC by the Community to finance relevant development projects". EU Commission Delegation to Zimbabwe (2004).

41 ACP/EU Partnership Agreement Article 96 paragraph 2 states that "if despite the political dialogue … a Party considers that the other Party has failed to fulfil an obligation stemming from respect for human rights, democratic principles and the rule of law referred to in Paragraph 2 of Article 9, it shall … invite the other Party to hold consultations that focus on the measures taken or to be taken by the Party concerned to remedy the situation".

42 EU Commission (2008).

43 In net terms, the real value of government social spending had fallen by a third between 2000 and 2002. *See* European Commission's "Co-operation between the Republic of Zimbabwe and the European Community: Joint Annual Report 2001-2002", Report of the National Authorising Officer and the European Commission Head of Delegation, p. 4.

44 EU Commission (2001).

45 This is a point noted by the EC delegation to Zimbabwe during 2006. It considers that the EU-SADC dialogue "has not been fully effective as a lever on neighbouring countries to maintain pressure on Zimbabwe". See EU Commission (2005).

46 In another passage, this ambivalence surfaces on land reform. Although seen by the Commission as "chaotic and counter-productive process", the land reform process "can be understood either as an issue manipulated by the government for electoral purposes, regardless of respect for the rule of law and human rights, or as *an attempt to implement the policy the ruling party stands for* [author emphasis]". EU Commission (2001).

47 Prior to the beginning of Article 96 consultations, the Commission made its views clear on the conditions for success. The essential elements of Cotonou would be restored once the government of Zimbabwe took concrete steps to abide by democratic principles and the rule of law (including freedom of the media and independence of the judiciary), respect for human rights was assured and an ending to political violence demonstrated, and swift implementation of the conclusions of the Commonwealth-sponsored Abuja Accord of September 2001, where Zimbabwe agreed to end

all illegal occupation of white-owned farmland. A key condition was the observation of the forthcoming elections by the EU and other international monitors. EU Commission (2001).

48 *See* European Commission's "Co-operation between the Republic of Zimbabwe and the European Community: Joint Annual Report 2001-2002", Report of the National Authorising Officer and the European Commission Head of Delegation.

49 EU Commission (2002).

50 Ibid.

51 The GAC considered that targeted sanctions would be imposed on Zimbabwe if "the government of Zimbabwe prevents the deployment of an EU observation mission starting 3 February 2002 or if it later prevents the international media from having free access"; "there is a serious deterioration in the situation on the ground, in terms of a worsening of the human rights' situation or attacks to the opposition" and "the election is accessed as not being free and fair". *See* European Union (2002).

52 European Union (2002).

53 BBC interview with Chris Patten, EU Commissioner for External Relations, BBC 4, 28 January 2002. http://europa. eu/rapid/pressReleaseAction.do?reference=SPEECH/02/31&format=HTML&aged=1&language=EN&guiLanguage =en.

54 EU Council (2002a).

55 European Union (2002a).

56 EU Council (2002a).

57 EU Council (2002b).

58 Ibid.

59 The specific regulation of the restrictive measures is detailed in Council Regulation of 18 February 2002, including a list of "Equipment for internal repression envisaged by Article 7" of the Common Position.

60 EU Council (2002b).

61 EU Council (2002a).

62 In its *Conclusions on Zimbabwe*, the GAC emphasised that "these targeted sanctions are aimed solely at those who the EU judges to be responsible for the violence, for the violations of human rights and for preventing the holding of free and fair elections (…) The sanctions are designed not to harm ordinary citizens of Zimbabwe or her neighbours, nor should they prevent dialogue between the EU and Zimbabwe to address its economic and other problems. The EU remains committed to provide humanitarian assistance to the people of Zimbabwe". In this regard, see European Union, General Affairs Council, Council Conclusions, Zimbabwe, 2409th Council Meeting, Brussels 18-19 February 2002 at http://www.consilium.europa.eu/ueDocs/cms_Data/docs/pressdata/en/gena/69471.pdf

63 EU Commission Delegation to Zimbabwe (n.d.) "The Meaning of the Suspension of EU-Zimbabwe Development Co-operation for the People of Zimbabwe".

64 EU Council (2003). *See also* European Union, Council Regulation (EC) No 313/2003 of 18 February 2003 Extending Regulation (EC) No 310/2002 Concerning Certain Restrictive Measures in Respect of Zimbabwe, 18 February 2003.

65 Declaration by the presidency on behalf of the European Union on the crackdown on the opposition in Zimbabwe, 7911/03 (Presse 96), 28 March 2003.

66 SADC (2003).

67 EU Commission Delegation to Zimbabwe (n.d.) "Position of the EU on Sanctions against Zimbabwe".

68 European Commission (2003:25–26).

69 EU Council (2004), EU Council (2005).

70 Declaration by the Presidency on behalf of the European Union on Freedom of the Press in Zimbabwe, 12697/03 (Presse 275), 18 September 2003.

71 Declaration by the Presidency on behalf of the European Union on the Adoption of the NGO Bill in Zimbabwe, 16249/04 (Presse 371), 22 December 2004.

72 The list now included the Director of the Central Intelligence Office (Happyton Bonyongwe), the Police Commissioner (Augustine Chihuri), the Commander of Zimbabwe's Defence Forces, the Chair of the Electoral Supervisory Commission, and several provincial governors.

[73] EU Council (2004). See also EU Council, Council Regulation (EC) No 314/2004 of 19 February 2004 Concerning Certain Restrictive Measures in Respect of Zimbabwe, 19 February 2004.

[74] European Commission (2005:2).

[75] The presidency would "urge the government of Zimbabwe to reinstate democracy, to respect the rights of its citizens, to reform [this] repressive legislation, to stop using the militia, the army and the police to intimidate civilians and to abide by its international human rights commitments". Statement by the Presidency on behalf of the European Union regarding the Human Rights situation in Zimbabwe, 24 March 2005.

[76] Declaration by the Presidency on behalf of the European Union on the Conduct of the Elections in Zimbabwe, 7789/05 (Presse 78), 5 April 2005.

[77] Declaration by the Presidency on behalf of the European Union Concerning the Recent Events in Zimbabwe, 9876/05 (Presse 139), 7 June 2005.

[78] From the same Resolution, the European Parliament "condemns the Mugabe dictatorship for its relentless oppression of the Zimbabwean people and expresses its profound disappointment at the refusal of regional actors such as the AU, the SADC and South Africa to take a more robust stance against the regime's abuses". Also of note, the Parliament "calls on China and other countries that continue to supply weaponry and other support to the Mugabe regime to desist from this and join the international community in its efforts to bring about change for the better in Zimbabwe". See European Parliament, Resolution P6_TA (2006) 0358.

[79] The example of Operation *Murambatsvina* between May and July 2005, when 700 000 people lost their homes is paradigmatic of this approach. Ostensibly designed to end illegal housing and informal economic activity in Harare, in practice this operation was deployed to punish peri-urban populations who were known to have supported the MDC. With Operation *Dzikisa Mitengo*, the government forced all businesses to reduce the prices of consumer goods by 50%, and in light of protest by traders and businessmen the government did not hesitate to imprison 8 500 people. See International Crisis Group (2010:3).

[80] The JOC was formed by ministerial level and chiefs of staff level representatives of the Ministry of Defence, Ministry of State Security, Police Commissioner, Chief of Staff of the Zimbabwean National Defence Force, head of the CIO and a representative of the "war veterans".

[81] EU Council (2008).

[82] Declaration by the Presidency on behalf of the European Union on Zimbabwe, 4 July 2008.

[83] Ibid.

[84] EU Council, External Relations Council, Council Conclusions on Zimbabwe, 2886th Council Meeting, 15 and 16 September 2008.

[85] As noted in a combined report by the National Authorising Authority and the EC Head of Delegation to Zimbabwe, following the restructuring exercise "it was agreed that the Micro-Projects and Decentralised Cooperation Programmes as well as a large part of the Health and Education Programmes would be maintained and only policy reform and institutional strengthening components were to be taken out of the programme". In net terms, the real value of government social spending had fallen by a third between 2000 and 2002. See European Commission (2002:4).

[86] European Commission (2002:31).

[87] European Commission (2005).

[88] "As a result of restructuring, approximately €18 million was identified as becoming rapidly available for re-commitment to extension of existing projects or for new projects. Additional funds would also later be released on conclusion of decommitment processes and closure of projects under the 6th and 7th EDFs". See European Commission (2002).

[89] EU Commission Delegation to Zimbabwe, "EC-Zimbabwe Cooperation: A Historical Perspective", Information Brochure, Harare, January/December 2004.

[90] EU Commission Delegation to Zimbabwe, "EU Support to Health in Zimbabwe", Harare, November 2006.

[91] The strategy was to address emergency needs (food, health, etc.) through International NGOs, UN agencies (particularly the WFP) and non-governmental organisations at a time when the Zimbabwean economy was already in a rapid downward spiral, having contracted 8.4% in 2001 and 12% in 2002. In fact, in 2001, 41% of Zimbabweans were living on less than US$1 per day. See European Commission (2002).

[92] EU Commission Delegation to Zimbabwe, "EC-Zimbabwe Cooperation: A Historical Perspective", Information Brochure, January/December 2004.

93 Including €18.5 million for health-related programmes; €6 million for micro-projects, community development and decentralisation; €22 million for food aid; and €15 million for humanitarian assistance in food security, water and sanitation. *See* EU Commission Delegation to Zimbabwe, "An Overview of EU-Zimbabwe Current Co-operation", Harare, January 2006.

94 EU Commission Delegation to Zimbabwe, "An Overview of EU-Zimbabwe Current Co-operation", Harare, January 2006.

95 European Commission, Directorate-General for Humanitarian Aid-ECHO, Evaluation of DG ECHO's Action in Zimbabwe, Final Report.

96 Ibid.

97 Ibid.

98 Ibid.

99 As noted by Clara Portela (2007:2), "… this feature is not unique to EU sanctions: general trade embargoes have been replaced by targeted or 'smart' sanctions also in the practice of the UN and other international actors. The unpopularity provoked by the acute humanitarian consequences of trade embargoes, such as those imposed on Iraq, brought about a preference for the use of targeted measures".

100 EU Council, "Basic Principles on the Use of Restrictive Measures", Paragraph 6, 7 June 2004. Furthermore, in deciding on restrictive measures, the EU notes "it is important to consider which measure or package of measures is most appropriate in order to promote the desired outcome". See EU External Relations, "Sanctions and Restrictive Measures" at http://ec.europa.eu/external_relations/cfsp/sanctions/index.htm.

101 *See* Sachikonye (2002).

102 Kibble has noted that the emergence of neopatrimonialist and clientelistic structures, side by side with the maintenance of a culture of intolerance and impunity, is a direct function of the way ZANU-PF conducted the liberation struggle. *See also* Kagoro (2003).

103 Several authors have reflected on the psychological motivations that may explain Mugabe's political survival strategy. A good example of this may be found in Blair (2003).

104 Sachikonye (1990:92–99).

105 As Portela (2007:1) poignantly notes, EU sanctions do not deprive their targets of essentials; travel bans can be circumvented; blacklisted individuals interested in conducting business abroad can resort to intermediaries; funds can be transferred to bank accounts outside Europe before the freeze comes into effect; and arms embargoes are usually issued late and targets always find alternative suppliers. In the Zimbabwe case, it was precisely the absence of such international consensus that prompted Mugabe to explore alternatives by "looking East", allowing him to keep the regime afloat and reduce the costs of sanctions.

106 Portela (2007:39).

107 EU Council, "Basic Principles on the Use of Restrictive Measures", Paragraph 5, 7 June 2004.

8
Conclusions

Martin R. Rupiya

For a number of African states, the transition to democracy since the 1990s has not been easy. In the post-colonial period, the one-party State morphed into perpetual institutions that criminalised everyone else seeking political office, as seen in the 1967 Arusha Declaration and Chama Cha Mapinduzi appropriating for itself sole political rights and the painful experience the country had to go through to reverse the unsustainable position in 1991 through the Presidential Commission on Single Party or Multiparty System in Tanzania, chaired by Chief Justice Francis Nyalali.[1] The documented experience of Tanzania, a founding member of the Organisation of African Unity (OAU) Liberation Committee, as well as Southern Africa's Front Line States (FLS), is important for other African states, particularly former liberation movement administrations still trapped in similar situations.

Political transition and democratisation challenges have been noted in Angola, Kenya, Mali, Central African Republic, Chad, Somalia, Tanzania, Sudan, Libya, Burkina Faso, Guinea-Bissau, Lesotho, Mozambique, Ethiopia, Eritrea, Madagascar, the Democratic Republic of the Congo, Rwanda, Burundi, Liberia, Sierra Leone, Cote d'Ivoire, Egypt and Zimbabwe, resulting in the African Union (AU) intervening on behalf of citizens, using tried-and-tested mechanisms of imposing a power-sharing agreement to preside over a transitional period, during which there are key changes to the constitution and the political conduct of the incumbency, and partisan institutions are weaned from seeking to perpetuate the status quo.[2]

This has been the emphasis of the series of intellectual discussions and manuscripts that have been put together in this book, focusing on Zimbabwe's military and its perceived veto power in the transition to democratisation during the transitional period from 2008 until 2013. Curiously, the major driving force for change on the continent, and in Zimbabwe, was located in the global economic demands – better known as the Economic Structural Adjustment Programmes (ESAPs) of the 1990s. Its origins had been associated with the World Bank report, *Sub-Saharan Africa: From crisis to sustainable growth* (1989), suggesting a new political environment and ethos. The new strategy, emerging from what later became known as the Washington Consensus, sought to provide the rationale and link between aid and governance.[3] In other words, without undertaking political deregulation and reform, also described as democratisation, a country would not qualify for international financial assistance. The immediate impact of the Washington Consensus democratisation on the African continent has shown the fragility of the African state and its lack of robust institutions and limited alternatives, generally located in the security establishment. Within half a decade of introducing ESAPs in over 30 African countries, the majority collapsed as political entities, while others were reduced to warring enclaves from Somalia and the former Zaire (now the Democratic Republic of the Congo), to more recently Mali and the Central African Republic.[4] Mark Duffield aptly captured this development in *Symphony of the Damned: New discourse, complex political emergencies and humanitarian aid* (1996), where he notes the subsequent "emergence of weak or failed states and warlords" in countries attempting to adopt the democratisation route of mature democracies. Samuel Huntington describes in *Third Wave of Democratization in the Late 21st Century*, the epochs that resulted in regions such as Asia and Latin America achieving new status; however, Africa appears to continue to be challenged and therefore lacks political stability and economic prosperity even in the future Fourth Wave.[5]

The objective of this book was, therefore, to analyse, monitor and comment on the unique democratic transformational challenges faced by the Government of National Unity (GNU) established in Zimbabwe under the auspices of AU Resolution No. 6, which was then translated into the framework of implementation through Southern African Development Community (SADC) facilitation known as the Global Political Agreement (GPA).

In the Zimbabwean case study, political deterioration has been gradual but almost unrelenting. Having experienced the negative impact of ESAPs during the 1990s, and blaming this on the ruling party, and with there being no evidence of policies changing course, the political opposition based on workers and other urban classes decided to establish an alternative political party: the Movement for Democratic Change (MDC). The February 2000 referendum on the Constitution became the first arena of political confrontation in which the ruling party, Zimbabwe African National Union Patriotic Front (ZANU-PF), "lost". Next was the national parliamentary election of June 2000, where again ZANU-PF's majority was whittled, returning to power with a majority of only five seats. Then, as the country prepared to host the March 2002 presidential election, the military commanders announced that they would not allow anyone without liberation credentials to contest the presidency, even if they won at the polls. This created a political crisis, resulting in the urgent intervention of former presidents Joaquim Chissano of Mozambique, Hassan Mwinyi and Benjamin Mkapa of Tanzania. Already in 2005, concern about governance through military operations had become a feature that was limiting the freedoms and personal security of citizens.[6] In retrospect, low-level mediation appeared to fail as, only in March 2007, after the Zimbabwe Police were shown on television beating and harassing political opposition leaders did the SADC call for an extra-ordinary summit in Dar es Salaam, Tanzania, where then South African President, Thabo Mbeki, was formally appointed as facilitator. Just months later, in March 2008, Zimbabwe hosted watershed elections that propelled it into the GNU. The significant development of the March harmonised election, which was soon followed by the violent June presidential run-off, was that the security establishment carried out its 9 January 2002 warning and blocked the succession of the MDC leader, Morgan Tsvangirai, because he lacked liberation struggle credentials. The political impasse was broken through the intervention of the AU calling for a power-sharing arrangement and the establishment of a GNU, to allow the country to reform its institutions for yet another free and fair election.

The transitional period following the inauguration of the GNU under Constitutional Amendment No. 19 has been an interesting period, which the research and discussion captured in this book has attempted to analyse. To this end, there are several key findings that readers are invited to review in order to better understand the arguments and lessons learnt.

First, the introductory discussion and chapter on command and control of the security establishment during the transitional period points towards a complex case study, replete with residual and historical liberation-struggle dynamics and rhetoric, including a regime change agenda by neo-colonial actors. Between 1980 and 2002, ZANU-PF had achieved the feat of capturing the State and completely transforming the civil service, judiciary, police and armed forces, as argued by Louis Althusser in *Lenin and Philosophy and Other Essays: Ideology and Ideological State Apparatuses*. The key lesson to draw from Althusser's assertion is that, every time partisan forces carry out an operation in the name of a political party, there is a direct correlation in which the same loses its national character. This is the context of the challenge facing Zimbabwean forces when used for partisan gain and why the SADC, in its last communiqué in Maputo on 15 June 2013, sought to compel a written undertaking from the generals that they would desist from playing a direct role in the politics of the country. The AU had expressed its deep regret and concern earlier, when faced with the results of serious human rights abuses that were committed with impunity. Because the political elite commanding the security establishment has been explicit in its use of the military, the chapter on command and control poses the challenge of what should be reformed now that the political objective has been achieved through military means? The military, as part of the electoral process of the former liberation movement, had been deployed in various dimensions of the electoral process, with responsibility for delimitation, the Electoral Commission, the voters' roll and registration, and campaigning. When political parties fail to address this, it leaves the country saddled with a militarised political party running civilian affairs. Nearly eight years ago, commenting on the nature of military operations in the governance of Zimbabwe, I had this to say (paraphrasing my work, but making the same point in contemporary times):

> *A military operation is blunt, indiscriminate and self-contained, and almost insulated from normal responsibility. During its execution, a military operation is immune from*

outside interference, except that communicated through its command structure. Once launched, it strives to complete its given task within the shortest possible time and perceives and treats any impediments as hostile. Finally, when the operation is complete, participants are immune from legal challenge(s), except through its political leadership and civilian administrative structures. Resorting to a military operation probably provides satisfaction (only) to those leading the process.[7]

A similar point is made by Abiodun Alao, who argues that the question of security remains uppermost in the minds of the Zimbabwean post-colonial political leadership, subjecting all else to the periphery.

Ndlovu-Gatsheni talks about the ethnic composition of the forces, drawn from a particular region and linguistic group, which has allowed such units to view and treat other ethnic groups as justified targets, culminating in the atrocities committed during the Gukurahundi operations in the Midlands and Western Matabeleland during the 1980s. His view is that this phenomenon still stalks the current composition of the Zimbabwean forces, and calls for an appraisal in which reconciliation and rehabilitation play a central part.

Engel alludes to the split foreign policy approach, first of the liberation movement and, later, in government and its coalition partners. The result is a skewed foreign policy tapestry that, in itself, becomes contested ground given the sanctions issued by the West towards ZANU-PF – a feature that remained in place during much of the transitional period.

Gomes Porto discusses the futile nature of attempting to impose sanctions without a coherent international position, such as a United Nations Security mandate.

The chance of success was further rendered unsustainable as a consequence of differing and shifting bilateral interests of the over 20 members in the EU towards Zimbabwe and Africa. Sanctions, therefore, appeared to be doing more harm than good. However, at the domestic level, smart sanctions or targeted sanctions, or whatever they are called, have been understood as sanctions – period – and welcomed as yet another frontier of confrontation and struggle. Many of the key actors viewed being on the sanctions list as a badge of honour, and succeeded in sending mixed signals to different constituencies, which included the Pan African community, who viewed those sanctioned as victims. Given the discussion of the subjective nature of post-1990s democratisation emerging from the now thoroughly discredited Washington Consensus, what lessons must Africa draw to fashion its own trajectory to multiparty democracy, without losing the advantages and benefits of the revolutionary armed struggle period? To this end, Gomes Porto's contribution is significant: if sanctions were meant to change the political conduct and behaviour of ZANU-PF and its leaders, then the record shows that these failed dismally. There was and continues to be no change whatsoever; in fact, this has been taken as a necessary challenge and battle to be won by maintaining precisely that which was viewed as abhorrent in terms of human rights abuse and operating in an environment absent of the rule of law.

Zondi's research asks a very pertinent question – one that former South African president, Thabo Mbeki, confirmed when invited to attend the inauguration in Harare: Where to with

SADC facilitation? Mbeki acknowledged that "Zimbabweans insisted he attend, as this marked the end of the negotiations" and, therefore, the political crisis. However, if we are correct in asserting that a military operation was substituted for a political campaign, it follows that the political crisis has not been addressed.

It is our hope that the complexity of the Zimbabwean case study is not lost on either the AU or the SADC. The research and analysis has not been about finding these bodies unable to impose a solution. Rather, the focus has been: Given the standard nature of the conflict-resolution mechanism available and deployed in the Zimbabwean crisis, what was the reaction and end result of the GNU? Some of the answers have been provided and, in some cases, research has pointed towards continuing challenges, particularly with former liberation movements when confronted with multiparty democratisation. Hence, is there value for the AU and SADC to begin to evaluate their standing intervention models?

---

[1] Rupiya (2006:31–33).

[2] Raftopolous & Alexander (2006:34–35).

[3] This included ideas from international financial institutions, the International Monetary Fund and the World Bank.

[4] Rupiya (2006:35).

[5] Scott London Book Review: Samuel P. Huntington *The Third Wave of Democratization in the Late Twentieth Century*, University of Oklahoma, 1992, at http://www.scottlondon.com/reviews/huntington.html. Accessed 3 September 2013.

[6] Rupiya (2005).

[7] Rupiya (2005).

Bibliography

ACP/EU Partnership Agreement. 2008. Available at http://ec.europa.eu/development/icenter/repository/agr01_eng.pdf. Accessed August 2008.

Adar, K.G., Ajulu, R. & Onyango, M.O. 2002. "Post-Cold War Zimbabwe's foreign policy and foreign policy-making process" in Adar, K.G. et al. (Eds) *Globalization and Emerging Trends in African States' Foreign Policy-Making Process. A comparative perspective of Southern Africa.* Ashgate, Aldershot.

Africa Confidential, Vol. 22(13), June 1981.

Africa Confidential, Vol. 23(11), May 1982.

Africa Confidential, Vol. 23(5), March 1982.

Africa Confidential, Vol. 44(4), February 2003.

Africa Institute. 1998. *Africa A-Z*. Africa Institute, Pretoria.

Africa Now. London. December 1983.

Alao, C.A. 2012. *Mugabe and the Politics of Security in Zimbabwe*. McGill-Queen's University Press, Montreal.

Alden, C. 2010. "A pariah in our midst: regional organisations and the problematic of Western-designated pariah regimes. The cases of SADC/Zimbabwe and ASEAN/Myanmar". (= Crisis States Working Paper. Series 2; 73). Available at http://www.crisisstates.com/download/wp/wpSeries2/WP73.2.pdf.

Alexander, E., McGregor, J. & Ranger, T. 2000. *Violence and Memory: One hundred years in the "dark forests" of Matabeleland*. James Currey, London.

Amnesty International, Zimbabwe. 2007. *Between a rock and a hard place*. AI.

Andrews, C. & Morgan, B. 2005. "Zimbabwe after the 2005 parliamentary election". London: House of Commons Library (= Library Research Papers; 05/58). Available at http://www.parliament.uk/commons/lib/rcsearch/rp2005/rp05-058.pdf.

AU Assembly (of Heads of State and Government). 2008. "Resolution on Zimbabwe", adopted at the 11th Ordinary Session, 30 June–1 July 2008, Sharm El-Sheikh, Egypt, Assembly/AU/Res.1 (XI).

AUC Chairperson. 2011. Report by the Chairperson of the African Union Commission on current challenges to peace and security on the continent and the AU's efforts "Enhancing Africa's Leadership, Promoting African Solutions" to the Extraordinary Summit of Heads of State and Government, Addis Ababa 25–26 May 2011. African Union, Addis Ababa. EXT/ASSEMBLY/AU/2.

Badza, S. 2008. "Zimbabwe's 2008 elections and their implications for Africa" in *African Security Review*, Vol. 17(4).

Bassett, T.J. & Straus, S. 2011. "Defending democracy in Cote d'Ivoire" in *Foreign Affairs*, Vol. 90(4) July/August 2011.

Bizos, G. 2007. *Odyssey from Freedom*. Random House, Cape Town.

Blair, D. 2003. *Degrees in Violence: Robert Mugabe and the struggle for power in Zimbabwe*. Continuum, London.

Bracking, S. 2005. "Development Denied: Autocratic militarism in post-election Zimbabwe" in *Review of African Political Economy*, Vol. 32(104).

Bratton, M. 2011. "Violence, partisanship and transitional justice in Zimbabwe" in *Journal of Modern African Studies*, Vol. 49(3).

Bratton, M. & Masunungure, E. 2007. "Popular reactions to State repression: Operation *Murambatsvina* in Zimbabwe" in *African Affairs*, Vol. 106(422).

Bratton, M. & Masunungure, E. 2008. "Zimbabwe's long agony" in *Journal of Democracy*, Vol. 19(4).

British Broadcasting Corporation (BBC). 2002. Interview of Chris Patten, EU Commissioner for External Relations, 28 January 2002. Available at http://europa.eu/rapid/pressReleaseAction. do?reference=SPEECH/02/31&format=HTML&aged=1&language=EN&guiLanguage= en.

Brown, W. 1999. "The EU and structural adjustment: The case of Lomé IV and Zimbabwe" in *Review of African Political Economy*, Vol. 26(79).

Burnett, P. 2007. "Zimbabwe: Is this the year?" in *Pambazuka News*, 295, 15 March 2007. Available at http://www.pambazuka.org/en/category/features/40373.

Catholic Commission for Justice and Peace in Zimbabwe. 1997. *Breaking the Silence: Building true peace in Zimbabwe*. Catholic Commission for Justice and Peace in Zimbabwe and the Legal Resources Foundation.

Cawthra, G. 2010. *The Role of SADC in Managing Political Crisis and Conflict: The cases of Madagascar and Zimbabwe*. Friedrich-Ebert-Stiftung, Maputo. (= FES Peace and Security Series; 2) available at http://library.fes.de/pdf-files/bueros/mosambik/07874.pdf.

Cheeseman, N. & Tendi, B-M. 2010. "Power-sharing in comparative perspective: the dynamics of 'unity government' in Kenya and Zimbabwe" in *Journal of Modern African Studies*, Vol. 48(2).

Chigora, P. 2007. "On crossroads: Zimbabwe's foreign policy and the West" in *Journal of Sustainable Development in Africa*, Vol. 9(1). Available at http://www.jsd-africa.com/Jsda/Spring2007PDF/ARC_OnCrossroads.pdf.

Chiroro, B. 2005. "Apathy, Fatigue or Boycott? An analysis of 2005 Zimbabwe Senate Elections". EISA Occasional Paper, No. 38, November 2005.

Chiwewe, W. 1989. "Unity negotiation" in Banana, C. (Ed) 1989. *Turmoil and Tenacity: Zimbabwe, 1880-1980*. College Press Ltd, Harare.

Cliffe, L. 2000. "The politics of land reform in Zimbabwe" in Bowyer-Bower, T. & Stoneman, C. (Eds). 2000. *Land Reform in Zimbabwe: Constraints and prospects*. Ashgate, Aldershot.

Commonwealth Secretariat. 2000. "The Parliamentary Elections in Zimbabwe 24-25 June 2000: The Report of the Commonwealth Observer Group". Commonwealth Secretariat, London.

Cross, E. 2009. "The cost of Zimbabwe's continuing farm invasions" in *Cato Institute Economic Development Bulletin*, Vol. 12, May 2009.

Dabengwa, D. 1995. "ZIPRA in the Zimbabwe War of Liberation" in Bhebhe, N & Ranger, T. (Eds). 1995. *Soldiers in Zimbabwe's Liberation War*. James Currey, London.

Deve, T. & Goncalves, F. 1994. *Whither the Opposition in Zimbabwe?* SAPEM, Vol. 7.

Duffield, M. 1996. *The Symphony of the Damned: Racial discourses, complex political survey and humanitarian aid*. Occasional Paper. Centre for Urban and Regional Studies, University of Birmingham.

Electoral Commissions Forum of SADC Countries. 2000. "Zimbabwe elections observer mission report: 24-25 June 2000". EISA, Johannesburg.

Electoral Commissions Forum of SADC Countries. 2008. "Observation statement submitted to the Zimbabwe National Electoral Commission". ECF, Gaborone. Available at http://www.eisa.org.za/PDF/zim2008sadcecf2.pdf. Accessed 15 November 2012.

Electoral Institute of Southern Africa, 2002. "Zimbabwe: 2002 Presidential Election Results" available at http://www.eisa.org.za/WEP/zimresults2002.htm. Accessed 23 September 2002.

Electoral Institute of Southern Africa. 2008. "The Zimbabwe Harmonised Elections of 29 March 2008 presidential, parliamentary and local government elections: with postscript on the presidential run-off of 27 June 2008 and the multi-party agreement of 15 September 2008". EISA, Johannesburg. (= EISA Election Observer Mission Report; 28) available at http://www.eisa.org.za/PDF/zimomr08.pdf.

Engel, U. 1994. *The Foreign Policy of Zimbabwe*. Institut für Afrika-Kunde, Hamburg.

Engel, U. (Ed). 2012. *New Mediation Practices in African Conflicts*. Leipziger Universitätsverlag, Leipziger.

Engel, U. 2013. "The changing role of the AU Commission in inter-African relations: The case of APSA and AGA" in Harbeson, J. (ed). 2013. *Africa in World Politics*. 5th ed., Westview Press, Boulder CA.

EU Commission Delegation to Zimbabwe. 2004. "EC-Zimbabwe Cooperation: A historical perspective" (information brochure). Harare, January/December 2004.

EU Commission Delegation to Zimbabwe. 2006. "An overview of EU-Zimbabwe current co-operation". Harare, January 2006.

EU Commission Delegation to Zimbabwe. 2006. "EU support to health in Zimbabwe". Harare, November 2006.

EU Commission Delegation to Zimbabwe. n.d. "Position of the EU on sanctions against Zimbabwe".

EU Commission Delegation to Zimbabwe. n.d. "The meaning of the suspension of EU-Zimbabwe development co-operation for the people of Zimbabwe".

EU Commission. 2001. "Communication from the Commission on the opening of consultations with Zimbabwe pursuant to Article 96 of the Cotonou Agreement", COM (2001) 623 final, 26.10.2001 EU, Brussels. Available at http://eeas.europa.eu/delegations/zimbabwe/eu_zimbabwe/political_relations/agreements/index_en.htm. Accessed 15 November 2012.

EU Commission. 2002. "Consultations with the ACP side concerning Zimbabwe pursuant to Article 96 of the Cotonou Agreement", 5243/02 (Presse 4), Brussels, 11 January 2002. Available at http://www.consilium.europa.eu/uedocs/cms_data/docs/pressdata/en/misc/doc.69086.pdf. Accessed September 2008.

EU Commission. 2005. "Co-operation between the Republic of Zimbabwe and the European Community: Joint Annual Report 2005". Report of the National Authorising Officer and the European Commission Head of Delegation.

EU Commission. 2008. Communication from the Commission, 26 October 2001, COM (2001) 623 on the opening of consultations with Zimbabwe pursuant to Article 96 of the Cotonou Agreement. Available at http://www.delzwe.ec.europa.eu/en/eu_and_country/com2001_0623en01.pdf. Accessed August 2008.

EU Council, External Relations Council. 2008. Council Conclusions on Zimbabwe, 2886th Council Meeting, 15-16 September 2008.

EU Council. 2002a. Council Decision of 18 February 2002 concluding consultations with Zimbabwe under Article 96 of the ACP-EC Partnership Agreement, 2002/148/EC.

EU Council. 2002b. Council Common Position of 18 February 2002 Concerning Restrictive Measures Against Zimbabwe, 18 February 2002, 2002/145/CFSP.

EU Council. 2003. Council Common Position of 18 February 2003, 2003/115/CFSP.

EU Council. 2004. "Basic principles on the use of restrictive measures". 7 June 2004.

EU Council. 2004. Council Common Position of 19 February 2004 Concerning Restrictive Measures Against Zimbabwe, 19 February 2004, 2004/161/CFSP.

EU Council. 2004. Council Regulation (EC) No 314/2004 of 19 February 2004 Concerning Certain Restrictive Measures in Respect of Zimbabwe, 19 February 2004.

EU Council. 2005. "Guidelines on implementation and evaluation of restrictive measures (sanctions) in the framework of the EU Common Foreign and Security Policy". 2 December 2005.

EU Council. 2005. Council Common Position of 22 February 2005 Extending Common Position 2004/161/CFSP Concerning Restrictive Measures Against Zimbabwe, 22 February 2005, 2005/146/CFSP.

EU Council. 2008. External Relations Council, Council Conclusions on Zimbabwe, 2865th Council Meeting, 29 April 2008.

EU External Relations. n.d. "Sanctions and restrictive measures" available at http://ec.europa.eu/external_relations/cfsp/sanctions/index.htm.

European Commission, Directorate-General for Humanitarian Aid-ECHO. n.d. "Evaluation of DG ECHO's Action in Zimbabwe, Final Report".

European Commission. 2003. "Co-operation between the Republic of Zimbabwe and the European Community: Joint Annual Report 2003". Report of the National Authorising Officer and the European Commission Head of Delegation.

European Commission. 2005. "Co-operation between the Republic of Zimbabwe and the European Community: Joint Annual Report 2005". Report of the National Authorising Officer and the European Commission Head of Delegation.

European Commission. n.d. "Co-operation between the Republic of Zimbabwe and the European Community: Joint Annual Report 2001-2002", Report of the National Authorising Officer and the European Commission Head of Delegation.

European Council. 2002. "Council Common Position of 18 February 2002 concerning restrictive measures on Zimbabwe" (2002/145/CFSP) available at http://www.sipri.org/databases/embargoes/eu_arms_embargoes/zimbabwe/145. Accessed 15 November 2012.

European Council. 2008. EU Press Release, 10316/08 (= Presse 163). EU Council, Brussels. Available at http://www.eusa.org.za/en/PDFdownload/Agreements/EU-SA_Troika_Slovenia_June_2008.pdf. Accessed 15 November 2012.

European Parliament. 2006. Resolution P6_TA (2006) 0358.

European Parliament. 2009. European Parliament Resolution of 16 December 2009 on restrictive measures directed against certain persons and entities associated with Osama bin Laden, the Al-Qaida network and the Taliban, in respect of Zimbabwe and in view of the situation in Somalia. 16 December 2009, Strasbourg.

European Union. 2002. Council Regulation (EC) No 310/2002 of 18 February 2002 Concerning Certain Restrictive Measures in Respect of Zimbabwe, 18 February 2002.

European Union. 2002. General Affairs Council, Council Decision of 28 January 2002, 2406th Council Meeting, Brussels 28 January 2002. Available at http://www.consilium.europa.eu/uedocs/cms_data/docs/pressdata/en/gena/69151.pdf.

European Union. 2002a. General Affairs Council, Council Conclusions, Zimbabwe, 2409th Council Meeting, Brussels 18-19 February 2002. Available at http://www.consilium.europa.eu/ueDocs/cms_Data/docs/pressdata/en/gena/69471.pdf.

European Union. 2003. Council Regulation (EC) No 313/2003 of 18 February 2003 Extending Regulation (EC) No 310/2002 Concerning Certain Restrictive Measures in Respect of Zimbabwe, 18 February 2003.

European Union. 2003. Declaration by the presidency on behalf of the European Union on the crackdown on the opposition in Zimbabwe, 7911/03 (Presse 96), 28 March 2003.

European Union. 2003. Declaration by the presidency on behalf of the European Union on Freedom of the Press in Zimbabwe, 12697/03 (Presse 275), 18 September 2003.

European Union. 2004. Declaration by the presidency on behalf of the European Union on the Adoption of the NGO Bill in Zimbabwe, 16249/04 (Presse 371), 22 December 2004.

European Union. 2005. Declaration by the presidency on behalf of the European Union on the Conduct of the Elections in Zimbabwe, 7789/05 (Presse 78), 5 April 2005.

European Union. 2005. Declaration by the presidency on behalf of the European Union Concerning the Recent Events in Zimbabwe, 9876/05 (Presse 139), 7 June 2005.

European Union. 2008. Declaration by the presidency on behalf of the European Union on Zimbabwe, 4 July 2008.

Freeman, L. 2005. "South Africa's Zimbabwe Policy: Unravelling the contradictions" in *Journal of Contemporary African Studies*, Vol. 23(2).

Gavin, M.D. 2007. *Planning for post-Mugabe Zimbabwe*. Center for Preventive Action, New York. (= Council on Foreign Relations Special Report; 31) available at http://www.cfr.org/content/publications/attachments/Zimbabwe_CSR31.pdf.

Gomes Porto, J. 2011. "Multipronged strategies for a multifaceted crisis? A critical reflection on EU policy towards Zimbabwe" in Gänzle, S., Grimm, S. & Makhan, D. (Eds). 2011. *The European Union and Global Development. An "Enlightened Superpower" in the Making?* Palgrave Macmillan, London.

Gomes Porto, J. 2012. "Mediators not in the middle: Revisiting the normative dimensions of international mediation" in Engel, U. (Ed). 2012. *New Mediation Practices in African Conflicts*. Leipziger Universitätsverlag, Leipzig.

Government of Zimbabwe. Ministry of Foreign Affairs. 2008. "Agreement between the Zimbabwe African National Union-Patriotic Front (ZANU-PF) and the two Movement for Democratic Change (MDC) formations, on resolving the challenges facing Zimbabwe". Harare, 15 September (mimeo). Available at http://www.zimfa.gov.zw/index.php?option=com_docman&task=cat_view&gid=61&Itemid=91. Accessed 12 November 2012.

Grebe, J. 2010. "And they are still targeting: Assessing the effectiveness of targeted sanctions against Zimbabwe" in *Africa Spectrum*, Vol. 45(1).

Hansard (Zimbabwe). 15 March 1983.

Hansard (Zimbabwe). 2 February 1983.

Harold-Barry, D. (Ed). 2004. *Zimbabwe: The past is the future*. Weaver Press, Harare.

Human Rights Watch. 2008a. *Our Hands Are Tied: Erosion of the rule of law in Zimbabwe*. HRW Publications, New York. Available at http://www.hrw.org/sites/default/files/reports/zimbabwe1108.pdf.

Human Rights Watch. 2008b. *Bullets For Each Of You: State-sponsored violence since Zimbabwe's March 29 elections*. HRW Publications, New York. Available at http://hrw.org/reports/2008/zimbabwe0608/zimbabwe0608web.pdf.

Human Rights Watch. 2009. *False Dawn: The Zimbabwe power-sharing government's failure to deliver human rights improvements*. HRW Publications, New York. Available at http://www.hrw.org/sites/default/files/reports/zimbabwe0809web.pdf.

Human Rights Watch. 2011. *Perpetual Fear: Impunity and cycles of violence in Zimbabwe.* HRW Publications, New York. Available at http://www.hrw.org/sites/default/files/reports/zimbabwe0311NoPage8Full.pdf.

Huntington, S. 1991. *The Third Wave of Democratization in the Late Twentieth Century.* Norman Press, University of Oklahoma.

Integrated Regional Information Networks (IRIN). 2006. "Zimbabwe: Government reports 150% drop in living standards" in IRIN NEWS, Harare, 6 December 2006.

International Crisis Group. 2000. *Zimbabwe at the Crossroads.* ICG, Harare. (= Africa Report; 22) available at http://www.crisisgroup.org/en/regions/africa/southern-africa/zimbabwe/022-zimbabwe-at-the-crossroads.aspx.

International Crisis Group. 2001a. *Zimbabwe in Crisis: Finding a way forward.* ICG, Harare. (= Africa Report; 32) available at http://www.crisisgroup.org/en/regions/africa/southern-africa/zimbabwe/032-zimbabwe-in-crisis-finding-a-way-forward.aspx.

International Crisis Group. 2001b. *Zimbabwe: Time for international action.* ICG, Harare. (= Africa Briefing; 5) available at http://www.crisisgroup.org/en/regions/africa/southern-africa/zimbabwe/B005-zimbabwe-time-for-international-action.aspx.

International Crisis Group. 2002a. *Zimbabwe: What next?* ICG, Johannesburg. (= Africa Report; 47) available at http://www.crisisgroup.org/en/regions/africa/southern-africa/zimbabwe/047-zimbabwe-what-next.aspx.

International Crisis Group. 2002b. *All Bark and No Bite? The international response to Zimbabwe's crisis.* ICG, Harare. (= Africa Report; 40) available at http://www.crisisgroup.org/en/regions/africa/southern-africa/zimbabwe/040-all-bark-and-no-bite-the-international-response-to-zimbabwes-crisis.aspx.

International Crisis Group. 2002c. *Zimbabwe: The politics of national liberation and international division.* ICG, Harare. (= Africa Report; No. 52) available at http://www.crisisweb.org/projects/africa/southernafrica/reports/A400800_17102002.pdf.

International Crisis Group. 2004. *Zimbabwe: In search of a new strategy.* ICG, Harare. (= Africa Report; 78) available at http://www.crisisgroup.org/en/regions/africa/southern-africa/zimbabwe/078-zimbabwe-in-search-of-a-new-strategy.aspx.

International Crisis Group. 2005a. *Post-Election Zimbabwe: What next?* ICG, Pretoria. (= Africa Report; 93) available at http://www.crisisgroup.org/en/regions/africa/southern-africa/zimbabwe/093-post-election-zimbabwe-what-next.aspx.

International Crisis Group. 2005b. *Zimbabwe's Operation* Murambatsvina: *The tipping point?* ICG, Pretoria. (= Africa Report; 97) available at http://www.crisisgroup.org/en/regions/africa/southern-africa/zimbabwe/097-zimbabwes-operation-murambatsvina-the-tipping-point.aspx.

International Crisis Group. 2006. *Zimbabwe: An opposition strategy.* ICG, Pretoria. (= Africa Report; 117) available at http://www.crisisgroup.org/library/documents/africa/southern_africa/117_zimbabwe_an_opposition_strategy.pdf.

International Crisis Group. 2007a. *Zimbabwe: An end to the stalemate?* ICG, Pretoria. (= Africa Report 122).

International Crisis Group. 2007b. Zimbabwe: A regional solution? ICG, Pretoria. (= Africa Report; 132) available at http://www.crisisgroup.org/library/documents/africa/southern_africa/132_zimbabwe_a_regional_solution.pdf.

International Crisis Group. 2008a. *Zimbabwe: Prospects from a flawed election*. ICG, Pretoria. (= Africa Report; 138).

International Crisis Group. 2008b. *Negotiating Zimbabwe's Transition*. ICG, Pretoria. (= Africa Briefing; 51) available at http://www.crisisgroup.org/library/documents/africa/southern_africa/b51_negotiating_zimbabwes_transition.pdf.

International Crisis Group. 2008c. *Ending Zimbabwe's Nightmare: A possible way forward*. ICG, Pretoria. (= Africa Briefing; 56).

International Crisis Group. 2009. *Zimbabwe: Engaging the inclusive government*. ICG, Harare. (=Africa Briefing; 59) available at http://www.crisisgroup.org/library/documents/africa/southern_africa/b59_zimbabwe_engaging_the_inclusive_government.pdf.

International Crisis Group. 2010. "A way forward for Zimbabwe" available at http://www.crisisgroup.org/ar/Key%20Issues/A%20Way%20forward%20for%20Zimbabwe.aspx.

International Crisis Group. 2010. *Zimbabwe: Political and security challenges to the transition*. ICG, Harare. (= Africa Briefing; 70).

International Crisis Group. 2011a. *Zimbabwe: The road to reform or another dead end?* ICG, Brussels. (=Africa Briefing; 173).

International Crisis Group. 2011b. *Resistance and Denial: Zimbabwe's stalled reform agenda*. ICG, Johannesburg. (= Africa Briefing; 82).

International Crisis Group. 2012. *Zimbabwe's Sanctions Standoff*. ICG, Johannesburg. (= Africa Briefing; 86) available at http://www.crisisgroup.org/en/regions/africa/southern-africa/zimbabwe/b086-zimbabwes-sanctions-standoff.aspx. Accessed 13 November 2012.

Jabri, V. 1990. *Mediating Conflict. Decision-making and western intervention in Namibia*. Manchester University Press, Manchester.

Kagoro, B. 2003. "The opposition and civil society" in Cornwell, R. (Ed). 2003. *Zimbabwe's Turmoil: Problems and prospects*. Monograph 87, Institute for Security Studies.

Kagwanja, P. 2006. "Power and peace: South Africa and the refurbishing of Africa's multilateral capacity for peacemaking" in *Journal of Contemporary African Studies*, Vol. 24(2).

Kagwanja, P. & Rupiya, M.R. 2009. "Praetorian solidarity: The state of military relations between South Africa and Zimbabwe" in Kagwanja, P. et al. (Eds). 2009. *State of the Nation: South Africa*. Vol. 5. HSRC Press, Cape Town.

Kanyenze, K. "The Zimbabwe Economy 1980-2003: A ZCTU perspective" in Harold-Barry, D. (Ed). 2004. *Zimbabwe: The past is the future*. Weaver Press, Harare.

Kasambala, T. 2007. *Bashing Dissent: Escalating violence and State repression in Zimbabwe*. Human Rights Watch.

Keesing's Contemporary Archives, July 1983.

Kibble, S. 2001. *Land, Power and Poverty: Farm workers and the crisis in Zimbabwe*. Catholic Institute of International Relations, London.

Kleiboer, M. 1998. *The Multiple Realities of International Mediation*. Lynne Rienner, London.

Kriger, N. 2005. "ZANU (PF) strategies in general elections, 1980-2000: Discourse and coercion" in *African Affairs*, Vol. 104(414).

Kriger, N.J. 2003. Guerrilla Veterans in *Post-War Zimbabwe: Symbolic and violent politics, 1980-1987*. Cambridge University Press, Cambridge.

Lancaster Agreement. Available at http://www.zwnews.com/Lancasterhouse.doc. Accessed 6 September 2001.

Lipton, M. 2009. "Understanding South Africa's foreign policy: The perplexing case of Zimbabwe" in *The South African Journal of International Affairs*, Vol. 16(3).

Lupogo, H. 2001. "Tanzania, civil military relations and political stability essays" in *African Security Review*, Vol. 10(1).

Lusaka Accord of the Democratic Republic of the Congo. 1999.

Lyman, P.N. 2006. "Zimbabwe: The limits of influence" in *African Renaissance*, Vol. 3(2).

Maroleng, C. 2004. "Zimbabwe: Reaping the harvest". Situation Report, African Security Analysis Programme. ISS, Pretoria.

Maroleng, C. 2004. "Zimbabwe's Movement for Democratic Change: Briefing Notes". Situation Report, African Security Analysis Programme. ISS, Pretoria.

Maroleng, C. 2005. "Zimbabwe: Increased securitisation of the State?" in *ISS Situation Report*, 7 September 2005.

Maroleng, C. 2005. "Zimbabwe's Zezuru Sum Game: The basis for the security dilemma in which the political elite finds itself' in *African Security Review*, Vol. 14(3).

Marongwe, N. 2003. *Conflict Over Land and Other Natural Resources in Zimbabwe*. Greenwood Park, Harare.

Masunungure, E. 2004. "Travails of opposition politics in Zimbabwe since independence" in Harold-Barry, D. (Ed). 2004. *Zimbabwe: The past is the future*. Weaver Press, Harare.

Masunungure, E.V. (Ed). 2009. *Defying the Winds of Change: Zimbabwe's 2008 elections*. Weaver Press, Harare.

Matlosa, K. 2009. "The role of the Southern African Development Community in the management of Zimbabwe's post-election crisis" in *Journal of African Elections*, Vol. 8(2).

Maudeni, Z. 2004. "Why the African renaissance is likely to fail: The case of Zimbabwe" in *Journal of Contemporary African Studies*, Vol. 22(2).

Mbaya, S. 2005. "Zimbabwe's land politics and the 2005 elections" in *Journal of African Elections*, Vol. 4(2).

Mbaya, W. 1980. "Ndebele rebellion gathering force" in *The Star* (Johannesburg), 23 July 1980.

McGregor, J. 2002. "The politics of disruption: War veterans and the local State in Zimbabwe" in *African Affairs*, Vol. 101.

McKinley, D.T. 2004. "South African foreign policy towards Zimbabwe under Mbeki" in *Review of African Political Economy*, Vol. 31(100).

Melber, H. 2009. "Southern African liberation movements as governments and its limits to liberation" in *Review of African Political Economy*, Vol. 36(121).

Meredith, M. 2002. *Mugabe: Power, Plunder and the Struggle for Zimbabwe*. Public Affairs, New York.

Mlambo, A. 2003. 'The ambiguities of independence, Zimbabwe 1980-1990' in Lee, M. & Colvard, K. (Eds). 2003. *Unfinished Business: The land crisis in southern Africa*. Africa Institute of South Africa, Pretoria.

Moorcraft, P. 1990. *African Nemesis: War and revolution in Southern Africa*. Brasseys, London.

Moorcraft, P. 2012. *Mugabe's War Machine*. Jonathan Ball Publishers, Johannesburg.

Moore, D. 2001. "Is the land the economy and the economy the land? Primitive accumulation in Zimbabwe" in *Journal of Contemporary African Studies*, Vol. 19(2).

Moss, T. & Stewart, P. 2005. *The Day After Comrade Bob: Applying post-conflict recovery lessons to Zimbabwe*. (= Working Paper, 72). Center for Global Development, New York.

Moyo, S. 2000. "The political economy of land acquisition and redistribution in Zimbabwe, 1990-1999" in *Journal of Southern African Studies*, Vol. 26(1).

Moyo, S. 2011. "Land concentration and accumulation after redistributive reform in post-settler Zimbabwe" in *Review of African Political Economy*, Vol. 38(128).

Moyo, S. & Yeros, P. 2007. "The radicalised State: Zimbabwe's interrupted revolution" in *Review of African Political Economy*, Vol. 34(111).

Mugabe, R. 1989. "The Unity Accord: Its promise for the future" in Banana, C. (Ed). 1989. *Turmoil and Tenacity: Zimbabwe, 1880-1980*. College Press Ltd, Harare.

Mugabe, R.G. 2001. *Inside the Third Chimurenga*. Department of Information and Publicity, Harare.

Mulikita, N.M. 2003. "A false dawn? Africa's post 1990s democratisation waves" in *African Security Review*, Vol. 12(4).

Musoni, F. 2010. "Operation *Murambatsvina* and the politics of street vendors in Zimbabwe" in *Journal of Southern African Studies*, Vol. 36(2).

Mutasa, D. 1989. "Unity Accord: A step forward in Zimbabwean political development" in Banana, C. (ed) 1989. *Turmoil and Tenacity: Zimbabwe, 1880-1980*. College Press Ltd, Harare.

Muzondidya, J. 2007. "The military business complex and the transition in Zimbabwe". (The death of quiet diplomacy and a new chance for Zimbabwe: Roundtable on Zimbabwe organised by the Human Sciences Research Council, Pretoria, 17 July 2007.)

Ndlela, D. 2003. "Zimbabwe's economy since 1990" in Lee, M. & Colvard, K. (Eds). 2003. *Unfinished Business: The land crisis in southern Africa*. Africa Institute of South Africa, Pretoria.

Ndlovu-Gatsheni, S.J. 2003. "Dynamics of the Zimbabwe crisis in the 21st Century" in *African Journal on Conflict Resolution*, Vol. 3(1).

Ndlovu-Gatsheni, S.J. 2006. "Nationalist-military alliance and the fate of democracy in Zimbabwe" in *African Journal on Conflict Resolution*, Vol. 6(1).

Ndlovu-Gatsheni, S.J. 2009. "Making sense of Mugabeism in local and global politics: 'So Blair, keep your England and let me keep my Zimbabwe'" in *Review of African Political Economy*, Vol. 30(6).

Ndlovu-Gatsheni, S.J. 2009. Do "Zimbabweans" Exist? Trajectories of nationalism, national identity formation and crisis in a postcolonial State. Peter Lang, Oxford.

Ndlovu-Gatsheni,, S.J. 2011. *Reconstructing the Implications of Liberation Struggle History on SADC Mediation in Zimbabwe*. South African Institute of International Affairs, Braamfontein. (= SAIIA Occasional Paper; 92) available at http://www.saiia.org.za/images/stories/pubs/occasional_papers/saia_sop_92_ndlovu_gatcheni_20110906.pdf.

Nel, P., Taylor, I. & Van der Westhuizen, J. 2000. "Multilateralism in South Africa's foreign policy: The search for a critical rationale" in *Global Governance* (6).

Nkiwane, S.M. 1999. "Zimbabwe's foreign policy" in Wright, S. (Ed). 1999. *African Foreign Policies*. Westview: Boulder.

Nkomo, J. 1989. "The significance of the Unity Accord and its future" in Banana, C. (Ed) 1989. *Turmoil and Tenacity: Zimbabwe, 1880-1980*. College Press Ltd, Harare.

Pan African Parliament. 2008. *Report of the Pan African Parliament Election Observer Mission. Presidential Run-Off Election and House of Assembly By-Elections. Republic of Zimbabwe, 27 June 2008*. (= PAP/S/RPT/76/08) PAP, Midrand.

Partnership Africa Canada. 2009. "Zimbabwe, diamonds and the wrong side of history" available at http://www.pacweb.org. Accessed 15 November 2010.

Peters-Berries, C. 2002. "The Zimbabwe crisis and SADC: How to deal with a deviant member state?" in Namibian Economic Policy Research Unit, et al. (Eds). 2002. *Monitoring Regional Integration in Southern Africa. Yearbook 2*. Gamsberg Macmillan, Windhoek.

Pieterse, J.N. 1997. "Deconstructing/Reconstructing of ethnicity" in *Nations and Nationalism*, Vol. 3(3).

Ploch, L. 2007. "Zimbabwe: Current issues and US policy", updated 21 June 2007. Congressional Research Service, Washington DC. (= Report-Nr.: RL32723).

Ploch, L. 2008. "Zimbabwe: 2008 elections and implications for US policy". Congressional Research Service, Washington DC. (= Report-Nr.: RL34509) available at http://fpc.state.gov/documents/organization/106142.pdf.

Ploch, L. 2010a. "Zimbabwe: The transitional government and implications for US policy. Congressional Research Service, Washington DC. (= CRS Report for Congress; RL34509) available at http://www.humansecuritygateway.com/documents/CRS_7July2010_Zimbabwe_TransitionalGovt_ImplicationsUSPolicy.pdf.

Ploch, L. 2010b. "Zimbabwe: Background". Congressional Research Service, Washington DC. (= Report-Nr.: RL32723) available at http://www.fas.org/sgp/crs/row/RL32723.pdf.

Portela, C. 2007. "Aid suspension as coercive tools? The European Union's experience in the African-Caribbean-Pacific (ACP) context' in *Review of European and Russian Affairs*, Vol. 3(2).

Portela, C. 2007. "The EU's 'Sanctions Paradox'". SWP Comments 18. *Stiftung Wissenschaft und Politik*, October 2007.

Potts, D. 2006. "Restoring Order? Operation Murambatsvina and the urban crisis in Zimbabwe" in *Journal of Southern African Studies*, Vol. 32(2).

Primorac, R. & Chan, S. 2007. *Zimbabwe in Crisis: The international response and the space of silence*. Routledge, London.

Raftopoulos, B. 2002. "Briefing: Zimbabwe's 2002 Presidential Elections" in *African Affairs*, Vol. 101.

Raftopoulos, B. 2006. "The Zimbabwean crisis and the challenges for the Left" in *Journal of Southern African Studies*, Vol. 32(2).

Raftopolous, B. & Alexander, K. (Eds). 2006. *Reflections on Democratic Politics in Zimbabwe*. Institute for Justice and Reconciliation, Cape Town.

Ranger, T. 2003. *The Historical Dimensions of Democracy and Human Rights in Zimbabwe, Volume 2: Nationalism, democracy and human rights*. University of Zimbabwe Publications, Harare.

Ranger, T. 2004. "Nationalist History, Patriotic History and the History of the Nation: The struggle over the past in Zimbabwe" in *Journal of Southern African Studies*, Vol. 30(2).

Riddel, R. 2013. *Why Did Robert Mugabe Win?* Jesuits Zimbabwe, Harare.

Robertson, J. 2007. "The State of the Economy". Paper presented at the "Zimbabwe at the Crossroads Seminar" Tshwane, October 2007.

Rotberg, R.I. 2011. *Beyond Mugabe: Preparing for Zimbabwe's transition: A report of the CSIS Africa Program*. Center for Strategic and International Studies, Washington DC. Available at http://csis.org/files/publication/110804_Rotberg_BeyondMugabe_Web.pdf.

Rukumi, C. 1987. "Gwasela: Bandit or dissident?" in *African Concord*, 24 September 1987.

Rupiah, M. 1995. "Demobilization and Integration: 'Operation Merger' and the Zimbabwe National Defence Forces, 1980-1987' in *African Security Review*, Vol. 4(3). Available at http://www.iss.co.za/Pubs/ASR/4No3?Demobilization.html.

Rupiya, M. 2005 "Governance through military operations" in *African Security Review*, Vol. 14(3).

Rupiya, M. 2005. "An examination of the role of the national Youth Service/Militia in Zimbabwe's elections in 2005" in *Journal of African Elections*, Vol. 4(2).

Rupiya, M. 2006 "The Nyalali Commission and security sector reform: 1992-2005" in Rupiya, M. et al. (Eds) 2006. *Civil Security Relations in Tanzania: Investigating the relationships between the State, security services and civil society*. ISS Monograph No. 128.

Sachikonye, L. 1990. "The 1990 Zimbabwean Elections: A post-mortem" in *Review of African Political Economy*, Vol. 17(48).

Sachikonye, L. 2002. "Whither Zimbabwe? Crisis and democratisation" in *Review of African Political Economy*, Vol. 29(91).

Sachikonye, L.M. 2005a. "Political parties and the 2005 elections in Zimbabwe" in *Journal of African Elections*, Vol. 4(2).

Sachikonye, L.M. 2005b. "South Africa's quiet diplomacy: The case of Zimbabwe" in Daniel, J., Southall, R. & Lutchman, J. (Eds). 2005. *The State of the Nation: South Africa 2004-2005*. HSRC Press, Cape Town.

SADC *Agreement on Madagascar*, 2009.

SADC Election Observer Mission (SEOM). 2008. Preliminary Statement on the Zimbabwean Presidential Runoff and House of the Assembly By-Elections held on 27 June 2008. SEOM, Harare. Available at http://www.eisa.org.za/PDF/zim2008sadc2.pdf. Accessed 15 November 2012.

SADC. 2003. Communiqué issued on 26 August 2003 in Dar es Salaam, Tanzania. Available at http://www.iss.co.za/af/regorg/unity_to_union/pdfs/sadc/communiques/HoS%2003.pdf. Accessed 15 November 2012.

SADC. 2004. "SADC Principles and Guidelines Governing Democratic Elections", adopted at the SADC Summit held on 16-17 August 2004 in Port Louis, Mauritius. Available at http://www.eisa.org.za/PDF/sadcguidelines.pdf. Accessed 16 November 2012.

SADC. 2007. Communiqué of the 2007 Extra-Ordinary SADC Summit of Heads of State and Government, 28-29 March 2007, Dar es Salaam. Available at http://www.dfa.gov.za/docs/2007/sadc0330.htm. Accessed 16 November 2012.

SADC. 2008. Communiqué issued at the First Extra-Ordinary SADC Summit of Heads of State and Government, 13 April 2008, Lusaka, Zambia. Available at http://www.zimbabwejournalists.com/story.php?art_id=3929&cat=4. Accessed 15 November 2012.

SADC. 2009. Communiqué. Summit of the Troika of the Organ on Politics, Defence and Security Cooperation, 5 November 2009, Maputo, Mozambique. Available at http://www.sadc.int/index/browse/page/624. Accessed 16 November 2012.

SADC. 2011. Communiqué. Summit of the Organ Troika on Politics, Defence and Security Cooperation, 31 March 2011, Livingstone, Zambia. Available at http://www.sadc.int/index/browse/page/858. Accessed 16 November 2012.

Saunders, R. 2011. "Zimbabwe: Liberation nationalism – old and born again" in *Review of African Political Economy*, Vol. 38(127).

Scarnecchia, T. 2006. "The 'Fascist Cycle' in Zimbabwe, 2000-2005" in *Journal of Southern African Studies*, Vol. 32(2).

Shaw, W.H. 2003. "They Stole Our Land: Debating the expropriation of white farms in Zimbabwe" in *Journal of Modern African Studies*, Vol. 41(1).

Shivji, I.G. 1996. "Problems of constitution making as consensus building: The Tanzanian experience". Paper presented at "Land tenure issues in natural resources management in Anglophone East Africa with a focus on the IGAD region". Addis Ababa, 11-15 March 1996. Available at http://www.mekonginfo.org/mrc/html/oss/sh2_lit.htm. Accessed 23 January 2006.

Silvester, C. 1995. "Whither opposition in Zimbabwe?" in *The Journal of Modern African Studies*, Vol. 33(3).

Soko, M & Balchin, N. 2009. "South Africa's policy towards Zimbabwe: A nexus between foreign policy and commercial interests?" in *The South African Journal of International Affairs*, Vol. 16(1).

Solidarity Peace Trust. 2003. *Shaping Youth in a Truly Zimbabwean Manner: An overview of youth militia training and activities in Zimbabwe, October 2000-August 2003*. Solidarity Peace Trust, Johannesburg.

Tendi, B-M. 2010. *Making History in Mugabe's Zimbabwe: Politics, intellectuals and the media*. Peter Lang, Oxford.

The Herald (Harare), 16 March 1983.

The Herald (Harare), 23 June 2008.

The Herald (Harare), 4 March 2000.

The New Vision (Kampala), 3 June 2000.

Thomas, N. 2003. "Land reform in Zimbabwe" in *Third World Quarterly*, Vol. 24(4).

Thompson, C. 2005. "Return to hell" in *The London Line* (London). 2 June 2005.

Tibaijuka, A.K. 2005. "Report of the fact-finding mission to Zimbabwe to assess the scope and impact of Operation *Murambatsvina* by the UN Special Envoy on Human Settlements Issues in Zimbabwe". United Nations, New York. Available at http://www.unhabitat.org/documents/ZimbabweReport.pdf.

Towriss, D. 2013. "Buying loyalty: Zimbabwe's Marange diamonds" in *Journal for Southern African Studies*, Vol. 39(1).

Tungaraza, C. 1988. "The transformation of civil military relations in Tanzania" in Hutchful, E. & Bathili, A. (Eds) *The Military and Militarism in Africa*. CODESRIA, Dakar.

UN Secretary-General (UNSG). 1992. "An Agenda for Peace. Preventive diplomacy, peacemaking and peace-keeping". Report of the Secretary-General pursuant to the statement adopted by the Summit Meeting of the Security Council on 31 January 1992. A/47/277 – S/24111, 17 June. Available at http://unrol.org/files/A_47_277.pdf. Accessed 12 November 2012.

UNDP. 2007. *Human Development Report 2007/2008: Fighting climate change: Human solidarity in a divided world*. Palgrave Macmillan. Available at http://hdr.undp.org/en/media/HDR_20072008_EN_Complete.pdf.

UNDP. 2008. "Comprehensive Economic Recovery in Zimbabwe: A discussion document". October 2008.

US House of Representatives, Committee on Foreign Affairs. Subcommittee on Africa, Global Health, and Human Rights. 2011. [Hearing] US policy toward Zimbabwe. Washington DC. Available at http://foreignaffairs.house.gov/hearing_notice.asp?id=1374.

US Senate, Subcommittee on African Affairs of the Committee on Foreign Relations. 2008. "The crisis in Zimbabwe and prospects for resolution". Hearing before the Subcommittee on African Affairs of the Committee on Foreign Relations. US Government Printing Office, Washington DC. (= Hearing United States Senate; S. HRG. 110-682) available at http://frwebgate.access.gpo.gov/cgi-bin/getdoc.cgi?dbname=110_senate_hearings&docid=f:46166.pdf.

US Senate, Subcommittee on African Affairs of the Committee on Foreign Relations. 2009. [Hearing] "Exploring US policy options toward Zimbabwe's transition". US Government Printing Office, Washington DC. Available at http://foreign.senate.gov/hearings/2009/hrg090930a.html.

US Senate, Subcommittee on African Affairs of the Committee on Foreign Relations. 2010. [Hearing] "Exploring US policy options toward Zimbabwe's transition". US Government Printing Office, Washington DC. Available at http://frwebgate.access.gpo.gov/cgi-bin/getdoc.cgi?dbname=111_senate_hearings&docid=f:56619.pdf.

World Bank. 1989. *Sub-Saharan Africa: From crisis to sustainable growth*. World Bank, Washington DC.

Youde, J. 2007. "Why look East? Zimbabwean foreign policy and China" in *Africa Today*, Vol. 53(3).

Zaartman, I.W. 1985. *Ripe for Resolution*. Oxford University Press, New York.

Zaartman, I.W. 2001. "The Timing of Peace Initiatives: Hurting stalemates and ripe moments" in *The Global Review of Ethnopolitics*, Vol. 1(1).

Zhou, E. 2002. *Socio-economic Implications of the Current Farm Invasion in Zimbabwe*. Friedrich-Stiftung, Harare.

Zimbabwe Europe Network (ZEN), et al. 2012. "Zimbabwe's Global Political Agreement Implementation. Four years on at best faltering ... at worst failing". Available at http://www.zimbabweeurope.org/sites/default/files/ZIMBABWE%20GPA%20IMPLEMENTTION.pdf. Accessed 16 November 2012.

Zimbabwe Global Political Agreement, 2008.

Zimbabwe Human Rights NGO Forum. 2007. *Political Violence Report*, June 2007.

Zondi, S. 2007. "SADC developmental plan and how it interfaces with the citizens of the region" in *Critical Dialogue: A public participation review*, Vol. 3(1).

Articles

"Arms ship not docking" available at http://www.thetimes.co.za/News/Article.aspx?id=752876.

"Botswana: Khama set to win elections, vows not to recognise Mugabe as Zimbabwe president" in *The Zimbabwean*. 17 October 2009.

"I don't regret what I said" in *The Namibian*. Available at http://allafrica.com/stories/200703270089.html.

"Let us all vote for land, peace and a democratic future" in *The Herald* (Harare). 12 February 2000

"Let us vote 'No' to dictatorship" in *Zimbabwe Independent* (Harare). 11 February 2000.

"Meeting to finalise cabinet line-up postponed" available at http://allafrica.com/stories/200809161237.html. Accessed 16 September 2008.

"Memorandum of Understanding" available at http://www.issafrica.org. Accessed 3 October 2008.

"Mugabe's costly Congo venture". Available at http://news.bbc.co.uk/2/hi/africa/611898.stm. Accessed 4 May 2007.

"Paradzai Zimondi, Head of Prison Services" in *The Herald* (Harare). 29 February 2008.

"President Robert Mugabe" in *The Herald* (Harare). 23 June 2008.

"SADC intervention long time in coming". Available at http://allafrica.com/stories/200703230677.html. Accessed on 3 February 2009.

"SADC leaders to discuss regional politics" in *The Herald*. Available at http://allafrica.com/stories/200703270089.html.

"SADC Summit divided" in *Business Day*, 23 January 2009.

"Solve Zimbabwe or risk blight on World Cup" available at http://www.monstersandcritics. com/news/africa/news/article_1285840.php/Tsvangirai_warns_Mbeki_Solve_Zimbabwe_ or_risk_blight_on_World_Cup. Accessed 8 November 2008.

"South Africa withholds aid" in *Business Day*, 27 November 2008.

"South Africa: Space invaders" in *The Economist*. 14 July 2001.

"Summit delivers no quick fix to Zimbabwe deadlock". AFP (IOL), 13 April 2008. Accessed 14 April 2008.

"The new Cabinet" in *Zimbabwean Independent*, 26 February 2009.

"Tsvangirai threatens to quit Zimbabwe deal after Mugabe seizes cabinet posts" available at http://www.guardian.co.uk/world/2008/oct/12/zimbabwe1. Accessed 13 October 2008.

"Zimbabwe Senate and Assembly Results". Reuters, 22 August 2008.

"Zimbabwe: A sinking ship – Mwanawasa" in *New Era*. Available at http://allafrica.com/ stories/200703220138.html.

"Zimbabwe: Constitutional Reform – an opportunity to strengthen human rights". Available at http://www.amnesty.org/en/library/info/AFR46/001/2000. Accessed 2 September 2008.

"Zimbabwe: SA Government holds on the line" in *Business Day*, 22 March 2007.

"Zimbabwe: The need to bear witness" in *Progressio*, 5 October 2007.

www.ingramcontent.com/pod-product-compliance
Lightning Source LLC
Chambersburg PA
CBHW081740270326

41932CB00020B/3344